Stranger to Caution

Monique Newby

People kept saying, 'Why don't you write a book about your sailing adventures?' It seemed such a romantic idea. But where to start?

By the time I met Peter, he had already experienced enough drama and disaster to fill several books.

As he described being asked to scuttle a 60-foot trimaran on the way to the Canary Islands, almost losing his life alone in the deep Atlantic and being pitted against many further challenges, I knew this was a story worth telling. So I began walking in my husband's shoes and discovered a true hero.

About the Author

Born and raised in Switzerland, Monique is a multi-linguist, an international recorded singer-songwriter and has appeared in numerous television programs worldwide. She has been published in Yachting Magazines and worked on documentary projects with *Third Eye Film Productions* in London.
Stranger to Caution is her first non-fiction sailing book with the sequel 'Slow Boat to Nashville,' soon to follow. As well as writing poetry and short stories, Monique is a keen photographer and kayaker. 'Mon péché mignon,' she says, 'is crème Chantilly and sometimes I sing in Italian in my sleep.'

About the Narrator

Born in Scarborough, Yorkshire, Peter Newby is an accomplished yachtsman and experienced shipwright. He is also a talented seascape artist who has exhibited in London and Dorset. He enjoys kayaking and says, 'I would happily paddle all the way around England to find the best cheesecake!'
Peter is a firm believer in eternal youth, regardless of the number of candles on his birthday cake. He delights in inspiring others to follow their dreams.

Stranger to Caution

I wondered if I would find my mermaid-bride amongst Neptune's myriad jellyfish strewn upon the ocean like rose petals at a wedding. I didn't want 'Captain Nemo' throwing the reception twenty thousand leagues beneath the sea!

This is a true story based on the life of Peter Newby. Some names have been changed to protect the privacy of others.

Self Published 2023

ISBN: 978-1-7391967-0-7

Cover ©2017
Lighthouse in the Mist
Painting by Peter Newby

moniquenewby.com
m.newbybooks@yahoo.com

CONTENTS

1. First Command - page 1

2. The Flight of the Dodo - page 15

3. The Uptown Girl - page 26

4. The Eyes of Suspicion - page 45

5. At Gun Point - page 63

6. Smoke over the Water - page 75

7. In the Trough - page 92

8. Scorpions and Beards - page 108

9. The Launch - page 134

10. Wall of Death - page 143

11. Déjà Vu - page 158

12. Armadas and Dolphins - page 174

13. Christmas in Morocco - page 190

14. The Woman in the Black Dress - page 204

15. Two Waves that Meet - page 229

16. Mid-Ocean Epiphany - page 242

17. Desert and Cuckoo Clocks- page 265

18. Whitewater Sailing - page 294

19. Butterfly with a Sting - page 309

20. Spilling the Gin - page 319

21. Farewell - page 345

Bon Voyage

1. First Command

I had much to prove to myself, aged 34. How could I ever forget my out-of-body experience on the operating table when I prayed for another chance at life. I thought of the fatal accident I was involved in when I was 19, the five years I had worked to repay my debts, and my estranged wife, Elisabeth. I felt sure sailing to Holland would be a fresh start to a new life.

Caroline was a 29-foot classic Tumlare cruiser-racer built in 1937. I had had my eyes on her for months berthed at Scarborough Harbour. When she came up for sale, I decided to sell my 19-foot *Scampi* and purchase the yacht. As I knew little about the Tumlare, I thought I would do a sea trial to Whitby before sailing across to Holland.

That day, I left Scarborough Harbour with a fair wind and was chuffed to see *Caroline* creaming through the water at an incredible speed of knots. I was amazed how the hull shape and sails were so well-balanced that I could steady the tiller with a bungee cord and leave her to sail by herself. As for making various course adjustments, all I needed to do was to alter the sheeting when necessary.

All went relatively well on my outbound journey. I spent the night in Whitby tied up to another yacht against the quay, went ashore for fish and chips and a pint of Guinness and turned in early. Although Whitby is only twenty miles along the coast from Scarborough, the weather in these waters can change dramatically in just a few hours, from calm to a full-blown gale.

On my journey back to Scarborough, the weather had something else in store. When I heard 'Force 3 to 4, 6 later,' announced on my radio, I wondered if 'later' meant tomorrow or today? How much time did I have left before the wind increased? *Caroline* was flying like a bird on the wing with her genoa set out to starboard and mainsail to port. It was exhilarating to play with the pure element of wind and sail; I felt like a true master in command. I had experienced speed on wheels, racing at over 100mph in Mallory Park and Ingliston circuits. However, speed on the water feels quite different. Sailing had become my new passion and certainly more affordable than being a self-sponsored racing driver. Besides, I thought my chances of survival would be far greater on the water than on a racing track. If only I knew.

The wind had increased by the time I was off Scarborough Castle. The seas were now towering behind me, and as I approached the harbour entrance, the waves were so steep that I couldn't leave the tiller to drop the sails; *Caroline* would have broached and keeled over. I needed to find shelter from the rollers, so I headed close for the outer harbour wall and into the bay, then lashed the tiller hard over to allow *Caroline* to turn in tight circles. Next, I started the engine. I took a sail down each time she came into the wind, but I had to hang on to the mast for dear life while she heeled broadside violently before completing the turns. Handrails on *Caroline* would have been a help.

Once I dropped both sails, I let her do two more circles while I tied the mainsail to the boom and secured the headsail to the prow. Then I motored gently into the harbour, shouting to the young boys fishing off at the entrance, 'Pull your lines in.' I had heard the exact words being shouted out to me as a four-year-old, fishing off the pier.

I made for *Caroline*'s cradle without a fuss. Looking at the holidaymakers promenading along the harbour felt unreal when minutes before, I was being tossed about as if going through the final spin of a washing machine cycle. What more was I to learn about sailing after today?

My romance with boats and the sea began as a boy when The Scottish Herring Fleet sailed into Scarborough each year, following the shoals southward along the East coast. Sometimes the Dutch Herring Fleet arrived at the same time with a hospital ship escorting them. To me, she looked like a Royal Motor Yacht with her tall, raked yellow funnel, masts fore and aft and clipper bow with a bowsprit. On her white hull amidships, she bore a large painted red cross.

One afternoon, as I was serving at the bar of the Wellington Hotel my parents ran, I asked the skipper from one of the Scottish boats how far offshore they went fishing. It must have struck a chord for the skipper said, 'Why don't you come with us tomorrow night, but you'd better ask your dad first. You'll need to dress warmly and be at the dock by six o'clock in the evening.'

Going to the circus wouldn't have been as exciting as a fishing trip on a herring boat! I quickly rushed to the kitchen to ask for my mother's permission. She would be the one to decide whether I could go.

The next day after an early teatime, I hurried to my room, put on some long trousers and a sports jacket, and ran down to the harbour. When I got there, I saw the whole fleet of herring boats, all tied up together on the quayside. I stared at the vessels in despair. Which one was it? Maybe this was just another broken promise from a customer. Then I suddenly heard, 'Over here *laddie*, hurry up.' Thankfully, the skipper had kept an eye out for me from the wheelhouse.

I climbed swiftly down the ten-foot steel vertical ladder and crossed the decks of three boats, stumbling against barrels, nets, and winches on the way. As soon as I stepped aboard the fishing boat, we cast off, and the ship headed out to sea. I felt like one of the crew standing next to the captain, watching the ruin of the Norman Castle fast disappearing behind us, and before I knew it, we were out of sight of land.

Until then, I hadn't paid much attention to the men and noticed they were flat-capped, weather-faced and spoke with a strong Scottish accent. The heavy drinking smell on their breaths was familiar to me from customers drinking in our pub. As we reached the fishing grounds, the men started shooting their nets. I could see their yellow aprons highlighted by the ship's deck lights. Then, as they began hauling in the squirming silvery catch, the skipper suggested I get some sleep. The cook took me to the crew quarters, down some steep steps. Then he made me a pint mug of hot cocoa which I could hardly hold in my hand.

If I drink all this, I'll need the loo.

He must have guessed what I was thinking and pointed to a bucket tightly secured in a corner. 'When you've drunk this *laddie*, have a nap in my bunk,' the cook said, nodding at what looked like a long cupboard without doors, closed off by a tartan curtain. 'You don't need to take your clothes off. Just remove your shoes and lie down on top of the mattress. Use the blanket if you're cold.'

I enjoyed the bitter-sweet taste of the cocoa made with hot water and condensed milk and finished it all. When I lay down, I couldn't get to sleep with the boat rolling and the throbbing engine vibrating through the hull. I felt my stomach turning with the stink of fish, diesel, the men's sweat, and the heat from the potbelly stove. Yet, despite it all, I finally dozed off.

I woke up feeling a gentle hand on my shoulder and the fatherly voice of the cook whispering, 'Okay, *laddie*, we're nearly there.' I got up quickly and followed him on deck, just in time to see us entering Scarborough Harbour. When we moored up the skipper said, 'All right, time to go home.'

It was six o'clock in the morning when I clambered once again across three decks and up the vertical iron ladder to the shore, leaving behind the smell and noise of the herring being unloaded. The streets in town were deserted except for the milkman in his milk float. I walked home in a daze, still feeling the motion of the sea through the pavement.

When I reached our front door, I put the key in the lock, let myself in, crept upstairs and went to sleep for an hour or two. Then I rose to my usual morning chore of making tea and serving it to my parents in bed.

'Oh! You're back!' my mother said as I walked into the bedroom with a tray. 'Was it all right?' she asked in between a yawn.

'Yes, thank you,' I answered, and that was that! But, for me, it was much more. I had gone to sea as an eleven-year-old schoolboy and returned as a seaman.

As I prepared for my forthcoming trip to Holland, my mother said, 'I'm worried about you sailing by yourself.'

I thought: 'What about the two shillings and sixpence you grudgingly paid the constable when he delivered a telegram on his bicycle, to inform you that a couple had brought your three-year-old boy to the police station, believing he was lost, when in fact, he was snatched from your doorstep.' I doubted my mother could fathom my angry reaction.

'You could take Bruce with you,' she insisted.

'I hardly know him,' I replied flatly. Bruce was my nephew. He visited his grandma from time to time, and whenever he talked to me, he looked down his nose. Was it because he was taller than me?

It was my first foreign trip to Ijmuiden, and I wanted to sail there alone. Some members at Scarborough Yacht Club thought me cocky to contemplate such a crossing with my limited experience; others volunteered to crew with me. Although I had studied navigation at night school and read many sailing books, (French yachtsmen Bernard Moitessier and Eric Tabarly were two of my greatest heroes), I was throwing myself in at the deep end. People say I am a stranger to caution. I felt sure I would develop my seamanship on the way.

My mother pressing me to take my nephew was unsettling. *Maybe, I should have somebody with me. It might even help mend family frictions.* So, I consented. *Let's hope he is good at brewing tea and making bacon butties.*

I didn't expect any help from Bruce, but I hoped he would cope with the motion to Ijmuiden, 130 miles away. As for me, I'm never seasick.

Keeping awake on an overnight passage to Ijmuiden wasn't going to faze me out. I had worked as a structural welder at Ward Brothers on many 16-hour shifts and sometimes even partied afterwards.

We weighed anchor at dawn from Scarborough Harbour. Although it was overcast, the shipping forecast only predicted occasional rain. At least the wind was lively and in the right direction. I thought this would do. Setting off into the open sea was far too exciting to worry about rain.

We sailed into the bay with *Caroline* cutting through the water with a clean wake. Looking at the speedo, she was showing a regular six knots. Although I was excited, I couldn't help feeling apprehensive. After all, we were taking on the North Sea with its enormous tides and unpredictable winds. Besides, sailing through the oil rig field could be tricky, even dangerous. The Americans once called the North Sea 'The Pond' until they lost several rig-supply ships to heavy weather.

As *Caroline* maintained her racing speed, drizzle turned into thick mist, and visibility dropped dramatically. *This weather is going to be challenging, not seeing any further than a few hundred yards ahead.* Fog is one of the most hazardous conditions at sea, and I didn't have a radar. We might as well have been blindfolded, playing Russian roulette where the rigs were the bullets! With only our ears to guide us, colliding with an oil rig became more and more of a concern. Standing at the bow was like playing blind man's buff with the fog as the blindfold. Who the hell would hear our handheld foghorn anyway? It was like whispering an order to the mechanic in a ship's engine room. Bruce and I still took turns complying with collision regulations. *Caroline,* meanwhile, lifted her skirt as she ran with the wind. At least we were making progress in this pea-soup fog.

Visibility showed no improvement halfway across to Ijmuiden. To assess our distance run, leeway, and tide accurately was hard to do using an old handheld radio direction finder, compass, and trailing log. I assumed that our position could be anywhere within a three-mile radius of my dead reckoning. In the distance, we could hear a rig's foghorn sounding 'U' as a warning in morse code. One minute, it resonated from the port side, the next from starboard, but I kept on course, misty-eyed, not in the romantic sense. One could hear water swishing past *Caroline's* hull and the wind whispering in the rigging between the deafening foghorns. I continued scanning through the liquid veil, ready to take avoiding action by pulling the tiller hard over if I got too close to a rig. Then suddenly, from above the mast, came this mighty blast that almost made me jump out of my skin. The sound was like a clap of thunder ringing through my ears. I was on an adrenaline rush, expecting to see a steel rig looming out of the mist at any moment. However, with such a responsive boat as *Caroline*, I felt sure that even if I got close enough to see the rivets in the rig's structure, I could still avoid wood against steel.

Thankfully, we didn't get to the nudging stage, but having run the gauntlet without being slapped on the face, I thought *Caroline* must have come close to one of the oil rigs for someone to fire a warning maroon. My heart stopped racing only when the sound of foghorns faded away in our wake.

As dawn broke, I identified the tall chimneys of Ijmuiden refinery towering above the low-lying fog. Relief was a feeble word to use after such an ordeal. The worst had been to sail through a rig-field which reminded me of the first time I rode a ghost train on Scarborough seafront as a little boy, clinging on with white knuckles. I thought of my navigation teacher at night school. He would have been proud of my skills as a navigator in such weather conditions.

After we had moored up in the canal, Bruce and I set off to go and buy some beers to celebrate. The shop was a mile and a half away. When we got there, we couldn't resist the discounted price of beer and bought twelve bottles. It was a windless, sultry June evening, and the weight we carried on the way soon took its toll. Bruce suggested we drink one bottle of beer each to lighten the load. A quarter of a mile on, I proposed the same. The farce lasted until we were back aboard *Caroline*. Then we jumped into the harbour with drunken bravado, frolicking about fully clothed. Fortunately, neither of us drowned that evening.

The following day, Bruce and I were sitting on deck like two sailors in the song, 'What shall we do with the drunken sailor,' when we noticed a trimaran making a grand entrance into the harbour. She was dwarfing every boat berthed inside. Minutes later, someone was standing on the quayside, looking down into *Caroline's* cockpit.

'Hello,' the man said in a Dutch accent. 'Have you sailed across from England? You must be a pretty good navigator to bring such a tiny boat over the North Sea.'

I shrugged my shoulders modestly. The man was looking at me intently, and I thought, *He must be mistaking my hangover for the air of an old sea dog.*

'I'm Hank,' he announced cheerfully.

'I'm Peter, and this is my nephew Bruce.'

Hank wore white slacks and a navy polo shirt. In his early forties, blond-haired, he looked dashingly handsome.

'You see the trimaran over there?' he said, pointing across the harbour, 'I built it myself.

We're heading for the Canary Islands at the end of the month. I'm looking for a navigator. If you're interested, come over for drinks - maybe in half an hour or so.'

'We'll be there,' I replied enthusiastically. I watched Hank walking away, bemused at such serendipity. The idea of navigating the 60-foot trimaran to the Canary Islands was beyond my wildest dreams. When we finished our Dutch coffee and had spruced ourselves up, Bruce and I strolled along the quay towards the *Albatross*. I felt like a teenager going on a first date - only the girl was a boat!

The sixty-foot trimaran was an amateur-built plywood yacht, sheathed in fibreglass. Although impressive in size, *Albatross* looked heavy in the water. What an ugly duckling! Like the dodo, I doubted she'd ever fly. As I pondered about the vessel, Hank saw us on the quayside and called out: 'Come aboard.'

Bruce and I walked across the large deck where tables and chairs were laid out.

'Make yourself at home,' Hank said playfully.

He introduced his wife, Elga. She was tall, slender, and had shoulder-length blonde hair. Dressed in a blue and white striped Guernsey, white trousers, and red high-heeled shoes, Elga embodied the demeanour of a yachtswoman at a Royal Yacht Club cocktail bar.

Hank poured champagne, and we clinked glasses. From the quayside, people were gaping at us, sipping our bubbly. I felt like an actor who had only just left the provincial stage to move into some cheap Hollywood movie set.

Pickled raw herring and amuse-bouche were served to accompany our drinks. Elga showed us how to eat the delicacy. She picked up a whole fish, sucked the flesh straight off the bone, and with the nonchalance of a courtesan, threw its head, tail, and skeleton over her shoulder into the water, shouting, 'Now swim.'

She asked me if I wanted to try some. I declined.

Hank had taken ten years to build *Albatross*, working in the evening as a DJ in a nightclub and boat-building during the day while his wife Elga managed a travel agency. They owned a warehouse apartment in Amsterdam by the canal and a mooring berth just below their place, giving them a seagull's eye view of their beloved *Albatross*.

After much merriment and frivolous banter, Hank said: 'Let's get down to business. Peter, how about you becoming the skipper navigator on *Albatross*?'

I was gobsmacked. I highlighted my limited skills, but it fell on deaf ears. Was Hank mistaking my concern for English modesty?

'You'll do fine,' he insisted. 'However, I can't pay you, but I'll cover your food and expenses.'

'Well, yes,' I replied, picturing myself at the helm of a sixty-foot trimaran.

'I assume you'll want to take your boat back to England first. My wife works for a travel agency. We can send you a ticket to fly you back to Holland. Once you join *Albatross*, you'll be the skipper and navigator, all the way to the Canary Islands.'

'Great,' I said. 'Where do I sign?'

He smiled mischievously. 'It'll be *Albatross's* maiden voyage. Up till now, we've only motored her on the Haslemere.'

Hank asked Bruce if he would like to join the boat as a crew. I was relieved when he said he needed to earn money before his next term at university. As for me, I had already taken unpaid leave for my trip to Holland. I didn't enjoy my job at the engineering firm, so I had nothing to lose. I was game to skipper this *dodo* to the Canary Islands, and I couldn't wait. This new command was the challenge I had been hoping for.

'Morning, Pete,' my boss chirped as I walked into the workshop a week later. 'How was your trip? You've obviously found your way back to Scarborough!'

I grinned at him, looking smug. 'Oh, great time,' I answered, 'but there's something I'd like to talk to you about.'

'What is it?'

'While I was in Holland, a chap asked me to skipper his sixty-foot trimaran to the Canaries.'

'When is the boat leaving?'

Surprised at his reaction, I said quickly, 'The end of the month.'

'I suppose you'll be wanting to give me a week's notice from now to get ready?'

The smile on his face confirmed that he approved of me seizing the chance. So, I replied, 'Yes please,' with a cheesy grin, thankful to him for being so accommodating.

A week later, a letter arrived from Holland. I opened it in anticipation and found a flight ticket. *So this is it; it's happening!* I felt a pang in my stomach. *Am I really up to the job as the navigator? But I found Ijmuiden in the fog! Yeah, I think I can do this!*

2. The Flight of the Dodo

Most trimarans have a light unballasted central hull and two hydro-dynamic outer ones to keep the main hull sailing upright. In Hank's trimaran, there was a double bunk with a shower and toilet in each outer hull. The wheelhouse, spanning the three hulls, was located forward of the master's cabin. On the starboard side, leading from the wheelhouse, was the galley with two fridges, an ordinary domestic cooker, and a double sink. To port were other quarters, with twin berths, a communal toilet, and a shower area. The saloon had a large table supported by the mast, which passed through the deckhead. Finally, there was another twin cabin with a forward anchor locker. I doubted *Albatross* was much of a sailing yacht with all that weight.

Kick, a lanky blond with unruly hair had seen *Albatross* taking shape through the years and had asked Hank one day if he could be crew. With some experience in dinghy sailing, Kick was keen to progress. His friends Jopp and Ingrid also planned to join as crew in Dover later. So far, it was Kick and me on the good ship *Albatross*. Hank and Elga were to accompany us as far as Ostend. She wanted to sample the open sea but couldn't afford the time off work to make the whole trip. They had spent a year of weekends motoring up and down the Haslemere. Hank had no sailing experience, but he had confidence in me navigating his *dodo* to the Canary Islands. But did he really?

Hank threw a farewell party on the day of our departure. The only attraction missing was a brass band. Relations and friends waved and cheered us as we cast off until *Albatross* was just a dot on the horizon. The weather, however, was far from ideal when we headed into an awkward swell and poor visibility. Hank could have postponed our departure but didn't want to lose face after such an extravagant send-off. When a light breeze sprang up, we hoisted the sails. For Hank and

Elga, it would be their first time seeing *Albatross* under canvas. We wallowed upon a featureless sea under a battleship grey sky with the engine switched off. Despite being a *rookie* at sailing, I noticed that all sheeting points would need altering once we reached Ostend. I saw Elga looking disheartened. She had waited so long to experience *Albatross* under sail! I assured her that we could soon sort out the rigging arrangements. Then, with the lack of progress, I proposed we start the engine. CLUNG! came the response.

After Kick and I tracked down the problem to a faulty battery lead, the engine roared into life. Earlier on, the speedometer had stopped working, and I had to pacify Elga by gently suggesting it might be seaweed fouling it. However, all looked promising, watching *Albatross's* foaming bow wave and turbulent wake. At a guess, she must have been doing eight to nine knots, but why were the two seaward buoys on our chart still out of sight? Then, when we switched the radar on to check our position, there were no blips on the screen. By the time we reached Ostend, the to-do list on *Albatross* wasn't going to fit on an A4 sheet. Finally, when we sighted the navigation buoys, I calculated that our speed was a disappointing four and a half knots when the consensus had been nine.

Hank was proud to be the sole designer, boat-builder, and owner of this palatial trimaran, but it appeared to me that he had designed his yacht on the back of a beer mat in a drunken stupor. After all, a sailing vessel only needs sharp and blunt ends; in Hank's case, multiplied by three with two poles sticking up! I watched him at the wheel, battling hard to keep a brave face while Elga complained about the years they had spent scrimping and saving. As if this wasn't bad enough, being scolded by his wife in front of the crew, the boat, for some unknown reason, suddenly stopped responding to the helm. I saw the look of horror on his face as he spun the wheel to port, then to starboard, to no avail. Elga hadn't noticed anything. When she did, she started screaming and bawling at Hank hysterically. 'Take me back to Amsterdam. That's it! I'm finished with this floating disaster, and I'm through with you.'

Hank tried hard to calm her down while Kick and I checked the steering cable. A bottle screw in the system had become slack, and with the vibration, it had unscrewed itself and parted. Everyone sighed with relief when Hank finally resumed control of *Albatross*.

It was dark when we arrived at the quayside that we had left nine hours ago. The place was deserted and just as well. Before we had even made fast to the pier, Elga was already scrambling ashore. She stormed off, screaming at Hank that she was going back to her mother. He followed her, pleading like a condemned man asking for mercy.

Hank reappeared on the jetty the following day as Kick and I were sorting out the rigging. He asked me to come to his flat and seemed agitated, so I dropped what I was doing and followed him. He never spoke until we got to the apartment.

'Peter, there are people in England who specialise in multi-hulls,' he said as he entered the living room. 'Do you think they'd buy *Albatross*?'

'Hank, I don't think brokers work like that. They're in the business of selling boats, not buying them.'

'I've got to do something,' he cried. 'Elga wants a divorce.'

Out of desperation, Hank scribbled down a few numbers from the sailing magazines I had lent him and rang some brokers. As the telephone conversations progressed, I could see the furrows in his brow deepening. As he was getting nowhere, he soon abandoned the idea. Next, he turned to me and said: 'Maybe if you're willing to sail *Albatross* to the Canary Islands for me, and Elga and I were to use the boat as a floating holiday home, she might feel better about it all.'

I nodded in acknowledgement, hoping Hank had resigned himself to that. But when he leaned over the coffee table towards the sofa where I was sitting, he said in a low voice as if I should be the only one privy to hear his words, 'Peter, if by chance you happen to lose my boat, I'll make sure you get ten per cent of the insurance claim.'

Before I could fully take in what he was proposing, Hank explained, 'Here is the plan: with a life-raft ready, and shipping in the vicinity, you could set fire to *Albatross,* but firstly, you would need to open all the seacocks, ports and hatches to ensure she couldn't be recoverable after she sank. Once in the life-raft, you would fire a few flares and wait for rescue.

His words were like Guy Fawkes asking me to light the fuse under the Houses of Parliament. I was horrified at such a foul plan, but I gave him the benefit of the doubt. It was the talk of a desperate man, and surely he didn't mean it?

'Hank,' I said, 'This will be my first command, and I'm not prepared to lose it. I'll take *Albatross* to the Canary Islands for you if you still want me to.'

Hank didn't seem the least embarrassed with what he had just asked me to do. He went to get a pen and paper and started to write an authorisation for me to skipper the yacht to the Canary Islands on his behalf, dated 28 July 1975. To validate the document, he took my passport details. With my lack of experience and all that had gone wrong, Hank may have thought I would lose *Albatross* anyway! But, as she was over-insured, my inexperience could be his way out.

Despite his despair, I felt confident I could achieve my mission. It would look good on my

CV to deliver a sixty-foot trimaran from Holland to the Canary Islands. Though dodos could never fly, maybe, with imagination, a hippopotamus with a tutu could be taught to dance. I might get *Albatross* to flap her wings and drift on the ocean current to the Canaries, after all!

When I returned to *Albatross,* I explained to Kick that each crew member joining the boat would have to pay into the food kitty. I also pointed out that I wasn't prepared to sail to a schedule. Yacht and crew would remain in harbour or at anchor during unfavourable weather. I thought it wise, whenever possible, to only sail in fair winds. *Albatross* had no self-steering gear, which meant the crew would have to hand-steer the whole time. So far, there was only Kick and me. He had been in touch with his friend Jopp who confirmed he and his wife Ingrid would be joining us in Dover later on. Then to our surprise, Hank decided to accompany us across the Channel. Kick, and I wondered why. Hadn't he told us he couldn't afford the time?

As we slipped the ropes from Amsterdam in the early morning, no one was standing on the quayside wishing us farewell - not even Hank's wife waving a handkerchief. While Hank looked subdued, Kick and I were just like two kids going to the funfair for the first time; both determined to try all the rides.

During the night, the weather started to deteriorate. With the forecast predicting a westerly force 6 to 7 imminently, we made a dash for Ostend. While we waited for better sailing conditions, the crew did some painting on deck. Kick and I giggled as we slapped the paint around like two circus clowns, getting as much on ourselves as the boat. When Kick noticed two girls walking past with backpacks, smiling at our antics, he hailed them and invited the girls aboard. They were American students visiting Europe on a three-week railway ticket. Over coffee, Kick asked if they fancied sailing with us to the Canary Islands. 'We'll go away and think about it,' the girls said. Later, one of them returned alone. 'My friend wants to carry on doing Europe,' she explained. 'We still have seven days left on our tickets, but I'm okay with that. I'd like to come with you.' Sam became our third crew member. Dressed in an oversize shirt and jeans, she seemed like a real tomboy. I thought yellow wellies wouldn't look out of place on her.

We left Ostend the following day. Hank was happy at the wheel, wearing his captain's hat, dishing out orders, 'Get me a coffee, make me a sandwich.'

He went quiet when he saw a supertanker bearing down on us. The ship must have been less than half a mile away. I noticed he was nervous and unsure of what to do next. Despite our inexperience, Kick and I knew more about sailing than he did. We looked at each other as a certain understanding bonded us without the use of words. Hank had been playing the 'know it all' ever since Sam joined the crew, ordering Kick and me like galley slaves. Didn't he realise that press-ganging of British seamen ended after the Napoleonic Wars!

Observing Hank and the horizontal skyscraper of a ship fast approaching, I noticed the perspiration on his forehead, like the sweat of an old metal box of dynamite about to explode. He looked at me, then Kick, expecting one of us might suggest what to do. But whenever we advised Hank about anything, he always answered, 'I know, you don't have to tell me, I was just about to do that.'

The ship was getting closer. Kick and I still said nothing, but we wondered what Hank had in mind when suddenly, he screamed out, 'What do I do next?'

In response to his plea, I shouted back, 'Don't panic, Don't panic!' And taking up the role of the butcher, *Lance-Corporal Jones in Dad's Army*, I started running from one side of the wheelhouse to the other, waving my arms in the air. Kick joined in, screaming, 'Don't panic, Don't panic!' in an exaggerated Dutch accent. Finally, Hank hollered, 'What do I do now, you bloody comedians?'

With the tanker's bow looming over *Albatross,* we stopped the charade. Then I said, 'With the tanker on our starboard bow, the vessel has right of way.'

'But power gives way to sail,' Hank retorted.

'Not when a vessel is restricted to a channel,' I answered. 'While we're motor-sailing, the tanker isn't obliged to give way. So I'd suggest you spin the wheel hard to starboard and please stop arguing.'

Hank quickly threw the wheel over, and the sixty-foot *dodo* painfully bore away to starboard, leaving the tanker to pass us at a safe distance before we resumed our course behind its stern.

Hank sulked for hours after that, but he handed me the wheel and, metaphorically speaking, the skipper's hat.

When we arrived in Dover, he went off to buy a ferry ticket home to Holland. Later, I asked him about expenses for charts and fuel. I anticipated more motoring than sailing with *dodo's* stubby wings and sizeable body. Hank took out his wallet and emptied its contents onto the chart table. He had a few guilders, which he quickly retrieved and left us with just enough English pounds to buy a few charts and a tank full of diesel. Kick and I looked at each other. 'Sorry guys,' Hank said. 'I'm broke - that's all I've got but I'll go straight back to DJ-ing and as soon as I've put some money aside, I'll send it on to you.'

Kick shrugged his shoulders, inferring we either take it or leave it.

'Okay,' I said. 'This should get us across Biscay. I'll keep all the receipts of what I spend for you to reimburse me later.'

Hank nodded. Having a sixty-foot trimaran to play with would be a learning curve. How exciting! Money was no longer my goal. Had it still been the case, I would have stayed in Scarborough to extract the maximum out of the divorce settlement. At least my mother recouped the money she had offered Elisabeth and me as a wedding present for the deposit on our bungalow. She did say: 'I don't want that woman to get away with a single penny of mine.' I was surprised by my mother's generosity in the first place. As for Elisabeth, had she known what her estranged husband was up to, she would have taken out a life insurance premium on me or asked Ladbrokes what the odds might be on reaching the Canary Islands with such a *dodo*.

3. The Uptown Girl

It had all started so innocently, giving the tall, blonde, smartly dressed young woman walking along the pavement a quick beep on my way to work each morning. Then, after a few days, she started to respond. We waved at each other for another fortnight until I was late for work one day. By then, she had already reached the bus stop. *What's the difference between ten or twenty minutes for being in trouble with the office manager.* So I stopped and timidly asked the stunning woman for a date.

She said, 'YES,' enthusiastically. I must admit this took me by surprise. I was only driving a modest cream Morris 1000, although it stood out with its two red stripes down the middle, bumper to bumper.

Was the woman into cars? Maybe she thought going out with a boy racer might be fun, while I felt like the downtown guy asking to date an uptown girl. We arranged where and when to meet before I drove off. I wondered what had prompted this beautiful stranger to wave back at me in the first place?

From our first date, Elisabeth and I believed we were in a serious relationship. However, we parted a few times during the eight years of our courtship. She didn't like competing with anyone, let alone the Mallock U2 I had built myself and was busy racing. So working away from home some of the time did little to help our relationship. But, stunning as she was and owning a sports car, she soon found other suitors.

One night, as I was completing an order (I had moved from widening wheels to manufacturing one-penny slot machines for the amusement industry), I heard a car rolling down the gravel path. I didn't expect my partner John or the two apprentices back to the workshop that night. I was surprised 'Blackie' hadn't barked, being a guard dog. Who could it be at this ungodly hour? Had I upset someone who was sending a henchman to sort me out? I strode towards the door and opened it with a jerk. Elisabeth was standing outside, her raincoat collar almost covering her face.

'What are you doing here?' I asked, startled.

'I'm pleased I've caught you,' she sighed. 'We need to talk.'

I wondered what the urgency was and felt a sense of dread.

'I don't know how to put this, but I'm pregnant. I don't know whether it's yours or Michael's.'

'How long have you been expecting?' I blurted out, stunned.

'Nearly three months!'

'But Elisabeth, we've been parted for six months!'

'Oh, is it as long as that? It must be Michael's then.'

How could she be so casual?

'I want an abortion and have already found a clinic in London.'

'Do your parents know?'

'No, I'll tell them I'm going to a hearing aid lecture through the hospital. I don't want my employers to know either.'

'This will be expensive. Is Michael footing the bill?'

'No, he doesn't know I'm pregnant. I don't want him to. We've already split up.'

I knew Michael. His parents owned a hotel in Scarborough.

'How are you going to pay for the abortion in a private clinic?' I asked, wondering if she had come to borrow money.

'A wealthy patient gave me a diamond ring as a generous gesture for my time with her. I sold it and got six hundred pounds for it.'

'Then how can I help?'

'I was hoping you'd say that. I'd like you to drive me down to London. I'll need to see two psychiatrists before booking the clinic. There's no one else I can turn to or trust.'

We drove down to London in Elisabeth's MG Midget sports car a few days later. The first psychiatrist's surgery was in Swiss Cottage. She went in alone while I stayed in the car. Although she was early for her appointment, it only took a few minutes for the psychiatrist to assess her mental state. I'm not sure whether she saw a consultant. I never asked. The other address was

Harley Street, which wasn't the place one expected to find a corrupt psychiatrist. When she returned to the car, I asked how it went. 'All the questions were loaded,' she replied. 'I just had to say yes or no.'

Armed with two medical documents that cost one hundred pounds, Elisabeth was granted a legitimate abortion in a private clinic of her choice. She made the appointment at one in Berkeley Square, and I wondered if the Rolls we saw parked outside belonged to the surgeon who would perform the operation. The booking was for the following week. I drove her down to the clinic in London on Monday and arranged to pick her up the following Thursday.

On Tuesday, I decided to leave my workload to go and visit her. I imagined she would be lonely and in need of support after surgery. Besides I still cared a great deal about her. I had bought some flowers and felt nervous when I walked into her private suite.

I found her looking desperately pale. Her eyes were dark and sunken. She smiled hesitantly, and her voice quivered when she thanked me for the roses. I kissed her on the cheek and then came to sit on the edge of her bed. I asked the usual questions, choosing my words carefully to spare her any further distress. Then, all of a sudden, she grabbed my hand with such insistence that I wasn't sure I wanted to hear what she was about to say. 'Peter, I want us to get married,' she announced with pleading eyes.

This announcement took the wind out of my sails. How could Elisabeth propose at such a traumatic time? I had no idea how to respond to such a plea and remained tongue-tied. The silence between us was deafening, and it seemed as if the clock by her bedside had stopped ticking. Elisabeth tightened her grip as if I was the only one in the world who could save her from falling into the abyss.

When I replied, 'Okay, we'll talk about it later,' my words felt like those of another person. In the past, Elisabeth had given me three or four ultimatums; either we get engaged, or we split up. So when I answered, 'I'm not ready to settle down,' we would break up.

On my journey back to Scarborough, I tried to understand what had happened that afternoon and couldn't come up with anything logical as to why I shouldn't marry Elisabeth. Was our sexual attraction enough to make a good marriage? Were we meant to be together? Then I thought of the advice millionaire Del Cooper had given me some time ago about marriage.

Del was a 5' 8" sixty-year-old who still had the allure of the prizefighter he used to be at the travelling fairs. When he was young, he boasted, he could take on two opponents in the ring simultaneously, knocking them both out, no matter how big they were. Although Del couldn't read or write, he owned an amusement arcade on Scarborough seafront. Every year he organised Scarborough Fair, and Elisabeth helped him with his correspondence. Fairground travellers usually wrote their requests for a pitch on the back of a sugar packet or a toothpaste box. Elisabeth never asked to be paid for her work. She didn't need to. Del was extremely generous, particularly at Christmas and birthdays. One day, he invited us to York Races, where we sat in his private box amongst all the gentry, eating caviar and drinking champagne. He even gave us pocket money to flutter on the horses.

Del had two sons and a daughter. I had met Alexandra and her friend Sue, a lovely brunette, at 'Two Bees' Night Club. I chatted Sue up, and we arranged to meet the following evening outside the Odeon Cinema at seven o'clock. At the time Elisabeth and I had parted once again. As I couldn't make our date and knew Sue wasn't on the phone, I called Alexandra at her home, hoping she could pass on my message to her.

Del answered the telephone. 'Who is it?' he asked gruffly.

I gave my name and told him I wanted to speak to Alexandra.

'She's not in,' he answered in a hoarse voice.

Undeterred, I rang again a few hours later. Del recognised my voice and said, 'I don't want a rake like you messing about with my daughter,' then he put the phone down on me.

Two days later, the door to my workshop suddenly flew open. Del strode in with a mighty crash, his face so red that had he been a traffic light, one would have hit the brakes. And he wasn't alone. On his tail was a gorilla of a man known as one of the local mafia henchmen.

'If you ever see this man with my daughter, break his arm,' Del yelled to his bodyguard.

'Shall I do it now, boss?' the brute barked, stepping towards me.

'No, not here,' Del shouted back.

My business partner John, a customer, and two chaps who rented some space in our workshop had conveniently disappeared, leaving me alone to deal with Del and his bodyguard. Although I felt intimidated, I still managed to pluck up the courage to face Del and explained that I had rung to ask his daughter to pass a message on to her friend Sue. My explanation infuriated him even more, and he started to remove his jacket, yelling out: 'You cheeky young whip. I'll sort you out myself right now.'

Luckily, the 6'6" Halloween nightmare pulled Del back and calmed him down.

'Don't bother with him, Boss,' the brute said, 'I'll sort him out later.' Then, turning at the door, Del shouted while wagging a finger at me, 'You've been warned to stay away from my little girl.'

The door crashed behind them; I heard the car revving up, then spinning wheels pebble-dashing the garage door as it tore off up the lane.

I had a friend who, at odd times, ran his antique business close to the line. I thought he might help me;

I didn't want the henchman to break my arms. So I told him what had happened and he put a name to him.

'Vince will never recognise you again,' he said. 'He isn't that smart. I must admit I wouldn't mess with him though. His nickname in certain quarters is the "Axe Man." When people owe money to the mafia and don't pay, Vince goes round and smashes their places up with his axe and anybody getting in his way.'

His explanation did nothing to pacify me.

'Okay Pete, there're two things you can do. I know some heavies in Leeds, who for the right money will put the willies up Del and even deal with Vince!'

I didn't like the sound of that.

'Alternatively, you can go to a magistrate's court and get Del bound over for threatening behaviour.'

I preferred the second option by far and quickly hatched a plan in my head. Later, I was in the police station, asking how to get someone bound over.

The desk sergeant asked, 'who is it?'

'Del Cooper,' I said.

One of the CID officers hovering in the background must have heard the name when he barged in.

'I'll deal with this,' he said to the desk sergeant, then motioned me to follow him down the corridor. 'Now, what's this all about?'

I told him about Del and Vince's visit to my workshop.

'Del wouldn't do such a thing!'

The officer's response was just what I had hoped for, and I felt sure this would get back to Del. Undeterred, I asked, 'Can you tell me how I can get someone bound over?'

'You've got to make an application to the magistrate.' I wouldn't be so hasty. I know Del, he isn't that kind of a person!'

I was surprised how quickly word reached Del. He called at the workshop the next day. He looked sheepish when he asked me to step out into the car park for a quiet word.

His demeanour seemed almost paternal.

'Look, son,' he said. 'It was all a mistake. There's no need to bother about this *binding over stuff*. Let's shake hands and forget what happened the other day.'

I sighed with relief and shook his hand.

'By the way,' he announced, 'I've got some engineering work for you in a couple of weeks.' His voice softened when he said, 'why don't you stop chasing money and women. Wealth isn't everything; it can split up a relationship. You might buy a big fast car, chase women, get drugged up, and then you're killed in a car crash, and that's the end of it!'

I thought, what a strange logic coming from a millionaire! Finally, he put his hand on my shoulder and declared, 'Elisabeth is a lovely girl. You should marry her.'

It was a glorious afternoon when I drove down to London to pick Elisabeth up from the clinic. She was waiting for me in the lobby when I arrived.

'Do I look all right?' she asked after we kissed gently on the lips.

You're fine,' I replied, thinking how drawn her face was. 'If people comment, laugh and tell them you had a good time in London, drank too much, and suffered from a hangover. Elisabeth still hadn't told anyone about the abortion. She had been focused on the wedding, while I hadn't even thought through the prospect of getting married.

'We could speed matters up if we paid extra to have the wedding banns read for next Sunday,' Elisabeth said excitedly.

She had already written her invitation list, thought of which flowers to order, who the best man and bridesmaid would be, the dress to wear, and what kind of reception to have. The telephone must have been red hot for the past two days in her room at the clinic. It seemed I was being carried along by a relentless tide of emotions. And I didn't know whether I would sink or swim.

'Elisabeth and I are getting married!' I told my mother the following day.

'What on earth for?' she barked, turning her back on me to carry on preparing lunch for the visitors. Maybe my mother was right, judging by how I felt when I walked towards the altar on our wedding day. Elisabeth was such a high-flyer, eager to climb to the upper echelon! However, I had agreed to marry her and promised myself, no matter what, to make a success of our marriage.

Six years passed. Elisabeth and I were now the proud owners of a bungalow in Lebberston, a cottage and land with planning permission in Flixton, a TVR sports car, and a boat. In my early thirties, my life was getting closer to where I wanted it to go. Then one night, as Elisabeth and I were sitting on the Chesterfield sofa with soft evening light pouring through the lounge windows, she suddenly announced, 'I've got something to tell you.' I knew by the tone of her voice that this wasn't going to be good news. Was she ill, I wondered?

'When I mentioned I'd been visiting my mum or my friend Judith while you were building the TVR, I was, in fact, seeing Gerald.'

I had met him. Elisabeth was the chief technician at the Hearing Aid Department at the local hospital, and Gerald was an *'Ear, Nose and Throat'* surgeon.

We had dined at his house once. He and his wife Helena had seemed a happy family with their three boys.

'Gerald is leaving his wife, and we're going to live together,' Elisabeth declared.

I stood up, dumbfounded, unable to speak.

The only other hobby Elisabeth and I shared apart from cars was horse riding on a Sunday afternoon. Then, one day, Gerald asked if he could join us on a hack. So I said to Harry, the owner of the riding stables and an ex-jockey, 'Can you give Gerald a quiet horse? He hasn't ridden before.'

'I'm not a riding school,' he barked with an impish grin. 'All I'll say is to tell your chap to keep his feet firmly in the stirrups, grip tight with his knees, and old Bessie will do the rest.'

The hack left the bridle path for a tarmac road on a steep hill. Halfway down, I noticed Gerald wasn't with the group. Unfortunately, the leader was too far ahead to raise the alarm, so I rode back up the hill to look for Gerald.

As I came over the brow, I saw Bessie in the middle of the road, with Gerald hanging over her right side. He had his left foot trapped in the stirrup, and his head was inches away from the ground. I quickly tethered my horse to a tree and approached Bessie cautiously. If she spooked and bolted, Gerald's head would be caved in by her hooves. And if a car came whizzing around the corner, it would be goodbye, Gerald. So I spoke to Bessie gently until I held the rein firmly in my right hand. She shook her head and snorted, but thankfully didn't move. As for Gerald, he was stunned. I got hold of him and with my left hand, humped him back into the saddle like a sack of potatoes. After I untangled his foot from the stirrup, Gerald leapt from the horse and collapsed on the ground. The urge to get as far away as possible from the animal gave him the impetus to crawl onto the wayside. I took his horse off the road while he sat on the grass, burying his head in his hands. 'I've had enough of this animal,' he declared. 'I'm not riding a horse ever again.'

'All right. Give me your car keys, and I'll take Bessie back to the stables. If you see the group, tell them what happened.'

'Poor old Bessie had quite a lather on by the time we got back to the stables. I wanted her to know that she couldn't just throw her rider off whenever she felt like it. It was the most exhilarating ride I ever had! Later, I drove Gerald's car to him and rode my horse sedately back to the stables.

Not long after the event, Gerald invited me to play snooker at the Grand Hotel. Halfway through our third game, I thought he looked bored. Was it because I was winning?

Finally, after missing an easy shot, he laid down his cue on the table, then said, 'Come on, Pete,' with a twinkle in his eye and a mischievous smile. 'Let's go and find a couple of nurses. You must know where they hang out on a night, being a local lad?'

'I don't know,' I replied abruptly 'and to be honest, I'm not at all interested.' There was an awkward silence, and then as soon as we finished our drinks, we went our separate ways.

Gerald had suddenly re-entered my life in a way that I would never have suspected when Elisabeth admitted their affair together. How was I to react? I was too stunned to say anything.

My silence must have disconcerted her, and she started to yell, 'Don't you just stand there! Say something! Hit me, get angry.'

I was far too bewildered to find words while Elisabeth continued shouting and getting more and more hysterical. She was now striking at me, but I parried her blows. Then, when I grabbed her wrists, she kicked and screamed uncontrollably. I had to do something, so I slapped her face, and she backed off, shocked out of her manic rage.

After Elisabeth had simmered down, she said: 'I despise you because you're like my father, always giving in to me. When I was little, I'd be so naughty trying to provoke him into hitting me, but he never did, and I got my own way every time. Why didn't you hit me sometimes instead of giving in? Aren't you enraged?'

'I'm not, but I feel betrayed and disappointed. I guess I haven't been much of a husband to you these last two years. I've tried to set us up in a comfortable position, building a bungalow for us and putting a TVR together for you. My ultimate dream of building a boat and sailing away seems to frighten you. I know it's not what you really want to do.'

The memory of our little yacht *Scampi* suddenly flashed through my mind one time Elisabeth and I sailed to Filey Bay. The sea that day was flat calm, and I used the outboard engine. On our return, a breeze had picked up, nothing much really, so I thought this would be the perfect opportunity to try the sails for the first time. With the wind on the beam, our speed was still slow. As we headed for Scarborough Harbour entrance, I made a course change and adjusted the sheets. *Scampi* heeled over, only slightly; the breeze wouldn't have blown the salad off a picnic plate. Elisabeth screamed like a demented banshee, 'I want to get off.' Her unexpected behaviour made it difficult for me to control the boat as I was about to drop the sails before heading towards the harbour entrance. I feared Elisabeth might lose her balance and fall overboard in such hysterics. I couldn't reason with her, so I shouted at her and ordered her to go below deck, where she stayed until we had moored. It was the last time I ever sailed *Scampi* with her. She warned me: 'I'll never set foot on a boat again unless it is the QE2.' What chance had I to sail away with her?

Elisabeth's confession of infidelity left me numb. All I could do was gaze at our elegant room, which seemed to glare back at me with irony. Our relationship was now in tatters. I was depleted. 'If it is Gerald you want, I won't stand in your way,' I conceded.

All of a sudden, the mood between us changed. Minutes earlier, Elisabeth was attacking me, and now she had her arms around me, begging me to make love. Was I about to become the adulterer in Elisabeth and Gerald's relationship?

The next day, she rose from our bed and then packed a suitcase, announcing she would be back sometime for the rest of her belongings. Days later, she returned. We talked about divorce. She and Gerald were having difficulty finding a new home, so I offered to sell them the cottage at cost price, thinking it would be quicker to clear the second mortgage than wait for a buyer. I also wanted to help them stay together.

It took a year to conclude the sale. All that time, Elisabeth and Gerald had lived in the cottage rent-free. I had given her the furniture in the house on the understanding that I would get the agreed value in cash from the estate. Sadly, her lawyer was smarter than mine, and I lost out on that too.

I remember the day she arrived with the furniture van. They cleared the whole house except for one bed, the cooker and the fridge. It wasn't worth her while taking up the fully fitted carpets as well - otherwise, she might have done so. However, Elisabeth left one single ornament on the sill of the bay window. It was a music box that played a theme from *Love Story* while two lovers surrounded by doves revolved around each other. For some reason, I flicked the switch as I watched her drive off. I saw her look up, and she met my gaze before she disappeared from view, following the furniture van in the TVR. I remained at the window, looking out over the fields towards the Wolds, the music still tinkling away melancholically. I thought about the good times we had shared and the hardships we had overcome, my racing accident, the bankruptcy, and my near-death experience on the operating table. Then, as the spring on the clockwork music box ran down and the tune became a blur, a sudden wave of excitement overtook me. I was once again the captain at the helm and felt the wind of optimism fill my sails.

One evening, the sound of the telephone startled me. The ringing echoed eerily through the empty bungalow. I wasn't expecting anyone to call and dreaded what I might hear when I picked up the receiver. 'It's Gerald,' came the voice. 'Peter, we've got to meet and discuss something.'

'Gerald, we've nothing to talk about, and there is no point in us ever seeing each other again.'

'No, Peter, you don't understand,' Gerald insisted. 'You remember when Elisabeth went for a week's course in London some months ago?' He referred to a time when she and I were still living under the same roof. 'She had an affair with the lecturer and was unfaithful to us both.'

I withdrew the receiver from my ear, astounded at what Gerald had said and shouted to him, 'You must be joking,' before slamming it down. *Please, Lord, don't let him send her back*, I pleaded as I put my hands together in prayer. But this wasn't the end. A month later, a letter arrived through the post.

Dear Peter,
If you're as lonely as I am,
please give me a ring.
Helena

I didn't try to find out if this was another of Gerald's dirty tricks or a genuine plea from his wife when I tore the letter up. Poor Helena, she handled the affair very differently from me. In the past, Helena had overlooked her husband's indiscretions as long as the family kept together. This time, Gerald went too far, and she had no idea how to fight back. She suffered a mental breakdown, and Gerald had her committed to an asylum.

Elisabeth did call once again asking me to meet her at the cottage. She had something important to tell me. She was insistent.

I arrived on my bicycle after riding from Scarborough. Elisabeth greeted me with a peck on the cheek and invited me in. We both felt awkward. I followed her into the living room, and she asked me to take a seat, but I declined. I was uncomfortable and had no idea what to expect when Elisabeth said, 'Two days earlier, a wheel fell off the TVR for no apparent reason. It happened when I was turning a corner at slow speed on my way back home from a clinic in Pickering. Gerald is accusing you of sabotaging the TVR and wants to report you to the police.'

'Surely, he's not serious,' I protested. 'I've no idea where the clinic is and which day you work there. Don't you think Gerald has caused enough damage in my life already, and now he is accusing me of attempted murder? Is it his way to make me the villain in our divorce?'

'I never thought for a moment that it had anything to do with you,' Elisabeth said plaintively. 'Gerald wants me to give you the TVR back. He's unhappy arriving at the hospital in his Volkswagen Beetle and me in the TVR.'

After that unwelcome meeting, I never saw or spoke to Elisabeth again.

4. The Eyes of Suspicion

'There's a swimmer in the water,' Sam cried out from the wheelhouse.

'Give a touch of reverse,' I shouted. 'We don't want to run him over.'

Kick looked in the direction I was pointing and yelled out, 'It's my friend Jopp!'

'Bloody Hell,' I said, 'Swimming across the Channel is one thing, but all the way from Holland raises the bar!'

I re-dropped the anchor and waited until Jopp had swum to the bow. From there, he climbed up the anchor chain like a marauding pirate. But he didn't have a *bandana* or a knife in his teeth!

'Didn't you receive my letter telling you Ingrid and I would be two days late?' Jopp asked Kick once he had regained his breath. 'I sent it *poste restante,* Dover.'

'Sorry, I never got it,' Kick replied.

'When we came in on the ferry and saw *Albatross* anchored in the harbour, I had no way of contacting you. So, Ingrid and I walked along the beach just beyond the ferry terminal. We were opposite the boat when I saw Peter pulling the anchor chain up. There was no alternative but to drop the suitcases, strip down to my underpants and run into the water, leaving Ingrid behind amongst the holidaymakers.'

Kick and I fell about laughing, imagining what people must have thought about the poor woman abandoned on the beach as she watched her man dive into the water. We launched the dinghy to go and pick up the forlorn Ingrid, still chuckling while the crowd continued enjoying the aquatic pantomime.

The following day, we set sail along the south coast. As I took my early watch, I prayed it would all go well. Being the skipper, I was responsible for everything that happened on the boat - what a big learning curve.

The crew were sound asleep when I tacked to clear a headland. There wasn't much wind, and the sea was relatively calm. Then as I put the wheel over to bear off from the rocky shore, *Albatross,* to my horror, started to sail in reverse as if possessed by a mind of her own. I yelled through the hatchway for Kick to hurry up on deck. I needed him to handle the headsail for me to complete the tack and, in so doing, stop *dodo* from being the first yacht ever to run aground backwards under full sail! *Albatross* certainly wasn't the boat for a single-handed sailor. We needed to find more crew members. So every time we stopped in some anchorage or harbour on the way, we invited people aboard for a party. Then, Kick and I would try to press-gang them into joining the good ship *Albatross.* We adopted the same tack in Plymouth. By then, poor Ingrid had had enough. Maybe Jopp realised his mistake. She suffered badly from seasickness and didn't really like sailing, so she decided to go back to Holland, leaving Jopp to continue the trip.

Two days later, we dropped Ingrid ashore in the dinghy, then Kick, Jopp, Sam, and I went to buy some beers from an off-licence. All we needed now was to find some fun-loving revellers. Being the most extrovert among us, Kick stopped two young women walking along the waterfront. 'We're having a party on our boat anchored just off the quay,' he yelled out. 'Come and join us!'

The women looked at each other, and before they could decide for themselves, Kick said, 'Don't you ever do anything on impulse in life? You might turn into boring old maids!'

'No, we aren't old maids,' the dark-haired woman replied boldly. 'And YES, we can be spontaneous. By the way, I'm Stella, and this is Susan.'

Stella had a sophisticated 'girl about town' look, unlike her friend who epitomised an off-duty member of the Salvation Army personnel in civvy clothes, which turned out to be what she was!

She appeared reluctant to accept the invitation on *Albatross*. But, eventually, she gave in. Kick could be very persuasive.

The six of us huddled together in our inflatable dinghy, only designed for a maximum of four people. On the way, Stella and Susan screamed and giggled with each wavelet splashing over the gunwales. Everybody had wet feet and soggy bottoms by the time we reached *Albatross*. Then we sat on the foredeck and drank beer. Kick began reciting The Ancient Mariner rolling his 'R's' like a Scotsman. We laughed so much that it hurt. Kick told the girls how we had all come together on this trip to the Canary Islands and how thrilling it was.

'Sounds fantastic, just taking off like that,' Stella remarked.

'It's gonna be an adventure of a lifetime,' Kick heralded. 'You shouldn't miss it!'

I looked at Stella and said, 'Why don't you come with us?'

'Are you serious?'

'Of course.'

'I work in a hairdressing salon at a department store in town, and if you come and see me tomorrow morning, I'll give you my answer.'

After the party, Kick rowed our guests ashore. I stayed behind tidying up, feeling excited about sharing my cabin with the gorgeous Stella.

The next day, I set off to go and see her. The hairdresser was located on the fourth floor of a large building. I took the lift up and walked across the smartly carpeted flooring to the salon. At the reception, I asked for Stella. She arrived shortly after. 'Could you wait until I have finished with a client?' she said.

With a polite but authoritative voice, she ordered the receptionist to make me a coffee. I thought this coquettish lady wouldn't give up her job running the salon for a trip on a boat with a bunch of buccaneers!

Stella returned before I had time to finish my coffee. 'Let's walk around the store and talk for a minute,' she suggested. As we strolled between the expensively priced furnishings, I wondered if I was in for a soft let-down?

'I've been to the doctor, got some jabs, given my notice in, and will be updating my passport tomorrow. So I'll be ready to leave the following day,' Stella announced.

I was speechless and only managed to splutter out, 'G-r-e-a-t.' When I regained my composure, I said cautiously, 'There might be a problem; the skipper's cabin only has a double berth.'

'I guessed as much, but as long as we take it slowly, she muttered, blushing.

Plymouth was our jumping-off point across the Bay of Biscay to Cape Finisterre. The weather seemed ideal to set off. Kick went ashore for some last-minute shopping. When he returned, he said, 'Would you believe it, I've bumped into a fellow Dutchman who has only just arrived on a catamaran after crewing across the Atlantic. He fancies joining us. His experience might be useful.'

'Is he willing to put money in the food kitty?' I asked.

'Yeah, sure.' Kick replied.

'Maybe we should meet him in the pub when we have our last drink ashore tonight,' I suggested.

'Then everybody can decide if we want him along.'

Max became our sixth crew member. He seemed to fit in well, although we all thought his stories seemed exaggerated. He told us his sister had married an Israeli man. He visited her in Israel just as the Six-Day War with Egypt broke out in 1967. Whilst there, Max decided to join the Israeli Army. One day, he found himself on the front line and trapped in an ambush. The vehicle somersaulted and threw him out as he drove his jeep over a landmine. Machine gun bullets and mortar shells were flying everywhere, blowing up several Israeli tanks while jet fighters rocketed into the enemy position all around him. The next thing Max knew, he was stretchered into the back of a field ambulance. He spent months in the hospital being treated for shell shock and shrapnel in his leg. He claimed to be suffering terrible nightmares. His long unkempt blond hair, haggard face, and scraggly beard didn't quite match the image of a young mercenary, but we were willing to grant him heroic status. Max also claimed to be a top mechanic and volunteered to service the engine and check out all mechanical equipment on board. He could squeeze easily into awkward places being skinny. Therefore, I was only too pleased to have his help.

We had a strong breeze just aft of the beam across the Bay of Biscay, which should have got our hippopotamus with a tutu dancing. But instead, she was only averaging four and a half knots of speed. It was a poor performance for a 60-foot yacht. She was sluggish and difficult to manoeuvre, wallowing on the ocean like a loaded sand barge. Then there was a problem with the crew and their unreliability in keeping an accurate log. I had caught Kick and Sam frolicking during one of their watches while *Albatross* sailed way off course. When I asked the pair how long the boat had been on that heading, they shrugged their shoulders. So I was more than relieved when I identified the flashing beam of Cabo Vilãin lighthouse after five days at sea.

While I sailed close to the towering cliffs during my watch, the sun was rising above the mountains. They looked menacing and awe-inspiring, with their tops backlit in gold and green sunlight while the cliff face remained in deep shadow. It was a pure indulgence to go over the time on my watch and catch the dawn, which is my favourite time of the day.

As I basked in the euphoria of the sweet smell of foreign land wafting down from the mountainsides and out to sea, I was jolted from my contemplative mood when a storm gust suddenly hit *Albatross* broadside on. The wind roaring in the rigging would have had the power to take the roof off a building. Under such impact, she heeled violently over to starboard. I thought *This is it. We are going to capsize.* I lost my footing and was thrown out of the open starboard door of the wheelhouse, then catapulted on top of the sheeting cleats of the mainsail and genoa, which stopped me from being cast overboard.

With no time to recover from the shock, I pulled myself up with the sheets, which immediately released them from their jam cleats all in one movement. This manoeuvre spilt the wind out of the sails and stopped *Albatross* from turning *turtle.* As she righted herself, her port hull hit the water with a thunderous thud, the spray reached halfway up the mast, and the wind cascaded it over the deck while the sails flogged like a huge sea dog shaking a rag. By then, Jopp and Kick were on deck in various states of undress, including Max, who was naked. Tossed out of his bunk in the port cabin, he had hit the deckhead as *Albatross* righted herself. Thinking that she was about to break up, he was ready to abandon ship. Then in no time, the four of us dropped the sails, and I started the engine.

What a hell of a morning wake-up call for the crew!

I didn't appreciate until then that the steep local topography could cause a *katabatic* force ten wind to funnel down from the mountains. To see the sun streaming down the valleys, cutting through the cliffs, felt like a gleam of salvation.

When *Albatross* rounded Cape Finisterre, we could just make out people clustering around the legendary lighthouse. I wondered if they were pilgrims who had walked *The St James' Way.* Their journey seemed in stark contrast with how we had sailed to the 'End of the World,' as it was believed to be in ancient times. I needed the past to heal and the adventure to test my courage. However, leaving the *Costa da Morte* could not come soon enough after our near-capsize.

And people think motor-racing is dangerous!

Kick was at the wheel when we motored into calmer waters, but it wasn't long before I noticed some disturbance ahead. I glanced at the chart, which indicated surface rocks at low tide, so I shouted 'rocks ahead' to Kick. Maybe he hadn't seen them; the genoa on the foredeck might have obscured his view beyond the bow. It was such a large bay to play with, but we had to find the one place with rocks just below the surface. The danger still lay ahead but we had enough time to alter our course. Then I noticed the puzzled look on Kick's face. *Albatross* was heading straight towards the rocks despite his desperate attempt to spin the wheel over to starboard to avoid them. Without a sign of panic, he quickly engaged the engine into reverse, and we halted short of the rocks.

What a narrow miss!

The crew settled down, thinking we were out of danger, but the respite was short-lived. The thrust of the propeller was now pushing us backwards in a big circle. Kick shifted the gear into neutral, but *Albatross* was still headed for the rocks in reverse. He tried the stop button for the engine as a last resort, but it powered on at full revs. So I scrambled to lift the floorboards, jumped down into the engine bay and pulled the lever on the fuel pump to starve the motor, which soon spluttered to a halt. Kick went to open the hatch to the steering linkage and found a broken cable that looked as if someone had deliberately weakened it with a hacksaw. He quickly fixed this with some bulldog clips. He glared at me suspiciously as he clambered out of the stern locker. With so much going wrong at once, did Kick believe me capable of foul play? Then, when I tried to start the engine, it didn't respond. There had been endless problems with the battery ever since we left Dover, and now it was dead as a *dodo*. Because *Albatross* sailed like a loaded sand barge, it took us well over two hours to tack into a safe anchorage off the village of Corcubión. By then, everyone had assembled on deck.

'This must be an act of sabotage,' Kick snarled, looking at me. 'Can you explain why the wires were disconnected out of the stop-solenoid on the dashboard? Then how come the split pin fell out of the gear linkage, not to mention the steering cable breaking.' I wished I hadn't told Kick about Hank offering me ten per cent of the boat insurance if I lost *Albatross*.

It was no use to protest my innocence; it would make me look guilty. I knew this only too well, being wrongly accused of something much worse in the past, which would haunt me for the rest of my life. I found myself thinking back to that fateful December day in 1962.

I was nineteen then and doing well, working as a salesman and driver, delivering bread from Scarborough to Hull. I bought an old MG Magnette sports saloon car and socialised with the sons of wealthy parents who owned their own vehicles. The drawback to the job was the five o'clock start, although I finished work between two and three o'clock in the afternoon after placing my order at the bakery for the next day. To enjoy some social life in the evening, I took a nap straight after work. Life was great until that dark foggy December morning.

I knew the road well across the Wolds to Hull and was used to driving in fog. Besides, the van could only do thirty-eight miles an hour at top speed, so there was no temptation for me to go faster at any time.

That day, as I negotiated a left-hand bend at a slow speed, I suddenly heard something loud hitting the side of my van. What on earth was that about? I stopped and quickly jumped out of the cab, leaving my vehicle by the grass verge on my side of the road. Although I had no idea what had smashed against the van, I sensed something awful had happened, judging by the impact.

I walked back along the road to go and investigate. At first, I couldn't see anything at all; then, in the heavy murk, deep in a ditch, I caught the dim glimmer of light on the opposite side of the road. My heart missed a beat. What was there?

As I approached, I saw a bicycle, then someone in a grey raincoat lying face down. Minutes ago, I was driving to my friendly customers, delivering bread, and now a man was lying by the side of the road. I froze to the spot and called out, but no sound came from my mouth. Was the man badly injured or dead? *My God, let this be a bad dream*, I cried aloud. I felt the dark dawn staring back at me in judgment, yet I couldn't bring myself to go and look where the man was lying.

Then, I heard the sound of a vehicle approaching which snapped me out of my confusion. I moved to the edge of the road, ready to wave the driver down. I heard him braking hard, and in the glow of his headlights, I could make out the outline of a bread van. I rushed to the cab door.

It was Dennis, a fellow salesman. I shouted to him that I had been in an accident and that someone might be seriously injured. He jumped out of his cab, and we both ran up to the edge of the ditch. By now, I was hysterical. 'Don't go there,' I begged him.'You can't help him. I think he's gone.'

Dennis didn't go and look. Instead, he told me to calm down, get back to my cab and put my indicators on. I should wait, he said, while he drove to the police station in the next village, half a mile away. I watched his rear lights disappear into the fog. For me, the end of the world had come.

I had no idea how long I remained by the roadside in total despair. Then I heard a siren and, as the patrol car drove nearer, I made a helpless gesture to the policeman in the direction of the cyclist. He parked his vehicle alongside mine and went to look in the ditch. Then he asked me to follow him to Beverley, five miles away. The ambulance arrived just as we drove off. I tagged along to the police station in a haze.

As soon as I arrived and parked my van, an officer ushered me into the interviewing room. At first, PC Watkins appeared sympathetic, but as questioning progressed, it became clear that he was keen to incriminate me. While he pressed on with more questions, I couldn't stop sobbing. Some of the theories I brought forward were self-condemning. I was so desperate to understand what had happened that I even suggested I might have fallen asleep or passed out. I explained I was driving with dipped headlights at the time as the main beam made it harder to see through the heavy fog. It was a relatively gentle bend; I indicated that the man could have been cutting the corner. He wouldn't have stood out against the bright reflecting posts on the opposite side in dark clothing and with a dim headlamp on his bike. I believed the cyclist was on my side of the road, and there was no way I would have seen him in time to avoid the collision.

PC Watkins offered me a cigarette. 'I don't smoke,' I said, thanking him for the gesture. 'It's a pity,' he replied. 'It would calm you down.' He lit himself one, then continued bombarding me with more questions. I wanted to ask about the cyclist, although deep in my heart, I knew the answer.

I must have been in the station for two or three hours when my supervisor Stan walked into the room. He put his arms around my shoulders and told me the cyclist had died. I broke down.

Then Stan left me, presumably to go and talk to the police. *Can there be life after this?* I wondered as I waited alone in the room for ages. Finally, when Stan returned, he explained that he had arranged with the police to accompany me to complete my bread round. He thought retaking the wheel would snap me out of my state of shock.

My legs were still shaking when Stan and I walked out of the police station. As we approached my vehicle, one of the officers shouted, 'You can have your van now. We've washed all the blood and brains off it.' His every word felt like another nail hammering into me, and despite his venom, I took the wheel, and Stan and I completed the delivery to my customers.

Meanwhile, the police had informed my employers of their intention to prosecute me for manslaughter or, at the very least, for causing death by dangerous driving. It would all depend on the evidence before the trial. As my company could be liable if I drove their vehicle and had another accident, they temporarily moved me to the bread-slicing machines in the bakery.

A few months passed before my case at York Assizes came up. I was to be tried by jury. My counsel had warned me that if the verdict went against me on the charge of dangerous driving causing death, I could be in prison for three to five years and banned from driving for life.

Until an officer called me to the witness stand, it all felt like I had nothing to do with the court case. It was primarily a battle between the bread company's barrister and the crown prosecutor, who seemed set to inflict the most severe charge against me. I wasn't from the Beverley area where the victim's family lived. They were known locally by the police, so it came as no surprise to see them taking their side. The more serious the charge against me, the greater the household would benefit from the insurance - providing the prosecution could prove that I was responsible for the accident. However, speeding had been ruled out as a cause.

The police had tested my van, which couldn't exceed 38mph. (The bakery's mechanics had fitted a speed governor function).

As I entered the witness box, everything went blurry until I could focus on the barrister, the crown prosecutor, and the judge. When the prosecutor proceeded with his interrogation, he asked in a condemning voice: 'Did you or did you not say to PC Watkins that you might have fallen asleep or passed out?'

'Yes, I did,' I replied with no hesitation. I remembered PC Watkins trying to catch me out at the first interview. Seeing the satisfied look on the prosecutor's face made me think that I had just signed myself to a five-year prison sentence. At this point, the prosecutor said, 'No further questions.' My barrister replied likewise.

When the judge rendered his summary of the evidence, he indicated to the jury that the whole affair had been an unfortunate accident with no conclusive proof to hold me responsible. He accused the prosecutor of using my statement as an admission of guilt by the incriminating way in which he had manipulated the question, 'Did you or did you not say to PC Watkins that you thought you might have fallen asleep or passed out?'

The prosecutor, addressing the jury in his final summary, seemed to base the case entirely on this assumption.

'The answer the accused gave isn't an admission of guilt,' the judge declared. 'The young man, in his heavy state of shock, was only putting forward a few plausible explanations for this fatal accident.'

The Court acknowledged the psychiatrist's statement, highlighting that it was not uncommon for a person to suffer a total memory loss following a tragic event. Forensics suggested that the cyclist had been on the driver's side of the road. The prosecutor couldn't find an answer and was desperate for one. While the Court took a recess, a policeman led me away to the holding cell. He would remain with me until the jury was ready to deliver their verdict. 'If they reach a quick decision,' the officer said, 'it's a good sign that things have gone in your favour.' After that, I could only hold my breath and pray.

A quarter of an hour later, a door opened at the top of the stairs, and an officer called out: 'The jury is coming back. Please bring the prisoner up.' The holding cell was in the courthouse basement. The several steps to the landing proved the hardest I had ever climbed. Was I heading to the gallows?

The policeman held my arm firmly as he guided me to the dock. The spectator gallery was packed. Had people come to see justice done or to watch a man about to be condemned?

When the jury resumed their seats, I felt my heart about to jump out of my chest. Then the judge asked: 'Have you reached a verdict?'

The jury's spokesman stood up and announced, 'We have'.

The Court remained cruelly silent. I felt the ground about to collapse under my feet, waiting for my fate to be revealed. Then I heard, 'NOT GUILTY,' echoing loud and clear around the courtroom. The words carried such an electric charge through my whole being that I had to grasp the side of the dock for support. I repeated, 'NOT GUILTY' several times in disbelief.

When I looked at the public gallery, only my mother, Dennis, and Stan seemed happy with the outcome. When permitted to step down, I quickly joined them, forgetting everyone else around me. We left the courthouse and hurried back to the car park. As I unlocked my car door, I confessed that there had been moments when I doubted I would drive back to Scarborough at all that day. Dennis was adamant from the start that I wouldn't be found guilty. How easy it seemed to trick innocent people through clever prosecutors and, as a result, wrongly convict them. I was almost another casualty that day.

Some years later, working on the site of a malting factory, once again as an electrician's mate, one of the electricians sitting opposite me in the tea hut asked without prompting.

'You're Peter Newby, aren't you?' I nodded, trying desperately to place his face.

Everyone was staring at us. Why had the man asked this question? Whatever he had to say, I knew for sure by the sickening feeling in my stomach that I wouldn't like it.

'You must remember me,' he pointed out, 'I was in the public gallery at York Assizes.'

His words put me right back to the edge of the abyss.

He paused, then explained, 'The cyclist who died in the accident was my brother-in-law.'

I nodded in acknowledgement.

'He didn't earn much at the flour mill. The kids now all have bikes. There is a new extension on the house, and the family are taking proper holidays. At least some good came out of it,' he added, sensing my distress.

I thanked him for his consoling words. The chatter then resumed, leaving me alone to finish my tea. Was he the messenger who had come to help me bring closure to this tragedy? I was only just twenty years old, and no matter what, carrying this heavy burden through a lifetime would be heartbreaking; I knew that for sure.

The memories of the tragic accident had cruelly resurfaced when Kick accused me of sabotaging *Albatross*. The atmosphere was tense amongst the crew. I had made a big mistake telling Kick about Hank's devious offer if I lost his boat. The eyes of suspicion were now resting on me, and there was nothing I could do to prove my innocence unless we caught the saboteur red-handed. I had a hunch about who he might be. Meanwhile, we were all in grave danger.

5. At Gun Point

I thought the crew on *Albatross* might cast me adrift in mid-ocean like Captain Bligh. It had all come to the boil. I needed to clear my head and go ashore. Stella and I had a pile of washing waiting, likely to occupy us for a few hours. Getting away from the boat might lighten the mood for us all.

After landing ashore with the dinghy, we noticed a ramp leading to a paved square. From there, we walked to a fountain surrounded by a circular trough. Stella and I dipped our buckets in and scrubbed our load of clothes. Then a woman in a black scarf and shawl rushed out of the nearby houses. She lifted her arms in the air, indicating that we shouldn't use the fountain. She beckoned us to follow her to where we thought there might be a launderette with machines and dryers.

Instead, we saw a large concrete bath with a washboard effect moulded into the sloping sides. A stream entered from one end and exited the other. A few women were already hand-washing their laundry, sheltered from the hot sun by a corrugated roof.

Stella and I found a vacant slot and got stuck in. The women around us were giggling amongst themselves. Were they seeing a man doing his washing for the first time and admiring Stella for getting me to do so? Then, I noticed the woman next to me looking unimpressed with my technique. She grabbed my shirt with firm hands and set about knocking the hell out of it, rubbing it with her clenched fists on the concrete ribbing. *My shirt is going to be a rag by the time she finishes,* I lamented to myself. Fortunately, before long, the woman handed it back to me with an air that said, 'This is how it's done.'

After rinsing our clothes where the stream flowed into the concrete bath, we laid them on the nearby bushes to dry in the sun. Next, I needed to call Hank to keep him updated on our progress and ask for payment of my expenses so far. I found a public phone and got through to him.

As I told him we had crossed Biscay safely, I thought I could hear a tinge of disappointment in his voice. Maybe it was my imagination. I had bought parts and equipment, including a starter battery, that Hank had promised to reimburse me, and when I asked for funds, he just retorted, 'I haven't had the time to put some aside yet.'

'The crew might jump ship if I don't get more money from you,' I insisted.

My warning had the desired effect. Hank instantly changed his tune at the prospect of us abandoning *Albatross* and promised to arrange an express bank transfer within a few days.

In Finisterre village, we moored *Albatross* to a concrete jetty to fill our tanks and wash the deck down. As Kick, Jopp, and myself set to, we saw a man on the quayside raving in Spanish. No one could make out why he was so agitated and angry. Fortunately, a bystander came to the rescue. 'He's the local mayor,' the man explained in English. 'There's been a drought this summer, and water is being rationed. You're only allowed to fill up your tanks.'

'Tell him I'm sorry,' I replied.

The helpful man was Portuguese and spoke good English. He was intrigued by *Albatross* and impressed by her size, although he implied that she lacked elegance.

'Under sail, she's a hippopotamus dressed in a tutu,' I remarked.

He laughed. Then the conversation switched to the political situation in Portugal. As it was our next destination, I asked if he knew something about the *Carnation Revolution* we heard mentioned on the radio. 'It's all over now,' he said. 'Despite what the papers reported, there were hardly any shootings. You'll have no trouble. You'll be most welcome, especially if you go to Oporto where I live.'

As we sailed into the commercial port of Leixões, we headed for the local Yacht Club, where the man in Finisterre told us we would be welcome to use one of their mooring buoys. 'There is hot water to shower in the club,' he mentioned too. 'You'll need to light the gas boiler and there are matches on a ledge above it.' If only nautical pilot books could add such information to lighten up their alarming piloting instructions.

After everyone had showered, we all set off to find a bus stop to Oporto. Jopp, using his Portuguese phrasebook, asked a young man for directions. He answered him in English and then gave us a sightseeing tour of the city, showing us the best places to stock up for the next leg of our journey to Madeira. We had a coffee at a terrace on a busy street. The conversation inevitably turned to politics. We wondered how the *coup* in Portugal had come about in such a harsh regime. The young man described his village in the mountains close to the Spanish-Portuguese border. 'In the past,' he said, 'guards boasted about the number of notches on their rifle butts, which indicated how many of their own people they had shot trying to flee over to Spain without papers. At that time, many Portuguese wanted to emigrate to find a better life elsewhere. It was virtually impossible to obtain a passport unless, in the words of *Woody Guthrie,* you had *the do re mi*.'

Oporto proved a fascinating city with its old trams trundling through the cobbled streets. Some of the houses seemed to lean jauntily against one another to remain standing. The balconies, adorned with washing, looked as colourful as the painted façades. Every street in the old town was bustling with people and traders. On our way, we came across an old lady sitting on her doorstep. She had a board on her knees with such a large fish that its head and tail drooped over on either side. With a knife at the ready, she peddled portions to passers-by.

It was late afternoon when Stella and I returned to *Albatross*, just as a woman in a dinghy was coming alongside. The rower was a plain-looking brunette with shoulder-length hair and a fringe. She was wearing black shorts and a grey T-shirt, which accentuated her sad demeanour.

'Hello,' she said timidly. 'I'm crew on a German sailing yacht moored close by. You appeared such a happy bunch that I'm hoping to hitch a ride with you.' The woman explained she was unhappy with her skipper, marooned in Leixões, and looking for a way out. We invited her aboard for a drink, and she told us her story.

Linda had replied to an advertisement in a local paper shop in Falmouth, *'Crew wanted to sail to the Canaries.'* She answered the ad, excited at the prospect of an adventure. At the time, she was a cash-strapped student, unsure of what to do next and decided to embark on the German boat. 'The trip went well until we reached Portugal,' she explained. 'Then the skipper made his move. I liked him well enough as a friend and took him at his word that our relationship would remain purely platonic. If I could make a getaway with you,' she pleaded, 'I promise to arrange a money transfer from England to put into the kitty once *Albatross* is in harbour long enough.'

Jopp, with a twinkle in his eye, offered to support her until then, and we all agreed Linda should join the crew. She returned to the German boat to pack her few belongings. Later that day, we picked her up before the skipper returned from his shopping trip in Oporto. She would hide below deck until *Albatross* left the following day to avoid any nasty confrontation with him. Her note to the skipper was brief: *'Gone back to England. Sorry, Bye!'*

We had agreed to slip the club moorings after lunch. However, Stella and I had spent too long at the cathedral, missed the bus from Oporto, and were late. The crew had already eaten their lunch but had left ours in the oven. Everyone was keen to go, but I insisted we eat our meal quietly before setting off. After all, I was the skipper on the good ship *Albatross*.

'Could we at least get underway?' Kick asked eagerly. Linda's skipper had been asking boat owners at anchor if they had seen her, which explained why the crew wanted a hasty departure.

'Okay, if you think you can manage,' I conceded. 'Get on with it.'

Someone started the engine, and we heard a great deal of commotion on deck. Stella sensed something was wrong. She looked at me, puzzled at my elusive attitude. She might have been right, but I wanted to finish my meal. 'If the crew are in trouble, they should sort themselves out,' I barked. There had been crew insubordination, possibly through Kick's suspicion that I might still try to scuttle *Albatross*; therefore, I needed to re-assert my credibility as a skipper. I expected the crew would require my help sooner or later.

Next, we heard the engine coming to a halt, followed by a big splash. I guessed somebody had dived over the side to try and untangle a mooring rope from around the propeller. Then came the creaking of rope blocks and turning of winches. Was this childish game of mine backfiring on me, letting the crew handle *dodo*? I rushed on deck and saw Kick hoisting the sails.

'What the hell is going on?' I asked.

'I thought it would be more fun to sail out,' Kick said, red-faced.

At that, I blew up. 'You've got to be joking. You know what a pig this boat is to sail. We'll never make it out of the harbour entrance against the wind without hitting a wall or worse, other boats, and we'll never claw off a lee shore under sail alone.'

I started the engine, but before putting it into gear, Kick screamed: 'Don't do that, the prop shaft is damaged.' Then Jopp, dripping from head to toe, said, 'While I was cutting the rope away from the propellor, I noticed the support bracket on the shaft looked as if it had been pulled out of the hull.'

'I can't believe what you intended to do!' I yelled at them angrily. 'You're putting the boat and ourselves at risk. We're not sailing to Madeira until we've sorted this out. We'll find somewhere to beach and see if I can do repairs.'

Albatross was now drifting onto other boats, and I had no option but to put the engine into gear.

Then I heard a tapping noise like a demented metronome clicking every time the propeller went round. The noise worsened when I increased the revs, so I throttled back until the tempo was *largo,* and we crept out of the harbour at a very low speed. While Max took the wheel from me, I consulted the chart to see where we could beach *Albatross* safely. Luckily, the river to Oporto was only a few miles away. There was a shallow lagoon formed by a sandbar on the landward side. I thought this could be a safe place to protect us from the ocean swell. We limped through the river entrance at a slow walking pace as I dared not go faster for fear of the propeller coming through the bottom of our *dodo.* Once inside, all hands were on the bow, helping me with eyeball navigation into the lagoon.

It was close to high tide when we dropped anchor. A fisherman in a rowing boat was approaching. He had a weather-beaten face and seemed highly agitated, babbling in Portuguese and making gestures. We understood he was warning us of the danger of running aground. Jopp threw him a packet of cigarettes and said, *Obrigado.* The fisherman then rowed away. What was all that about?

It would be an hour before the tide receded enough for me to start work and for the damaged area to dry out. I could then do the repairs needed. As the boat was going nowhere, we all decided to go ashore and explore the surroundings. The seven of us behaved as if we were on a school trip visiting the seaside. We played at who could skim a stone across the water the most times, then raced each other along the deserted beach. There were no signs of habitation, not even a beach hut as far as the eye could see. With a knotted handkerchief on my head and trousers rolled above my knees, I showed the crew how to paddle *Yorkshire East Coast* style in the cold Atlantic Ocean.

When we returned to *Albatross*, the tide was out, but we were in for a surprise. Two soldiers with machine guns slung over their shoulders were gazing up at the boat, and there was a truck parked on the beach above the strandline. As the men heard us approach, they swung their guns off their shoulders and held them at the ready. Thankfully, they weren't aiming their weapons directly at us - at least not yet! Then an officer jumped out of the truck and marched towards us, pistol in hand pointing to the ground. Kick, always ready for a joke, put his hands in the air and shouted, 'Don't shoot, Don't shoot. I surrender!'

Luckily, the officer saw the funny side and even struggled to keep a straight face until he said in perfect English: 'You're illegally beached on military property. What are you doing here?'

'We've serious underwater damage,' I explained. 'We're here to carry out some emergency repairs. I'm the delivery skipper.'

'Regardless of your situation, you'll have to leave on the next tide,' the officer stated, 'and if you don't, the vessel will be impounded. Two of my men will stay here to ensure nobody goes ashore.'

Kick's jokes quickly ended when he realised the gravity of our predicament.

'This is what the old fisherman had tried to warn us about,' Jopp remarked. I could read the words on the girls' faces, 'What another fine mess you boys got us into.'

We paddled to *Albatross's* stern to assess the damage. I knew this was serious when I saw that the propeller P-bracket had pulled its bolts out through the hull, and water was dripping from the hole. And I was the only one with fibreglass experience.

Fortunately for us, Hank had left five gallons of resin and a roll of fibreglass matting aboard. I thought this might be enough to ensure a permanent repair, but I would have to work fast. The P-bracket was directly underneath where Stella and I slept. I was horrified when I lifted our mattress board and saw the seabed through a hole in the hull. One saving grace in Hank's design was that he had built many separate compartments in the main hull. Luckily, the area under our berth was the only place flooded and not the whole boat. There was a gas blowtorch on board, which I applied to the saturated area until it ran out of fuel. I prayed that the section would be dry enough for the resin to bond to the hull.

The officer, meanwhile, had driven off, leaving the two soldiers on guard. They were to remain on the beach until we floated the following morning. The crew invited them on the boat out of sympathy. With sign language and a phrasebook, we suggested they sleep in the saloon until daybreak. By then, we would hopefully be ready to exit the lagoon. One of the soldiers produced a bottle of spirit to thank us for our hospitality. I soon noticed that they preferred our beer. We all tried their well-intended gift. 'This stuff is like drinking bleach. It's almost pure alcohol, good for lighting barbecues!' Kick remarked.

After the damaged area had dried, I mixed the catalyst and resin. Then I propped the bracket in its correct position underneath the hull, reinforcing the complete section under our bunk with multiple layers of matting and resin. But I told Kick and Stella to drag me up on deck quickly if I should pass out because of the fumes. It was late by the time I finished. All we could do now was wait and see what happened once we floated. Whatever the outcome, we still had to move, 'hole or no hole'. Then we all turned in, including the two soldiers.

I awoke when I heard the boat stirring with the incoming tide. I got Stella up to check if my emergency repair under our bunk was watertight. Thankfully, it was holding up and feeling dry. Kick rowed two sleepy soldiers ashore just before daybreak. When he returned, I lifted anchor and gingerly motored out of the lagoon. The soldiers waved us farewell with their machine guns in the air, and it felt as if we were parting with old friends. Then, as we cleared the river entrance, Kick and Jopp hoisted sail, and I switched the engine off. I checked my repair once more and finding no water leaks, I set our course for Madeira.

6. Smoke over the Water

The crew had little to do but found much to say on the long haul to Madeira. And there was a burning question on everybody's lips. What had brought each of us together? Stella was the first person to volunteer. She had broken up with a possessive boyfriend and was tired of working as a manager at the hairdressing salon, seeing the same customers every week. She knew there was no prospect of further promotion for her and had nothing to lose when she took the snap decision to leave everything behind and embark on an adventure with us. On her return to Plymouth, she promised herself a fresh start.

Sam had travelled around Europe and was still at college in San Diego, studying biology. With a sparkle in her eyes, she said, 'I just fell for Kick; he's tall, slim, blond, outgoing and full of fun, and I thought it'd be neat to sail an ocean.'

Kick had dropped out of university. Over the years, he had seen *Albatross* taking shape, and as she came to near completion, he had asked Hank if he needed a crew. Kick's sole ambition was to sail his way around the world, then later, build a boat.

Jopp studied at the same university as Kick. He had a degree in Art and Design and was between jobs. Being mad about boats, he must have persuaded Ingrid, against her better judgment, to come sailing when Kick invited him. None of us knew if they had fallen out or whether Ingrid had been gracious enough to let Jopp fulfil his dream when she left *Albatross* in Plymouth. His relationship with Linda had now transcended beyond the platonic stage. After all, he had agreed to cover her share of the kitty and, as he pointed out when Linda joined the boat, the only berth available was in his twin cabin.

As for me, I was still feeling raw after my marriage break-up, disillusioned about the business world, and haunted by the cyclist's death.

Then there was Max. He no longer took his watches and had become a recluse. He went without food for days, and everyone tried hard to humour him, hoping he would snap out of his despondency. Even Kick, gregarious and full of fun, failed to bring him out. 'Leave me alone,' Max would say to him, 'I'm still suffering from shell-shock.' Had he been taking medication and suffering from withdrawal symptoms? Was he even capable of committing suicide? Everyone felt wary, expecting something awful to happen sooner or later, but nobody could put their finger on it!

For three days, we sailed on a beam reach. Even for a flightless bird, our progress was astonishing. Then the breeze died down, and our speed dropped, so we played at coaxing *dodo* into sailing faster. We stripped our beds with the warm morning sun and used the sheets as makeshift sails. Kick hoisted his shirt like a spinnaker whilst we all held on to our hats, pretending to feel the acceleration. Our endearing hippopotamus with a tutu looked more farcical than ever. We even laughed and joked when a supertanker crossed our bows. It was amazing to see the ship's forward section submerged as she crashed through the massive Atlantic swell. *Albatross,* meanwhile, glided over the waves as if she was a Rolls-Royce driving up and down the rolling South Downs at a stately pace.

As we made for Funchal, I homed in with my handheld radio direction finder on the airport aero-transmitter beacon, which had a range of three hundred and fifty miles. This beacon helped me navigate safely to a sheltered bay off a small village where we dropped anchor. Although mountains surrounded us with vineyards on the lower slopes, Funchal wasn't far from the place.

As provisions were getting low, we all went ashore except for Max, who stayed in his cabin.

We found a grocery store in the village square with a bar in the backroom. Customers could only access it through a door behind the counter. The inside was sparse, with just a table and two chairs, a few crates of beer, and a large wooden barrel. Unanimously, we opted for wine. The proprietor, portly and jovial, placed six glasses on the counter, which I thought could have done with a good clean. Then he filled a white enamel jug with blood-red wine from the barrel and topped our glasses up generously. When he brought a tray of sundry tapas, we tucked in with *gusto*. Using sign language and a few Portuguese words, we understood from him that the wine was produced locally. Being his only customers, the proprietor focused all his attention on us until a man of short stature joined us at the bar. He wore a brown suit with wide lapels, 1930s style, with a striped shirt and polka dot tie. His 'Al Capone' gangster trilby hat, half-covering his wrinkled face, made me wonder if he was a member of the local mafia? But the bizarreness of his demeanour didn't stop there. With his trousers rolled up above the knee, one could see his bare feet stained the same colour as the wine in our glasses. I was no longer sure about ordering more wine. His feet, bunions and all might have trodden last year's grapes that produced the wine we were drinking.

It was tempting to linger on the beautiful island of Madeira, but the longer one stays in a place, the harder it is to leave; sailors call it *harbour fever*. Before we lifted anchor, however, I promised Stella a visit to the Reid's Palace Hotel, featured in one of Dennis Wheatley's novels she had been burying her head in since she joined *Albatross*.

We had a long walk to the hotel, and when we reached its grand entrance, Stella suddenly decided she wasn't going inside. She was in a T-shirt, shorts, and flip-flops and felt far too underdressed for the grandiosity of the place. I was in shorts too. But I hadn't come all that way only to see the outside of such a famous location. So I walked through the foyer, then into the sumptuous dining room, all set for silver service. Although there were no diners, a waiter in uniform with a white linen napkin over his raised forearm was standing to attention at the far side. Sadly because of Stella's timidness, she missed seeing the celebrated setting of one of the scenes in the novel she was reading.

The wind was fair and warm when we set sail on our last leg of the journey to the Canary Islands. While Stella was at the helm in her yellow polka dot bikini, the rest of the crew were on the foredeck, basking in the sun. I took refuge at the stern, not feeling particularly companionable that morning. I felt melancholy watching the wake of the yacht on the water. I thought how different my life would have been if I had joined the Royal Navy. Unfortunately, it wasn't to be. I had a perforated eardrum through mastoiditis, which stopped me from pursuing this direction. Then I wondered what I would do after delivering *Albatross* to the Canary Islands. With the sea in my blood, I wanted to make it a way of life. Although I had no idea how to achieve this, I believed I would find a way.

As I pondered about future adventures, my reverie was abruptly interrupted when I heard Stella yell, 'I can smell smoke.' I ran to join her in the wheelhouse and shouted out to the others, 'Fire, Fire!'

The crew on the foredeck quickly tumbled into the main cabin. Black smoke was billowing out from under the door of Max's quarters. When Kick turned the handle, he found the door locked, so he banged his fists against it, screaming to Max to open up.

Max didn't reply. The acrid smoke thickened, and we could hear him coughing. Getting no answer from him, Kick aimed at shouldering the door, but Hank had made such a stout job of it that Kick immediately bounced off.

Desperate to contain the fire, I ordered everyone to stand back. I grabbed a fire extinguisher, using it as a battering ram and struck the door lock. My first attempt failed, but with the second, more desperate and forceful blow, the door splintered around it and burst open. Max's cabin was thick with smoke which almost made me choke. A sleeping bag was alight on the floor, and I saw

Max standing close by, trying to beat the flames out with a shirt. I pulled the safety pin out of the extinguisher and aimed at the fire. With a prolonged blast, I managed to quench it. Then when I felt the boat and crew were safe, I asked Max, 'What the hell has happened here?'

'I must have fallen asleep while smoking a cigarette,' he replied between coughing bouts. Then he pushed us aside and scrambled up on deck for fresh air. Was Max telling the truth when he said it was an accident, or had he tried to set *Albatross* alight? What about Kick? Perhaps he thought I had arranged with Max to split my share of the boat's insurance. If only I hadn't told him about Hank's offer.

When I got up the following day, it was a shock when I suddenly felt a stabbing pain in my intestines. I grabbed the wooden pole that supported the ceiling in my cabin and clutched it like the stick a surgeon would have put in a seaman's mouth before cutting a limb off at the Battle of Trafalgar. *Am I going to bleed to death? There is no blue light at sea to get me quickly to a hospital.* We were still more than a hundred miles from the nearest land. My memory drifted back to when I was rushed to Scarborough Hospital seven years earlier.

'Everything will be all right,' my mother said, trying to reassure me. But why was the ambulance doing 70 mph in a built-up area, sounding its siren? 'We're late for our tea break!' the paramedic said, jokingly, guessing that I would be alarmed.

After we got to the hospital, a nurse gave me a stomach pump, which felt as if she was pushing a fireman's hose down my throat. I asked why she was putting me through such torture. 'You can't eat anything if we operate on you this afternoon,' she explained. Nurses and doctors were flying around, looking concerned. They had already taken a blood sample, and I had a saline drip in my arm until a blood match could be found. Then they wheeled me into a general ward, claiming my condition had stabilised, whatever that meant. Finally, after several days of X-rays and being prodded and poked, they announced they would operate.

Ten days later, they removed my stitches, leaving a twelve-inch vertical scar across my stomach. They had found nothing abnormal and decided to send me home. Everyone thought, maybe it was just one of those things. After a week, I began eating solid food, and the bleeding returned. This time the doctor told my mother, who was staying at our bungalow, to call for an ambulance straight away.

It was back to endless probing and X-rays from every possible angle, held upside down, strapped to a table as the head of the X-ray machine was fixed. 'We don't have to do this very often,' the radiologist said.

I thought *just as well!*

Then the bleeding from my anus worsened, and I found myself with a drip in each arm to keep up with the loss of blood. I couldn't move and was only allowed an egg cup of water every hour. I watched the clock relentlessly, and if the nurse was late, I soon reminded her. It seemed the future didn't exist beyond the next cup of water. All my bodily functions happened in bed, and I found it most humiliating when the nurses had to clean me up. The only light relief came when the pretty trainee nurse put a screen around my bed. She gave me a thorough bed bath, telling me how she liked hairy men. I won't mention what part she was washing at the time.

What stopped me from feeling aroused was the lack of blood. I didn't have any spare to pump up *John Thomas!*

Whenever they brought a new supply of blood in, I couldn't resist asking the nurse if it was the right blood group and where it originated. 'I must admit you've depleted our local stock,' one of the nurses said. 'An ambulance is having to bring us more blood from other parts of the country.' I wondered how long this would go on. By then, my mental state had worsened after so many blood transfusions. I often broke into tears without provocation. Was this the beginning of the end? Before I became ill, I worked all hours as a foreman in an antiquated engineering workshop, paying my debts back.

One Sunday evening, I couldn't keep the egg cup of water down. Every time I retched, my whole body racked with pain even though I hadn't eaten anything solid for over ten days. Finally, someone called a nurse; she drew screens around me, which meant an emergency operation. Wheeled away for the second time, I was given the anaesthetic injection and asked to count. I tried hard to delay going through the operating theatre doors, thinking this could be my ultimate one-way trip.

Total emptiness, no light, nothing, just a complete void. Where is my body? I want to get back to my body, God or whoever is listening. I've only been chasing money and fast cars; surely this can't be what life is all about! In twenty-seven years, what have I achieved spiritually? Nothing! Please, God, grant me another chance. I want to experience a more fulfilling life. Let me get back to my body. I want to try again. I begged and begged as I sank deeper into the void.

When my eyes began to focus, the sun was filtering through the windows of the Graham Men's Surgical Ward. I felt the tubes up my nose and down my throat, and something inside my intestines. It was like an ache after too many abdominals at the gym. Then I heard a voice which seemed to echo from the other side of a mountain calling out, 'Mr. Newby.' As the sound drew nearer, I realised a nurse was standing next to my bed. 'It's all over, and you're going to be all right,' she whispered reassuringly.

Despite her comforting words, I remained frightened, wondering if I would live up to the promise I had made to God before re-entering my body. Then as soon as I could walk about the ward, the nurses asked me to help count up some of the patients' water-intake charts. I had been exceptionally good at mental arithmetic before the operation and could add figures faster than most people using a mechanical adding machine. I was now slow. When I mentioned it to the nurse, she said, 'You'll pick up soon.' Then she told me with a smile that I cost the NHS more than an arm full of blood.

It had taken forty-two pints of blood to keep me alive. Before my discharge, the surgeon visited me at the ward. 'I'm sorry we had to operate on you twice,' he said. 'I've never dealt with such a condition before, having to remove a non-malignant tumour the size of a pea. To locate it, I had to feel every bit of your thirty foot of intestines. The tumour had burst a blood vessel and caused a massive haemorrhage.'

Before the surgeon left me, he asked if he could submit my case to the medical journal *The Lancet.* Of course I was happy for him to do so. After all, he had saved my life.

And now, I was aboard *Albatross,* lying in my bunk, terrified that I could bleed to death. There wouldn't be a 999 on-call this time, and even if someone were listening on the emergency channel

16, what could they do to help. So all I could do was pray, *Please, God, don't let me die.* I thought of the crew and how shocked and horrified they would be at finding me. What an ordeal for them if they had to bury me at sea?

Meanwhile, I had left Kick and Jopp in charge. They took sun-sights throughout the day, teaching themselves celestial navigation while Max still confined himself to his cabin. From my quarters, I could hear them arguing about our present position.

Thankfully, I felt better, and the debilitating pain I had suffered disappeared altogether. There was no time to waste reasserting control of the good ship *Albatross.* Meanwhile, there had been disagreement between Kick and Jopp. They were two university graduates having trouble understanding the mathematics of celestial navigation. I knew I might struggle too. So I decided to stay with my long-wave portable radio and *Consal* paper chart. I was familiar with this method, although I suspected it would soon become obsolete with the advent of other navigation aids.

Tenerife's aero-beacon signals were not as powerful as those in Madeira. Still, I had the relevant chart that showed the positions of long-wave radio beacons along the Spanish and Portuguese coasts. The signal lines radiating from the beacons formed a latticework, and the morse code of dots and dashes gave me the converging lines and a position. All I needed were the correct paper chart and a long-wave radio receiver. It had moderate accuracy, and I held more faith in my method than Kick and Jopp's sextant work. Providing we kept to our present course and weather conditions remained the same, I estimated we were two days from the Island of Tenerife, which meant a discrepancy of one hundred miles between their reckoned position and mine.

Kick and Jopp suggested a course change to align with their estimation. I immediately overruled them, much to their disgruntlement. By now, everyone was on tenterhooks as we couldn't concur. It was two against one. I reminded the pair that I held the ultimate responsibility as the skipper. They had agreed to this when they joined *Albatross* - paid or unpaid! I thought of sea captains in bygone days. How did they feel, having to make unpopular decisions for their men? Would I become another Captain Bligh, threatening to hang the mutinous crew from the yardarm, only to be cast adrift in an open boat?

The following day, Sam, who had been keeping a watch for dolphins on the foredeck, suddenly yelled to us, 'I can see land.' This new sighting brought everybody on deck, but not all the crew seemed convinced it was land looming ahead. 'It's just an unusual cloud formation on the horizon,' Kick and Jopp declared.

'No, it's the top of Teide Mountain you can see above the cloud-line,' I pointed out. 'We're eighty miles from Los Cristianos in Tenerife, and the course I insisted on keeping is taking us straight to our intended destination.'

Kick and Jopp didn't like it. The awkwardness was like an elephant on board threatening to tip the boat over. Moreover, the pair failed to comprehend that one could see a mountain from that far away. Still unconvinced, they consulted the Reeds Nautical Almanac, where they came across a paragraph stating that, in the right conditions, mariners can recognise the snow-capped peak of Teide up to one hundred miles away.

The next day, the crew's spirits lifted when we approached the northern tip of Tenerife, and before nightfall, I dropped anchor in Los Cristianos. It was the beginning of October 1975. The journey from Holland had taken us almost two months.

The *dodo* had landed, or should I say, the hippopotamus with a tutu had performed her version of Swan Lake! So far, *Albatross* had escaped the evil swamp monster but hadn't turned into a beautiful swan. The two-thousand-mile aquatic pantomime had been played out, leaving the cast to decide what to do next.

As I was leaving *Albatross*, Kick rang Hank to ask if the remaining crew could take her around the islands while waiting for him and his wife to arrive. Hank insisted the boat stay in Los Cristianos until their arrival. Max, by then, had secretly jumped ship. He must have been afraid of Kick's cousin's letter arriving in Los Cristianos while he was still aboard.

Before we left Portugal, Kick had asked Max which place he was from in Holland. Kick said, 'I have a cousin there. I'll write to him about the coincidence of you both living in the same town.' Max looked uncomfortable at the time and had swiftly changed the subject. Then, when Kick checked his mail the day after we arrived in Los Cristianos, he found a letter. 'Guys, you've got to listen to this,' he said when he joined us on deck. His cousin was warning Kick about Max and hoped his letter would reach him before something terrible happened aboard *Albatross*.

Two of Max's girlfriends had died in car accidents after he did maintenance on their vehicles. Forensics had examined one of the cars and found the brake pipes partly sawn through. The police suspected Max of murder or, at the very least, manslaughter, but before they could prove him guilty, he fled the country. As for a sister living in Israel, it was all invented - Max was an only child. Kick apologised for suspecting me of being after the ten per cent of Hank's insurance payout.

Then, we each started to recollect incidents that inexorably linked Max to the misadventures. He was the swamp monster who had tried to turn us into dead swans.

‘Peter,’ Sam asked. ‘When you burst into Max’s cabin, was he trying to beat the flames out or fan them with his shirt?’

‘Fanning more like it!’ I said.

‘I suspect the cable to the rudder was cut when Max pretended to do maintenance on the steering gear and engine while crossing Biscay,’ Kick added.

‘I saw him messing about with the dashboard,’ Sam said. ‘Could that have caused other problems like the wires being pulled out of the stop button?’

‘And how about when *Albatross* went backwards and we couldn’t stop the engine because of the missing split pin in the linkage to the gearbox?’ Kick resumed. ‘My cousin has suggested that we had a psychopath with us.’

‘It seems we only survived because everybody reacted quickly to Max’s sabotage,’ Stella concluded. ‘No one would have guessed that behind Max’s haggard face, was a dangerous man.’

While they waited for Hank’s arrival, Kick and Jopp bought a fifty-five-foot trading schooner built in Scotland in 1903. They paid ninety pounds for the old yacht. At that price and with no engine, I don’t need to detail her condition. Kick thought that by adding a few patches to the old sails, they would easily make it to the West Indies. However, there were so many cracks in the deck one could see sunlight illuminating the leaking bilges. I hoped for their sake that it wouldn't rain on the way. Kick mentioned the yacht was only taking in two or three bucketfuls of water a day.

'The planks can open up when buffeted by the waves,' I warned him.

Nothing seemed to deter Kick's enthusiasm, even after telling him about all the horror stories I had heard of old wooden boats springing planks and sinking. The crew were already hand-sewing patches onto the old cotton sails.

I didn't wait three weeks for Hank's arrival or paint and varnish his boat as he expected. For my part, I had delivered his yacht to the Canary Islands. Unfortunately for Hank, he had used mild steel instead of stainless for the rigging and deck fittings, and after two months at sea, *Albatross* was covered in rust streaks and looked ready for the scrapyard. He never covered all my expenses for the journey, and now I had run out of money. However, there was still plenty of food left on *Albatross* to last the crew until Hank's arrival, so Kick offered to lend me the English sterling he had on him, which amounted to forty pounds. Adding to what Stella had, it might be just enough to get us to Barcelona, steerage class, then to Paris on the Magic Bus, and hopefully to London by night train and ferry. The journey back home would be a debriefing after our sailing odyssey. What was I returning to anyway? I had no money, no job, but I still had one asset, my boat, *Caroline*. Perhaps uncertainty could be my elixir to new ideas, for I had developed a bad case of wanderlust. Undoubtedly, the antidote would be another adventure soon, and I couldn't wait.

7. In the Trough

The lights of Tenerife were fading fast into the distance. As I watched the ship's wake, I felt all churned up like the turbulence from the propellors. How could I return to the mundane after such adventures? My romance with Stella had ended too. I looked at her pretty face and slender body and wondered if she was the real cause of my sadness. The thought must have echoed with hers when she said, 'We both know that once we've reached England, this will be it. Don't take me wrong, this was a great adventure and I've loved every minute with you, but it is the last time I'll ever set foot on a sailing boat. I know your real mistress is the sea.'

What could I say? Stella never showed any interest in sailing and had spent most of her time burying herself in a book. How different we both were. She could never share my passion, yet I hoped there might still be that spark between us. Sleeping in separate cabins was bound to push us further apart. We kissed gently on the lips, then left the upper deck to go and find our respective quarters.

When I got to my cabin, there was only one top bunk free, just above a man with skin so dark it looked midnight blue. Half-lying down on his bed with his shoes on, reclined on one elbow, he was talking to a chap wearing a wide-brimmed, trilby hat. His loud flowery shirt clashed with his white, red, and blue striped trousers. The third fellow wore a black suit. He had undone the collar button on his white shirt and loosened his tie at the neck. I saw him watching everybody's moves from his bunk through half-closed eyes and sensed his stare when I placed my clothes in the remaining locker.

The men looked like shady characters in a thriller, and I wondered if someone would murder me in my sleep. Thankfully, I awoke to see another day after a restless night. I collected our picnic from my locker and hurried to meet Stella on deck for a breakfast of sardines and stale bread, yet again.

When we docked in Las Palmas, there was an hour to spare to replenish our store before the ferry left. The next leg, from Gran Canaria to Malaga, through the Straits of Gibraltar, was the most extended passage.

On our second day at sea, the man in the dark suit asked me if I spoke Spanish. 'No hablo Español. I'm English,' I answered.

'Can I have some of your bread and wine?' he asked, struggling with his speech. Stella and I only had three bread rolls, some cheese, and a half-bottle of the cheapest red wine, so I gave him a roll and the wine.

'Gracias,' he said before climbing back into his top bunk.

I quickly put our remaining supplies in one bag and rendezvoused with Stella up on deck to share another of our meagre breakfasts. As usual, I found her reading one of Dennis Wheatley's novels. 'I'm sorry, I gave some food to a chap in my cabin,' I told her. 'He had such a pleading look on his face. I know we can't feed three people, so you'd better put the bag in your locker from now on.' I mentioned the Mafia characters in my cabin, and Stella told me about the women in hers.

There was a beautiful young Mexican who she thought might be the partner of the man I had described to her, dressed like Pancho, the sidekick to the Cisco Kid. The other woman was in her forties and looked like a Spanish nun. Stella had little to say. So I left her to *Dennis Wheatley* and went off to explore. In the saloon, some people were eating, others were playing cards. I recognised the dark-suited man from my cabin sitting alone at a table among the diners. He caught my gaze, and called me over before I could look away.

'Do you play chess?' he asked cheerfully.

'Yes, sort of,' I said casually. I had played the odd game on *Albatross*. Although neither Kick, Jopp, nor myself were particularly good at it, we all matched each other's abilities. There were board games in the saloon for passengers to use. The man grabbed a chess set, and we played two games. I won both times. We chatted for a while, and I mentioned my adventures sailing to the Canary Islands. He seemed intrigued. Then he asked me for a chance of revenge in the afternoon, and we agreed on a time to reconvene.

After a quick lunch with Stella, I went to meet my mysterious 'chess-mate.' At one time, alone in the cabin, I had peeped inside his partially open locker. He had no luggage, no change of clothes, nothing.

When I entered the saloon, I found him sitting at a table with a chessboard. His keenness made me wonder. Was he after something? When he saw me, the man jumped up from his seat and invited me to join him. I noticed his English had improved from our last meeting. We started a game, and as I was about to make him checkmate, he interrupted my move, keen to talk.

'I used to work for an airfreight company in Tenerife Airport, but I had to run away,' he said with eyes like a puppy dog begging for food.

I looked over my shoulder, but no violinist was approaching our table. The man continued:

'As I searched through some papers in the office one day, I uncovered a Mafia smuggling ring. I saw strange characters and officials exchanging money and knew what that meant, being a witness to these dealings. The police had already questioned me, but I was too frightened to say anything. I thought the Mafia would be after me. I had to make a run with nothing else but what I had in my wallet, which was just enough to buy a ticket to Barcelona.'

'What a thing to happen,' I exclaimed, wondering where this was leading to.

'I need to get out of Spain before either the Mafia or the police catch up with me,' he said with a dramatic gesture.

His story would have been the perfect opening chapter in a crime thriller.

'Can you help me get out of Spain without a passport?' he finally asked.

'I wouldn't know how to,' I replied. 'Besides I've had to borrow the money for the ferry. My girlfriend and I are living on bread and sardines.'

He didn't comment, and we resumed our game. This time, after four or five moves, he had me checkmated.

'You're not a worthy opponent,' the man blurted out sarcastically. He stood up, pushed his chair away, and departed like an impatient fisherman losing his catch. Later that afternoon, I saw him again, sitting at another table. He was drinking coffee and cognac, playing chess with someone else who might be prepared to help him out of his situation. Was he genuinely desperate or just a con man with an exciting story? He never revealed his name or asked for mine.

It was a chilly morning when we disembarked in Barcelona. Outside the railway station, touts were flaunting tickets to travellers for the intriguing Magic Bus. These buses ran on licence plates from some obscure country and travelled the whole of Europe, Asia, and Africa, with no road tax or insurance. The only one heading to Paris that day was ten pounds a ticket which Stella and I just managed to pay.

On our way, the bus only stopped to drop off or pick up new passengers or when someone was desperate for a loo. When the changeover came, the driver slid out of his seat to let his relief driver take over the wheel, with the vehicle still cruising at one hundred and ten kilometres an hour. It was a wonder that we got to Paris in one piece. As we left the bus, the driver was already touting for more passengers to fill our seats on his way to Denmark.

When we got to the railway ticket counter, Stella and I realised we hadn't the money in the kitty for a boat train to London. So I asked a young backpacker if she knew a cheaper way, apart from trying to swim across the Channel.

'I've only taken the night train,' she replied.

'We don't have enough for the fare,' Stella explained. 'I can't get money from my bank account until I reach England.'

'How about me buying the tickets?' the girl said. 'You can repay me when we get to London tomorrow morning.'

She was our guardian angel.

The following day, Stella cashed a cheque, paid the young student back, and lent me some money for my train ticket home to Scarborough. Then, we kissed on the cheek, wished each other good luck, and parted. Although I knew that Stella and I were neither soul mates nor in love, I still felt sad and depleted. Was it about her or the adventure on *Albatross* coming to an end?

On my way to Yorkshire, listening to the 'clickety-clack' of the wheels over the lines, my memory took me back to my childhood. I pictured my mother putting me on a train in Scarborough and being picked up by my uncle Lewis in Leeds. I remembered feeling very grown-up for a seven-year-old. We were still in the age of steam, and one time I saw *Sir Nigel Gresley*'s *Mallard* pulling out of York Station with slipping wheels and billowing steam covering the whole platform. As I reminisced, my mind flipped back to the model railway set I had as a boy.

It was nearing Christmas when a regular customer of our pub came in with a sad story. He had just been put out of work and had no money to give his family a good celebration. He begged my father to buy his son's train set as he no longer played with it. My father agreed. I wondered if it was to help his customer or reward me for working so hard in the bar for meagre pocket money.

The train set was mounted on a six-by-four foot board. Thrilled at that, I persuaded my parents to let me have a room in the attic. I bought wood with my pocket money, and with the aid of a customer, I built a three-foot-wide tabletop height shelf to fit around the room. I made hills with tunnels out of *papier mâché*, trees out of grape stalks, and leaves out of glued-on sawdust. I bought second-hand tracks wherever possible. I could never afford electric points, so I made a system of strings leading back to the control position to operate them by hand from under the boards. All pocket money, birthday and Christmas presents went into this model railway. By the age of fifteen, my ingenuity had developed to such an extent that people thought my layout worthy of any professional railway modellers. Then one day, home from work, I popped my head into the room in the attic and found the place empty. The only evidence left of my train set was the holes in the wall where I had fastened the layout boards. I felt numb seeing such desolation and rushed downstairs to confront my mother. She was in the kitchen cooking.

'Where's my railway set?' I cried out, my heart pounding with anger.

My mother replied without the slightest compassion. 'We're a bit hard up and I'm not sure how we'll get through this winter. Besides, the only interest you seem to have now is girls. Aren't you too old for a train set? Anyway, we sold it.'

The 'Anyway, we sold it' caught me off guard, and I was dumbfounded at such a callous reaction. I had poured every penny I earned into my train set, not counting all the hours of work I had dedicated to it. I felt that my parents had stolen it all from me, including my adolescence. I couldn't believe they were capable of doing this to me. It seemed that neither my feelings nor my accomplishments mattered to them. Even though I was overwhelmed, shocked and distraught, I still couldn't tell my mother how devastated I felt at being dispossessed of what I had worked so hard to achieve. I doubted they got very much for it, considering how little they respected the labour and zeal I had put into this model railway layout.

Perhaps I was selfish not to sympathise with my parents' financial situation, but it hurt me so much that they never even asked me beforehand. We didn't have the kind of relationship where I could discuss my feelings, so they remained locked in.

Once in Scarborough, I stayed at my mother's house while pondering my next move. My father had since died. It wasn't going to be an easy time. I knew my mother wanted me to settle down and look after her, but I had other plans.

When I checked my yacht *Caroline*, moored in Scarborough Harbour, I heard myself saying: 'Sorry old girl, you're a lovely boat but not ideal for carrying me across oceans. I'll have to find you a good home.'

I set about enquiring at the yacht club and browsing in magazines and newspapers for a replacement, but nothing in my price bracket suited my purpose. *I could try the yacht brokers in Southampton and stay with my half-sister Eileen. I might even ring Stella in Plymouth and ask if she could put me up for old time's sake.*

I stayed two nights at Eileen's but found nothing suitable in Southampton. So to save money, I hitch-hiked to Plymouth. I waited a while to get a lift and was dropped twenty miles further on at a lay-by. I had better luck when a truck driver stopped and gave me a ride.

'I've already passed you once,' the trucker said. 'I stopped for a break and this time you were easier to pick up.'

We had plenty to talk about on the way to Plymouth. Jeff had been in 'special services' during the Korean War. The subject sprang up after I mentioned an American officer in the news accused of killing a whole village in the Vietnam War.

'This is nothing new,' Jeff stated. 'When I was in Korea on mopping-up exercises in the jungle, I saw children in villages pulling a pin on a hand-grenade and blowing up, not only themselves but the soldiers who had offered them chocolate. When we went to places harbouring the enemy, there wasn't even a dog left alive by the time we moved out of the area. Don't misunderstand me, it was a case of us or them. War is wrong - it's a shitty business!'

Jeff dropped me in Plymouth, and we shook hands like best friends. Next, I looked for a telephone box to ring Stella. When I got through, I said, 'Hey Stella, I thought I'd call to see how you're doing.'

'Where are you?' she asked awkwardly.

'Here in Plymouth.'

'Oh, you could have given me more warning,' she replied. 'I'm not free at the moment. But, I tell you what, wait for me in the café opposite Dingles at 2 pm.'

When we met, we kissed on the cheek. I felt Stella didn't seem overly pleased to see me. I suspected she had met someone new.

'I can put you up in my flat for a couple of nights and if I don't catch up with you before you go, just leave the key under the mat.'

And that was that.

With much to do, I set off on my quest to find a boat in my price range. I saw a *Tumlare* similar to *Caroline,* in one yacht broker, for sale at one thousand five hundred pounds. I decided to go in and check the specification and see what I could ask for mine. Inside was a young couple enquiring about the same boat. How lucky was that! I left the broker and waited outside.

When the couple came out, I shouted, 'Excuse me, I overheard you asking the broker about a *Tumlare*. I've one for sale if you're interested?'

'Well,' the man exclaimed: 'We'd love to buy your *Tumlare* but I'm afraid we don't have the money. We're only dreaming about it but all our funds are tied up in a boat in kit form. We have a hull without a deck in our back garden, a keel in some field in Poole, and a mast still at Kemps. We don't even have the financial resources to put it all together!'

'What boat is it?' I asked.

'It's a *Sadler* 25 cruiser-racer with eight-foot beam,' he replied. 'Should be a flyer, if only we could get it together. To be honest we'd rather be sailing a boat than building one! Otherwise, we'd buy yours if we could.'

I don't know what came over me when I said, 'Why don't we just do a straight swap then?' My words must have surprised them as much as they did me. They glanced at each other, nodded, then replied, 'Why not?'

We agreed to meet in an Italian restaurant in the evening.

I arrived early at La Trattoria and had only been sitting at a table for two minutes when Reverend Michael and his wife made their entrance, both looking cheerful. During dinner, Michael announced they were willing to do the exchange. Jeannette handed me an itemised A4 list that included everything from the oil lamp to the mast and keel. Earlier in the afternoon, I had researched the *Sadler* 25 and was impressed with the design.

Michael and Jeannette seemed keen to swap boats. So I asked him about the deck on the *Sadler.* He hadn't mentioned it at all. 'Well, I wanted a wooden deck but I'm sure *Sadlers* could supply you a fibreglass one,' he said.

I looked through the inventory and agreed to the deal, providing *Sadlers* could fit a fibreglass deck. I was prepared to pay for it. We shook hands on the agreement, and Michael promised to contact *Sadlers* the following day. However, he insisted that *Caroline* matched the description I gave him for the negotiation to go through. I believed Michael would be impressed by her condition.

When he called *Sadlers*, the factory agreed to sell me a deck moulding and fit it at a special price as it had a slight defect on the gelcoat.

Michael arrived in Scarborough with a Land Rover and trailer to collect *Caroline* a week later. He was very impressed with her and trundled back to Oxford, a happy new owner. Then the following week, Michael returned what was now my S*adler*'s hull to the factory in Poole. Later that day, he phoned me with bad news. *Sadlers* wouldn't fit the deck moulding because Michael had cut off the original mounting flange from the hull to fit a wooden deck.

'The deal is off,' I said. 'We had an agreement that *Sadlers* would fit a new fibreglass deck. Could you please bring *Caroline* back?'

'Peter, don't be hasty. Give me twenty-four hours. I'll sort something out,' Michael pleaded.

He rang the next day. 'Peter, here's the deal. If you're willing to pay another three hundred pounds to *Sadlers*, they will cast you a brand new hull with a deck as agreed. The yard foreman wants to buy your hull and the new one can be completed within a month. All you need to do is ring Martin Sadler and say 'yes.' What do you think?'

'Okay Michael, it's a deal.'

When I called Martin, I asked him for a red hull since he was casting me a new one.

'We only do white or pale blue,' he replied, 'but as it's just a case of buying red pigment, I don't see why not!'

As soon as I got the word that the new hull was ready, I borrowed a trailer, and then my mother's eccentric neighbour Roy offered to drive me down to Southampton to pick the hull up from *Sadlers* with his large American V8 Chevrolet station wagon. He and his wife Liz ran a residential home next door to my mother.

Thin, wiry with curly brown hair, Roy was a dapper dresser. He loved to flirt with the ladies, young or old. When in men's company, he spoke with authority, giving the impression that he was a country squire or a retired businessman.

So Roy and I set off in his Chevy with his two eldest sons and their au-pair Joyce. Philip was eleven and Thomas ten. In Poole, we collected the shiny red hull from *Sadlers* and the mast from *Kemps*, and by the time we had finished loading up, it was too late to travel the three hundred miles back to Scarborough. After all, we had set off at 5 am that day. Anyway, Roy had planned for the five of us to sleep in the station wagon. His Chevy was very much like a stretch limousine without the boot. Not far from *Kemps* was a forested area, which seemed a suitable place to spend the night. Joyce worked her magic, cooking a three-course meal on a two-ring camping stove, and we all sat on the grass on rugs, eating our supper. We sang *'What shall we do with the drunken sailor'* and any other songs we remembered until the boys could no longer keep their eyes open.

We turned in, which was very much like a game of sardines. Around midnight, we all woke up to the sound of a vehicle coming alongside us and two doors slamming hard. A powerful torch was shone into the Chevy, blinding us, and then we saw two men glaring in. They wore light-coloured trilby hats and safari jackets with badges on the breast pocket. 'You can't stay here, it's private land,' one shouted through the partially open window.

'We're causing no harm,' Roy said in a sleepy voice.

'If you don't move straight away,' he barked, 'I'm calling the police and I'll have you arrested for trespassing.'

We had no other option but to go. Fortunately, we found a country lane close by, parked on the grass verge, and managed to get some sleep.

Everything went well on our way back north. Then on a steep hill, thirty miles short of Scarborough, the Chevy began to overheat. Roy stopped at the roadside to let the engine cool down, topped up the radiator with water from a stream and left the cap off. He gently nursed the vehicle back to my mother's place just as the motor gave up. Luckily, it got us back, and Roy wasn't fazed at all by his loss, to my immense relief. 'It was a bloody good adventure,' he said. 'Anyway, the Chevy was on its way out.'

Then with Roy and the boys, we pushed and pulled the trailer into my mother's backyard. I had carefully measured the width of the gate and knew I could just squeeze the hull through if I took the double doors off the hinges. When the boat was in, my mother only had a small area for hanging her washing. It was the start of my new project, a big empty hull. Michael had named the original hull *Ellis of Tamar* as he intended to keep the boat on the River Tamar. *Ellis* was the name of Michael's wife's great-grandfather, a sea captain on square riggers. I thought the story was romantic, so I decided to keep the name even though it was a new hull.

There was much to do, putting this boat together. First, bulkheads would need to be glassed in, then hatches and windows fitted on the superstructure, including mast and rigging. I had experience in fibreglass work when manufacturing amusement machines. Building a boat would be another learning curve. But, it was the way I approached things.

I would also have to earn money to complete *Ellis* and go off cruising. As the divorce proceedings were still in progress after all this time, I decided to accept a six-month contract in Saudi Arabia following an introduction from my friend Jeff Lawson, which landed me the maintenance manager position on a battery chicken farm near Riyadh. Another career shift for me! I am never afraid of hard work, especially if it means adventure in the end. I pictured myself hoisting *Ellis's* sails off Scarborough Bay and setting out on a long voyage with no return date. Working in Saudi Arabia would help me achieve that.

8. Scorpions and Beards

The heat was oppressive walking across the tarmac towards the terminal building. I quickened my pace to escape it radiating from the aeroplane's engine, only to realise it was the ambient temperature. *How on earth am I going to cope with this climate?*

After clearing customs and passport control, I was picked up in a taxi and dropped at a hotel in Riyadh for the night. A minibus would collect the company's recruits the following day to take us to the farm site, one hundred kilometres south of the city. I turned in early, thankful for the air-conditioning in the room and felt reasonably confident that no scorpion would join me in my bed.

I woke up in a cool room. Outside, the sun must have been beating hard. After a spot of breakfast, I made my way to the lobby, where a small group had assembled. We greeted each other cautiously. After all, we weren't about to go on a school trip. It would be more like hard labour, working in the desert.

The minibus left the hotel on time and headed out of the dusty city. I became lost in the landscape of endless dunes and rugged rocky outcrops. Now and then, a lonely palm tree oasis punctuated the stark scenery. I thought of *the green, green grass of home* I had left behind and remembered my father when he sang *Cool Clear Water* in the Wellington Hotel my parents had once run. He loved the song which went:

He's a devil, not a man,
and he spreads the burning sand with water
Dan, can ya see that big, green tree?
Where the water's runnin' free.
And it's waiting there for you and me.

My father, Dougie, had a good voice and enjoyed singing cowboy songs. Customers arrived early to hear him sing and play the guitar. Then as soon as the 'smoke room' filled up, he would stop entertaining and come and help my mother and me behind the bar. I was twelve years old, working as an underage barman. That night, we could no longer cope with all the customers, but my father was enjoying himself far too much to notice. My mother lost patience. 'I'll sort your dad out, leaving us struggling like this,' she said. 'He should have been here half an hour ago.' I saw her filling a glass of water and heading for the 'smoke room' with a face as sour as curdled milk, and I knew what she intended to do.

My father was in full flow,, singing the last verse of *Cool Clear Water,* when she marched in.

'Dougie,' she cried angrily, 'I'll give you cool, clear water,' and with an accurate toss, she threw the water straight at my father's face, then stomped out. The floorboards groaned under her feet. An eerie silence hung heavily around the room as if the world had pressed pause. Then my father, as a true professional, smiled at his audience, and everyone roared with laughter.

My parents didn't speak to each other for a week after that. As we ate at the dining table, my father would say, 'Tell your mother such-and-such,' and she would reply, 'Tell your father so-and-so.' I was like a mouse mediating between two elephants! I never understood how they could sulk at each other for weeks. However, from then on, our 'smoke room' was packed from seven o'clock onwards. Everyone believed the water on Dougie's face was part of the act, and they expected an action replay each night.

Father never sang *Cool Clear Water* again, even on request.

My thoughts jolted back to the minibus when it hit a pothole. I stared at the dusty road and the desert with its unending waves of dunes traversing the lonely landscape. The vehicle stopped to let a herd of camels and their drovers cross the highway. I was pleased with the distraction it brought to our journey, although the men looked menacing, carrying long-barrelled rifles on their shoulders and double bandoliers of bullets across their chests. I asked the driver to allow me out to take a picture.

As I prepared to click, I noticed one of the men lowering his weapon to his waist. He was standing like a turbaned sheriff telling 'Billy the Kid' to get out of town.

'He's probably worried about the flash from your camera spooking the animals, or he doesn't want you to capture his soul,' the driver explained in perfect English. 'Please step back on board. I want to deliver the same number of people I've picked up from the hotel.'

We drove on as soon as the road had cleared. My heart missed a beat every time an oncoming truck came whizzing around the bend on our side, only to swerve away at the last second. It seemed as if these vehicles were playing desert dodgems.

Covered with multi-coloured illustrations of 'the Arabian Nights,' they looked like fairground attractions cruising at high speed.

The man sitting next to me must have noticed my unease. He offered me a handshake and introduced himself as Bill.

'You ain't seen nothing yet,' he said. 'Saudi is a very different world. Let me illustrate the logic of the Saudis so that you're prepared. When you hire a taxi involved in a crash, you'd better grab your bags and run. Otherwise you could be blamed for it because the driver wouldn't have had the accident if you hadn't hired the taxi.'

His comments did nothing to reassure me.

'There was an incident about a Saudi businessman,' Bill continued. 'He committed suicide by jumping off the top of a five-storey building, smashing onto the roof of a car. He died on impact. The police arrested the car owner for killing the businessman because he landed on his vehicle. Fortunately, the judge dropped the case against him.'

'Thank Goodness,' I said, shocked by such an alien law. Then, wanting to lighten the conversation, I asked Bill if he got a squirt of water up 'his' from the toilet bowl to wash his bottom. He nodded and said with a grin, 'Saudi will be quite a culture shock for you!'

The large farm complex was surrounded by an irrigation system of canals fed from a spring.

Abundant vegetation grew alongside the banks where, to my surprise, giant palm trees had matured over the years. They offered canopies of much-needed shade, although no vegetation reached further than a few metres from the water. The desert took over beyond this point.

There were six farms on the site. The one allocated to me was the same as the others. Each had six battery chicken houses. They all stank to high heaven with billions of flies. The whole place had come to a grinding halt, including the automatic extractors which removed the droppings from the hens' cages. In the number one house, the poor chickens had to be re-homed, and thousands of rotten eggs kept exploding at random. In comparison, even the stink bombs of young boys' pranks would have smelt like sweet roses.

The number two, three, and four houses were barely working, engulfed by a mountain of excrement. Only the fifth one was operational after a fashion. The sixth one had been stripped for spare parts to keep the others running. I wondered what I had let myself in for. I had signed a six-month contract for sun, sand, and sex - they forgot to mention the shit, the heat, the flies, the scorpions, the snakes, and the poisonous spiders!

A Scarborough firm originally built these farms for the Saudis to operate. They had tried to manage them with imported labour, mainly from

Syria, Iran, and Yemen. Nobody could blame the workers for their lack of 'know-how.' They had no concept of mechanics and modern machinery. Some of them had been shepherds, goat herders, or simple fishermen before working on these farms. Then, when everything came to a grinding halt, the Saudi Management asked the company to return and rebuild the place.

They brought me in as an engineering manager to bring my six houses back into full production. I immediately got stuck in, up to the armpits in manure, to try and achieve this monumental task, working alongside ten locals and six English workers. Whenever I thought life would be easier for me, shit would happen even without a fan!

I shared a villa and a bedroom with Jeff and James. Four other engineers occupied the two remaining bedrooms. All of us got on swimmingly well. James was funny, astute, and well-read. He wore glasses and told everybody he used to have brown hair but left the grey stage out to go straight into pink! Some people didn't get it at first - that James went bald young. He told us stories of his Navy days when he served as an armourer on an aircraft carrier.

His favourite was about the Admiral of a Fleet who arrived by helicopter to carry out an inspection one day. The Admiral was renowned for staging bizarre emergencies to test the crew's reactions. Walking across the flight deck with the waiting helicopter flanked by saluting ratings on either side, he suddenly threw his hat at one of the crew, 'a hairy-arsed stoker,' as James put it, shouting, 'It's a bomb.' Thinking on his feet, the rating took a running kick at the hat, which went flying over the side into the deep blue - gold braid and all! The startled, open-mouthed Admiral was obliged to say, against every sinew in his body, 'Well done that man!'

Every Friday - the equivalent of our Sunday - several white Nissan pick-up trucks packed with locals flocked to the farm complex as if on a day to the seaside. They picnicked by the canals and bathed in the water. Even though the sea was three hundred miles away with no river nearby, there were fish in it. Around the perimeter of the farm was the wind-driven sand. When we drove into the desert to the manure tipping place, we often came across the carcass of a donkey or a cow. The area attracted desert foxes and critters that looked like gerbils. A large pack of wild dogs, likely to have been abandoned by their owners living in the nearby town, frequently roamed around the farm's outer fences.

Each morning the six managers breakfasted on double-yolkers and beef cut like rashers of bacon. We bought the meat at the local supermarket, labelled 'English Breakfast.' No shops sell pork in Saudi Arabia. Little Abdul, a Yemeni, brought me a tray full of double-yolkers each day after packing eggs. I pitied the poor hens. Their eyes must have been watering, laying such large eggs!

Abdul addressed me as 'Mr. Peter.' I knew he was keeping a few eggs for himself in place of poor wages, and it was his way of thanking me for turning a blind eye.

One evening, back from work, I found chaos in the villa. Four of my colleagues were running around the place screaming. I wondered if the sun had finally got to them.

'It's a sidewinder!' I heard James shouting. I thought it must be a potent cocktail drink, seeing the gang in such a state.

'What is a sidewinder?' I asked. 'Is it the juice of one lemon, a bottle of whisky, one of rum and two of vodka, stirred but not shaken!'

'It's a deadly poisonous snake, you bloody idiot,' Jeff barked as he charged about the room. With his sweeping brush, he looked like a wizard trying to jump back on his runaway broomstick.

I am not a coward, but I didn't want to add to the confusion, so I shut the front door and stayed outside. Anyway, I didn't have a broomstick myself!

After a risky chase across our villa, Jeff finally pinned the snake down with his sweeping brush while another chap chopped its head off with a spade - much to James's disapproval.

Days later, James, Jeff, and I were tucking into our double-yolkers, beef and toast, when I felt something crawling up my left leg. Before I could react, I received a sharp and painful bite. I drew back my chair to look for the crawler but saw no sign of it. Disgruntled at having their breakfast interrupted, James and Jeff helped me look for the creature. Finding nothing, we carried on eating, but I was on high alert. Just as well. Soon after, I felt something creeping up the same leg again. This time I was swifter and managed to brush it off. When it tried to scurry away, I stamped on it so hard that it looked like I had flattened the spider with a steamroller. By then, my leg had swollen. James said, 'You know that with some poisonous spiders, once bitten, the person only has a few minutes left to live. Maybe we won't even get you to a hospital in time!'

I knew they were winding me up, but just in case, I went to fetch an envelope, scooped the invertebrate up and put it inside, sealing it with the date and time, then gave the envelope to Jeff.

'If I collapse,' I said, 'take me to the hospital and show the doctor the remains of the spider.'

My heartbeat had shot up, and the mark on my leg had spread. To the touch, the area felt numb, and it looked as if I had been stung by a six-inch mosquito.

My pulse took a while to settle down. However, I survived the bite without medical intervention, and the red mark soon disappeared.

Weeks later, I found out about the creepy-crawly from the truck driver delivering spare parts to our farm from England. He showed me a nasty scar on his face and explained that it happened on one of his trips across the desert. One night, stifled by the heat, he decided to sleep under his truck. In the morning, when he woke up, he had a hole in his cheek the size of a pea. The doctor he visited in the next town thought it might have been a flesh-eating spider that had injected his cheek with venom to anaesthetise the area, only to return later to feast on his skin without him being aware. The driver's account appeared to solve my spider mystery.

At the start of the New Year, which falls on my birthday, I decided to shave my beard off. James, the site electrician, bet me a tenner that I couldn't leave half of it on for a day. I took up the challenge. Friday was my day off, so I had a fair chance of winning as I planned to potter around the villa where I lived with the other managers. It was a small complex, a mile away from the farm and five miles from the nearest town across the desert. Two families lived nearby. They were courteous and kind but had the dreadful habit of chucking their household rubbish as far as possible from their back door. That day, all the Brits in the complex started a big clean-up. We bagged everything we couldn't burn and loaded it up into the truck, ready to take to the farm rubbish tip after we had finished clearing. Most of us dressed in shorts, but I always wore ankle-length suede boots with steel toe caps in case I stepped on a scorpion or a snake.

In the middle of our frantic activity, we suddenly heard Franky's voice yelling: 'F**king scorpion!' I guessed he must have been stung. I had tried numerous times to discourage him from wearing open sandals but to no avail. Franky belonged to my team, and therefore I was responsible for him. I rushed over to see what was wrong. His foot had swollen up, and he couldn't put it down for the pain.

'I'd better take you to the doctor in the local town,' I said, helping him into the pick-up, then we drove off.

The traffic came to a halt on the way. Half of Al Kharj, the nearest town, was heading for a picnic by the canal. The pick-up vehicle next to us was going in the opposite direction. Inside were father and son in the front cab and mothers, grandmothers, and daughters sitting on benches, on either side of the cargo area. The women wore veils except for a girl, who must have been under fourteen years old, and therefore not obliged to wear one. I had the window wound down with my arm leaning on the door when the girl turned her head and looked at me. For some reason, her prolonged stare prompted me to glance back at her and smile, forgetting for a moment that I had shaven half my beard. She let out a scream, which unnerved me. I was an infidel who had smiled at her. No matter how innocent my action was, I could be in serious trouble. Luckily, the road ahead had cleared by then, and I drove off with my rear wheels spinning.

When we got to the surgery, I supported Franky with his arm over my shoulders as he hopped on one foot. The waiting room was empty. The young Egyptian receptionist gave us a dubious stare, then, stern-faced, ushered us straight into the consulting room. The doctor, also Egyptian, looked smart in his beige suit, shirt, and tie. He was sitting behind his desk like a king on his throne. With a hint of a smile, he asked us to take a seat. I helped Franky to a chair and sat next to him. Poor man, he looked feverish and in urgent need of attention. Still, the doctor took no notice of him. I couldn't understand it, even when he put his elbows on the desk and peered into my eyes, crying out, 'Why?' Then it dawned on me when he stroked his chin. I saw the puzzled look on his face and realised he was referring to my odd shaving habit. 'I've made a bet to stay the whole day like this,' I explained.

'Oh yes, you're English, aren't you,' he exclaimed as if to justify my eccentricity. Then he remembered his patient. After examining Franky's foot, he gave him an injection, prescribed some painkillers, and directed us to the nearest pharmacy.

'You should be careful about yourself,' the doctor warned me as we were leaving. 'Beards are mostly worn by holy men. People might be offended when they see you with half a beard.'

I thanked him for his assistance and advice. Then we left the surgery, and I helped Franky back to the pick-up truck.

'I know you're self-conscious about your beard but I can't go in,' he said as we pulled up outside the pharmacy.

'It's okay, Franky. Don't worry.'

I marched into the pharmacy and handed the prescription over to the chemist. The man stared at me like a camel caught in a car's headlights. I smiled and shrugged my shoulders, trying to put him at ease. He quickly turned on his heels and disappeared into the far end of the premises. When he returned with the painkillers, he laid the box on the counter and, with his eyes fixed on me, pushed it my way as if he was loading a mousetrap with a hair trigger. Then as I moved to pick the prescription up, he withdrew his hands quickly as if wanting to avoid getting them trapped. I said, 'Shukraan.'

I closed the door behind me but could still sense his stare. I strode briskly back to the truck, belted up, engaged first gear and then glanced towards the pharmacy. Through the glass door, I noticed his eyes glaring in my direction.

I stepped on the gas, and we made our getaway like two robbers from a bank heist. I shaved the other half of my beard the following morning.

However, James, to this day, still owes me. After all, I won the bet despite my ordeals.

The complex had a repair workshop with four local mechanics working full time. Three of my trailers were in the process of being repaired. The men had borrowed parts from the other two to get at least one going. The farm was fully mechanised except for the egg collection, so we couldn't switch the auger off for long as the scraper mechanism that disgorged the waste into a waiting trailer outside would crash. With the shortage of trailers, the manure spilt out onto the ground, creating enormous stinking pools that took hours to shovel up. It should have been transported across the desert, then spread over the sand and left to dry before being bagged and sold as fertiliser.

When I went to collect my repaired trailer at the garage that day, another manager had taken it. So I told Franky, and he said, 'Come on Gov, let's go and sort this out.'

Franky was short but built like a pocket-weightlifter. He had a gypsy look about him and was a man with a past. If Franky wasn't busy winning medals at amateur boxing championships, he robbed banks and cracked safes. The law caught up with him, and he served time in prison. While behind bars, his wife had an affair with the detective who had arrested him. After his release, Franky had a quiet word with this six-foot brawny

CID man, who landed up in hospital. Before the authorities could arrest him for assaulting a police officer, Franky fled and took up a six-month contract here on the farm.

When the police found out, they ordered his employers to fly Franky back to England. I told the company that he was my best worker, willing to do anything to help, so they pleaded his case and vouched for his exemplary conduct. Moreover, sending him back to England halfway through his contract would be uneconomical. Finally, the police relented, and Franky was allowed to complete his term.

Franky was now ready to help me retrieve the stolen trailer, and I agreed with his plan. I took the wheel, and we bounced along the desert track with him holding tightly onto the tractor's hydraulic lifting arms.

When we arrived at the offending farm, we saw someone loading my trailer. Undeterred, Franky and I proceeded to hitch it to our tractor. Then George, who ran the farm, hurried out of one of the buildings with four men in tow.

'I need this trailer and you are not taking it away,' he bellowed. Then to confirm his intention, he started to let the tyres down to stop me from driving the trailer off. Quick as a flash, Franky grabbed George by the scruff of the neck and the seat of his pants and carried him towards a stinking pool of manure. 'Put me down, let me go,' George yelled as he thrashed his arms and legs like a horizontal *Hokey Cokey* dancer. So Franky heeded his plea and dropped him down into the wet manure. Witnessing Franky's feat of strength, George's men had no stomach for further confrontation.

As we drove off with the trailer, we saw George back on his feet with his face and body covered in goo. He swiftly wiped his face revealing two white eyes, then started jumping up and down like an outraged stooge in a slapstick comedy act. 'I'm going to report you and Pete,' he shouted, brandishing his fists. 'You're both in for it.' We could still hear him howling halfway back to the farm.

'That's the last time anyone will dare to take one of our trailers once this gets out, Franky,' I said proudly. We were in stitches and couldn't stop ourselves.

An inquest ensued over the incident, but the managers laughed when they heard our side of the story. George walked away from the meeting room in disgust. 'The George incident' became something of a legend. Meanwhile, 'the trailers saga' continued.

When another of my trailers broke down, I couldn't take it anymore. I felt management was failing us. They couldn't appreciate the hardship we were all experiencing, especially with the shortage of trailers. The tipping mechanism was a recurring problem that prevented my team and me from getting the excrement away from the farms. I felt sure somewhere in Riyadh sold spare parts for hydraulics. Since none of the other farm managers, including George, appeared willing to tackle the matter with senior management, I had to take action.

One day, I filled my broken trailers with manure and lined them up side by side in the management car park, directly underneath the air-conditioning intake for the offices. I wanted the bosses to experience the full effect of our steaming, foul-smelling cargo. It would be the mother of all aromatherapy treatments for sure!

As I positioned my third trailer, one of the under-managers rushed out of the office. 'Pete, get these bloody trailers out of here for God's sake. We've got the message. They are stinking the place out. We'll be sending a man into Riyadh with instructions not to return until he has the parts you and the other farms need.'

My antics worked for a while, and we received spare parts for our trailers. Then a new project manager flew out from England intending to 'break eggs with a stick.' He made matters worse with his inflated managerial skills. He didn't appreciate the conditions on the farms. Being so far removed from the stench and flies, he would have needed a half-a-mile long stick to break any eggs! I had trained my team through practical demonstrations by working alongside them and never asked anyone to do what I wouldn't do myself. As a result, four out of my six houses ran like clockwork; the other two were almost fully operational. I also set up a preventative maintenance programme.

My friend Jeff followed the same principles. Neither of us was ever frightened to roll up our sleeves and get stuck in, unlike the other managers who just wanted to manage the farms from a distance and drink tea in their office.

The new manager then decided to send some of my team members to work on other struggling farms. As a result, mine was now in danger of reverting to the chaos I had found it in four months ago. Battling against such a harrowing situation had taken all my resolve not to let it get me down. With less staff, I wouldn't be able to keep up with my maintenance programme now, no matter how hard I kept working.

We attended a daily nine o'clock farm managers' meeting as part of the new regime. Some of us thought that a weekly one would have been ample. During these sessions, we reported any pending problems and made comments. Unfortunately, management never took the issues we raised at meetings seriously, so I had to pick up the gauntlet and challenge them once again.

One morning, I arrived earlier than usual for the meeting, carrying a bucket with a clean white cloth over it. I hid it under the mahogany conference table where I was sitting and waited for the session to start.

'You're keen this morning, Pete,' my friend Jeff said as he entered the room, followed by the others. I didn't let on.

After everyone had taken their seat, the meeting started in the usual format.

When my turn came to report on my progress from the previous day, the project manager asked, 'Do you have anything for us today, Peter?'

'Yes,' I replied with confidence. 'I've been complaining at these meetings about my dwindling workforce for some weeks, and I still haven't received any replacements. I feel that the management is unaware of the situation on my farm. I have the most houses in production in the complex but, without sufficient workforce, they will revert to cages full of excrement producing billions of flies. Now, if you'll permit me, I'd like to offer you a practical demonstration of what my men and I have been battling through to resurrect these houses.'

Everyone looked puzzled as I reached for the bucket under my seat. I lifted the cloth covering it and laid it on the table before carefully putting the bucket down to avoid scratching the polished surface. I had deliberately filled it with the ripest manure I could find on the farm. The evil-smelling fumes were rising like ectoplasm at a seance.

'Right,' I announced. 'I'd like to illustrate the conditions under which my team and I've been working to bring the six chicken houses up to full production. Without men to keep up the maintenance programme, future operatives will suffer this hellish labour again. Let me demonstrate. In the bottom of this bucket is a spanner.' I plunged my arm up to my elbow to retrieve it. 'And this is what we've to contend with when repairing machinery.' I held the spanner aloft like a trophy and cried, 'Revolting isn't it!'

The slime dripped from my elbow to everyone's disgust; some pushed their chairs away from the repulsive sight and obnoxious stench; the ones with the weakest stomachs clasped their hands over their noses to stop themselves from retching.

'Yes, I feel you've expressed the predicament you're in extremely well, Peter,' the manager said through his handkerchief. 'You can be assured that I shall do my utmost to resolve this situation, but for now you may be excused from the meeting to go and clean up.'

'Thank you very much,' I replied with a hint of sarcasm. 'I'm accustomed to the smell and if you don't mind I'll stay like this until the end of the meeting. I don't want to miss anything.'

I casually wiped my arm with a rag while the foul odour continued to assail the audience's nostrils. The meeting concluded much sooner than usual. *What will I have to come up with next to get more workers, tools, and trailers?*

Three days later, two recruits arrived on my farm. One of them was a handsome 'man about town' called Adrian. He was only nineteen years old, a little naive, and on his first trip abroad. His main interests in England were football, meeting girls at the disco, and drinking with his mates at the pub.

As many Brits did, Adrian went to Riyadh on his first day off. There he met an Arab of his age called Abdul. The two of them hit it off right away, so much so that Abdul offered to pick Adrian up from the farm the following Friday on his day off. Some 'old hands' had forewarned him about other sexual orientations. As we were all curious about Adrian's new friend, some of us waited for Abdul to arrive that Friday. 'Do you have cast-iron underpants on?' someone said to Adrian with a cruel grin on his face.

'Do you think he's still a virgin?' another chap asked. 'If he is, it won't be for long, and when he returns and is walking funny, we'll know what he's been up to!'

'No, you've got it all wrong,' Adrian protested. 'We're mates, just like back in England, going to football matches and pubs together.'

At that moment, Abdul drove up in his open-top-silver-grey Mercedes sports car. His immaculate white headdress was flowing in the wind, contrasting with Adrian's western apparel. It seemed evident from the way Abdul greeted Adrian that he had received an Oxbridge education. Adrian looked pretty dapper as he hopped into the Mercedes cavalierly without opening the door.

'He must have seen James Bond doing this kind of stunt in a movie,' I said to the guy sitting next to me on the wall. The two youngsters drove off, accompanied by wolf whistles and jeers.

'Don't be late, and remember that if you aren't home by twelve, the Mercedes will turn into a pumpkin, *Cinderella*!' I shouted.

There was no sign of Adrian in the morning, and I began to worry about him. Then by late afternoon, he re-appeared looking rather sheepish and bedraggled. 'Oh, look at what the camel has dragged in,' I remarked. 'What the hell has happened to you, Adrian?'

'Oh, you won't believe it, Pete,' he replied, distraught. 'I should have listened to you guys.

After we left the farm yesterday, Abdul drove to Riyadh to show me all the sights and then invited me back to his place. He said, "I've some single malt whisky." Abdul lives on the third floor of a luxury apartment building. His flat is all Persian carpets and futuristic furniture. He even has a concealed cocktail cabinet. Anyway, he poured us a drink and came and sat close to me on the six-seater sofa. I thought this was strange, but I shouted, "What the f**k are you doing" when he started to stroke my hair. I jumped up and spilled my drink on the carpet. Abdul became impatient when I retreated behind the settee.

"There's nothing wrong with a kiss and a cuddle," he remarked, grinning while chasing me around the room. We looked like two kids having a game and a giggle, but I wasn't laughing. I didn't have my bloody cast-iron underpants on, did I!

So I dashed for the nearest door, which happened to be the bathroom and locked myself in.

At first, Abdul tried to coax me to open the door while I frantically looked for an exit. His pleading soon turned into raging demands. I thought I'd be no match for him. He was taller than me and looked like he worked hard at the gym in the complex.

"Open this door, damn you!" Abdul started to yell. "It's payback time. You don't think I wined and dined you for nothing!" I felt sure Abdul was going to rape me. I was so scared that I climbed up on the toilet seat and opened the window as wide as possible. There was a soil pipe running down to ground level. I abseiled down until the pipe started to come away from the façade and then I went into free fall the last two metres before landing in a heap at the bottom. Finally, I jumped over a perimeter wall and ran.

I remembered Abdul's flat was close to the city centre where the company had an office. I managed to find it and huddled in the doorway with my collar turned up until the office opened at nine o'clock, then I borrowed some money for a taxi.'

'I think you ought to go and get some sleep,' I suggested, taking pity on Adrian. 'I'll see you tomorrow morning.' I spared him the inevitable "I told you so."

Adrian wasn't the only one to experience the 'ups and downs' of Saudi. Sometimes, the flies and smell proved too much, and I was ready to chuck it all in. One day, going to the market in Al Kharj, I walked past a fully veiled Saudi woman sitting cross-legged on the stony ground. All I could see of her were her brown, begging eyes. She had two dozen small tomatoes and a few peppers displayed on a tea cloth in front of her. I crouched down with my wicker basket and indicated I wished to buy all the tomatoes. 'How much?' I asked in Arabic.

With a finger, she wrote the price in the dust. I handed her the correct change, and she added two extra peppers to my purchase. Was it my sun-bleached blond hair, blue eyes, shorts, and large suede boots that made her say, *Baksheesh,* or was it her way of giving me a discount? Divorced women either sold a few tomatoes at markets or were driven into prostitution to survive, being shunned by family and friends.

On my way back to the farm, I took the usual shortcut across the desert, only this time I hit a sand drift. The vehicle halted, and the spinning wheels buried themselves up to the axles. Fortunately, I was well-prepared for this, carrying several scaffolding planks in the back of the truck. I jacked one side up, shovelled sand into the hole the wheels made, and then lowered the vehicle down onto a couple of planks. I did the same on the other side. Once back in the cab, I gunned the engine hard and drove over the planks to firmer sand, then stopped to go and retrieve them, keeping a wary eye open for wild dogs.

I was exhausted after all that digging in the searing sun. The wind-blown sand was stinging my eyes and clinging to my sweating body. Once back inside the vehicle, I broke down. There were so many obstacles on the farm, and now the vet refused to give me more fogging chemicals to kill flies. I howled out of the window like a wolf to the desert, crying aloud: *This is it, I've had enough. I'm packing it all in.* When I returned to my senses, I reminded myself that I was here to earn money for my next adventure, so I turned the ignition on and drove off.

I remembered the many discussions amongst my colleagues over Coca-Cola and *Sadiki* (*Sadik'* means friend in Arabic). It is illegal alcohol brewed in home-built stills by ex-pats, but *'Sadiki'* is no friend to anyone if wrongly distilled. People go blind. Some of my fellow workers talked about building their dream home or starting new businesses once they made their pile, though I suspected a few would waste it away like the old cowboy song, 'Cigarettes and Whisky and Wild, Wild Women.'

My time in the Middle East had thankfully drawn to an end. As I settled down on my seat in the air-conditioned cabin of the plane back to England, I asked myself how I coped with scorpions, spiders, poisonous snakes, billions of flies, the heat and the chicken shit?

My dream to build a boat and sail away still held firm, especially now that I had the money. I imagined casting off for the open sea, the wind filling my sails, and Saudi Arabia a far distant whisper in the rigging. Oddly enough, there is no word for "PLEASE" in Arabic, but there is one for "GOODBYE," so I said, *Ma'assalama* to Saudi Arabia, as the plane took off.

9. The Launch

Curtains twitched more than usual that day when a twenty-ton mobile crane reversed down the lane to Mrs Newby's house with only inches to spare. The other surprise came when a shiny red hull was plucked out of her tiny backyard, loaded onto an antiquated launching trailer, and towed away by a Land Rover. Very few people knew that I had been building a boat behind the high brick wall. At last, my mother could reclaim her backyard, now that *Ellis* was about to receive her saltwater christening. I was happy as an admiral in a bubble bath, a glass of champagne in hand, playing at submarines.

It was a short drive downhill to Scarborough Harbour. On the way, I thought of my friend Roy and the two glasses appearing on the deck of *Ellis*, followed by his head peering over the gunnel announcing, 'Time for G & T, Pete.' How much his enthusiasm and banter had lightened up the mighty task of putting a yacht together. Roy left his mark, too, signwriting *Ellis of Tamar* on her bow.

When my mother saw the name, she sulked for days. Mum expected that I would call the boat *Irene* after her. Maybe she thought I owed it to her, using her backyard for nearly a year. Changing a boat's name is considered bad luck amongst the yachting fraternity. Reverend Palmer had already named his even though it was still in kit form.

Despite her disappointment, my mother was happy to smash the bottle of champagne on *Ellis's* keel while the lighthouse watchman lowered her into the water with the harbour crane. After three months of full-time boatbuilding, *Ellis* was now afloat. Amongst the raucous cheers from Roy, other friends and well-wishers, my time of glory had finally come on Friday 8 July 1977.

Ellis was a cruiser-racer, fitted with a two horsepower outboard motor mounted on a sliding bracket. Her interior was sparse with a two-ring paraffin-wick stove, a sink and a chemical loo. However, one of my design features, which I considered my luxury, was an instant slide-out double-berth in the saloon.

I was just as sparing with navigation aids. I had a compass, a Seafix Radio Direction Finder, a depth gauge and a log. I had no VHF radio as I wanted to sort myself out if I got into trouble. I would never choose to put anyone else at risk. With this in mind, I purchased a brand new life-raft which was the most expensive item in my inventory. It would be my life insurance. Finally, I bought a plastic sextant and a book to teach myself how to take sun-sights. With *Ellis's* pillar box red hull, red and yellow striped spray dodgers, and matching mainsail cover, she stood out amongst the white yachts and the occasional blue ones moored in Scarborough Harbour. One night, as I was drinking a beer at the yacht club, the Commodore said with a plum in his mouth, 'I presume the new yacht in the harbour is yours. Which circus do you belong to?'

'Fred Karno's,' I replied, grinning.

Roy and his wife, Liz, invited me over to a get-together to celebrate *Ellis's* launch. When I arrived at their house that evening, the party was already in full swing. Fortunately, I knew most of the guests.

Liz was a charismatic petite blonde. She had been a sister in the Casualty Department at Scarborough Hospital. When she was younger, Liz ran with the local nobility and spoke like one of them.

Roy was inventive but far too laid back, so Liz mostly managed their residential home. He worked at Plaxton Coach Builders, often going to Scarborough seafront during his lunch break, and on a beautiful day (these were few and far between), he would say to himself, 'What the hell, I'm taking the afternoon off.'

Liz had many stories about her days working as a sister, and that evening she was keen to share some of them. She mentioned a young couple going to a police station 'knotted' and an ambulance taking them to the hospital.

The subject matter got her audience very excited. Someone then remarked, 'The poor buggers, they must have pretended to be dancing on their way there.'

'You could say they waltzed into the station,' I ventured. 'And if the young man had been aroused en route, the dance would have moved into a quick step!'

Everyone roared with laughter, then Liz explained in medical terms that the bell-end of the boy's penis became trapped by the young girl's virginal cord. Maybe she wanted to curtail the crude remarks. But they didn't stop there.

Another person asked, 'Did you throw a bucket of cold water over them as they do with dogs?' The jokes were out of order.

'I've got a more bizarre story,' Liz continued, eager to recapture the limelight. 'We had a young woman admitted for a drug overdose. She was passed out on a trolley, naked under a sheet. I saw a group of doctors taking turns at drawing the linen back - then walking away laughing. Curiosity got the better of me so I went and took a peek. You won't believe it! The young woman had *mild and bitter* tattooed on her breasts and on her stomach *keep off the grass* and *pay as you enter*.'

Everyone giggled except me. When the cacophony died down, I couldn't stop myself from asking, 'And was there a hunting scene tattooed on her back?' All the guests stared at me, stunned.

'How did you know that?' Liz asked, sounding shocked. Then, before I could protest my innocence, she said, 'Come on Peter, confess your murky past.'

I wasn't going to tell everyone how I knew about Sally's tattoos. It was no use trying to justify myself either, so I retreated under a barrage of jeers and went to get a drink from the bar in another room. Sally's life story was all too sad for a party, but Liz mentioning her set me thinking about the day our paths crossed.

I had accepted a welding job, which I could only do on a Sunday. So I asked Jeff to help. He worked for me during the week, widening wheels for racing cars. I arranged to pick him up in the morning from his girlfriend's house. I gasped when he gave me the address. It was a notorious council estate and one of the worst in

Scarborough. People spoke of the police chasing villains through the houses of Newcombe Road and finding their patrol cars up on bricks with all the wheels stolen on their return. The prospect of visiting such a place did nothing to reassure me when I set off that Sunday.

I drove down Newcombe Road, crouched over the steering wheel, ready to dodge bullets or even a half-brick thrown through the windscreen by a toddler. I looked at the house number Jeff gave me. There was litter of all kinds in the street, including broken toys, and the houses stood in various states of disrepair. Cardboard and plywood replaced the broken windowpanes here and there. Some properties looked like scrapyards, full of rusty old cars on bricks with windows smashed and bonnets open. The corner shop I drove past had steel shutters over the windows, and I saw the owner behind the counter with two big Alsatians holding vigil.

I arrived at the address, which was one of the houses with cardboard replacing the window panes. When I tried to ring the bell, the push button was missing, leaving bare wires protruding, so I knocked on the front door, which needed more than a lick of paint. I knew Sally's brother Malcolm by sight. He came to answer the door.

'Hello, Pete. Come on in and sit down,' he said, pointing at the old settee. 'Jeff won't be long.'

I thought I'd seen better settees thrown on bonfires on Guy Fawkes night! I also noticed someone had torn off all the skirting boards around the room, leaving an untidy gap between walls and floorboards. They must have done that on a frosty winter night when the coal ran out! As for the curtains, there were more holes in them than a string vest. Finally, in the corner was a television on a tea chest.

While I waited for Jeff, sitting uncomfortably on the edge of the settee, Malcolm asked me if I wanted to see his motorbike. I followed him into the kitchen, where I saw it partially dismantled, standing in a pool of oil in a corner. There were pots, pans, jars, and packets littering every other surface. On the opposite side was a pile of coal up against the wall. I asked him why the coal was there? 'The neighbours would nick it if we left it in the outside coal house,' he explained. Like the skirting boards, the door had been chopped up for firewood.

How hard life can get for some people!

My jaw dropped when Jeff walked down the stairs with his girlfriend. I thought, *this is Cinderella and Jeff is the Prince taking her away from all this!*

The woman had blonde hair down to her waist and wore a tight skirt which seemed more like a curtain pelmet, but she had the legs to go with it. Her body-hugging V-neck sweater revealed well-formed breasts. I was still under the spell when Jeff introduced me to his 'princess' who stopped chewing gum long enough to say, 'Hello Pete,' in such a broad accent that it instantly dispelled my romantic vision of her.

Jeff asked, 'Is the job still on? I'm ready.'

'Yes, if you're up for it?' I replied, bewildered.

'There's one thing,' he said hesitantly. 'I've got a problem with my car. Can you tow me to the workshop? I'll fix it after we've finished the job.'

'Sure, I've got a rope in the back of my van.'

'One more thing, can you give Sally a lift into town? She doesn't like travelling in a car that's being towed.'

'No problem!' My vehicle was a souped-up Minivan with twin-carburettors and a high compression cylinder head. It was painted white with a broad orange stripe down the centre, matching my Mallock U2 racing car.

Sally climbed down into the Minivan. Her skirt was so high that she couldn't have shown any more thigh if she had been naked. I pretended not to notice. She chatted away cheerfully, chewing at the same time. Then, when I caught her looking out of the side window, I quickly snatched a glance at her thigh. She had an impressive tattoo of a snake entwined around a six inch dagger. I dropped her off near the Wimpy Bar and carried on to the workshop.

While Jeff and I untied the tow rope, I said, 'Sally has a tattoo on her thigh!'

He laughed, then said, 'Yeah, and she's got *mild and bitter* on her breasts.'

'Oh really!'

'There's more. On her stomach is an arrow pointing to the "furry bit" that says, *pay as you enter* and *keep off the grass.*'

'Jeff, you're having me on.'

'And that's not all, she's got a hunting scene on her back with men in red coats on horseback and you'll never guess where the fox's tail is disappearing to?'

'All right, Jeff. I almost believed you up till now!' He gave a cheeky chuckle before slipping into his overalls.

I asked him later why he was dating such a wild girl. 'Sally's got a heart of gold,' he said, 'and boy does she know how to.'

Jeff's romance with Sally was short-lived. After they parted, she went down the slippery slope of drugs and rock and roll. She survived three overdoses and finally died in a car crash.

The flashback into Sally's life was suddenly interrupted when I heard Liz say, 'Come on back to the party, Peter! We are all missing you.'

Now wasn't the time to feel sad about the beautiful Sally's demise. After all, I was here to celebrate my upcoming adventure, which was only a tide away.

10. Wall of Death

Sir Francis Chichester and Sir Alec Rose were heroes of mine, but I had no intention of trying to emulate their achievements, and neither did I plan to sail around the world non-stop. All I wanted was to enjoy my journey of discovery, regardless of the destination. As I prepared for my solo voyage, my mother tried to persuade me that I should take Eileen's son Bruce along again. I wasn't keen at all and made her aware of it. The situation soon turned into an emotional battle. There was already so much tension within the family that, in the end, I relented. My nephew and I weren't particularly kindred spirits, but hopefully, he would miss his home comforts and jump ship sooner rather than later.

As I accommodated myself to the idea, I recalled the day I overheard my mother talking to her friend Vera Gray about 'Auntie Eileen' getting married. My mother was arranging the wedding reception at the Wellington Hotel and complaining about the cost and trouble, organising it all for her daughter Eileen. I suddenly felt my head spinning at the mention of 'my daughter Eileen.' This revelation was like sinking into a quicksand of lies. Until then, I thought I was my mother's only child. Why conceal the truth?

After Vera left, I went and cornered my mother. 'I've just heard you talking to Vera Gray about your daughter Eileen,' I said in a condemning voice.

'Yes,' she answered curtly.

'This means that Eileen is my sister and not my auntie.'

'Didn't I tell you?'

The only word that came out of my mouth was 'NO,' and before I could ask her why nobody ever told me, she had turned on her heels and was walking away.

How could my mother have kept such a secret and deceived me like this for so long? Learning Eileen and I had the same mother set my mind buzzing with questions. Could I trust that I was my father's son? He had left to go and fight the war in India in 1942.

I was three years old when I saw him for the first time. Tall for my age, blue-eyed with blond hair, I bore him no resemblance. There were so many questions I wanted to ask my mother, but I knew she would have said that at fifteen, I couldn't possibly understand.

Did my father know about Eileen being my half-sister? My grandparents had raised her as their daughter. In the 1930s, my mother would have been frowned upon for being pregnant out of wedlock. Eileen was nine years older than me. I remember her once babysitting me when I was three, then later wearing her Wren Navy uniform. But why wasn't I told that Eileen was my sister?

I recalled the day my mother had asked me to join her in bed, which was most unusual. Mum wasn't usually affectionate, but I felt her warmth, tucked in next to her and wondered why she was making such a fuss? It was just after the summer season of 1949. I was six years old. My father was working away, weeks at a time, while Mum managed the boarding house at 24A Newborough. I still pictured the attic bedroom, the patterned wallpaper peeling off from the sloping ceiling, and the pile of clothes draped over the brass-knobbed bed frame. There was the smell of urine too. My parents often used the chamber pot as the bathroom was two floors down, and they frequently forgot about emptying it.

My mother began telling me what a sickly baby I had been and how I only survived because of her intensive nursing. I also should have had two brothers, but they died soon after birth. Then she said, as if giving me an order, 'I hope you look after me when I'm old, just like I cared for you when you were a baby.' Her voice sweetened when she finally asked: 'Would you like a brother or a sister?'

'NO,' I replied sharply. I couldn't imagine having to share the odd cuddles, rare toys, or sweets with another sibling. Maybe my mother had tried to tell me about my sister Eileen then. But, although the rift remained between us, I was willing to forgive and forget and agreed to take Bruce on my voyage.

After a few sea trials in Scarborough Bay, *Ellis* and the crew were ready to cast off. Bruce and I slipped out at first light, leaving her berth under sail and then tacking across the narrow harbour. With the wind on the nose, *Ellis* virtually stopped dead at the entrance, so we pulled ourselves along the harbour wall until we were clear of the pier. There wasn't a soul standing on the quayside to wish us farewell that day. I hadn't told any of my friends when we might be leaving. With the ebb tide in our favour and the predominant westerlies, I was more than ready to sail down the east coast in style, even with Bruce tagging along. I put in a tack towards the beach, waved to an early morning dog walker by the water's edge, and then tacked again at a 90° angle before heading out to sea.

We coast-hopped to Poole Harbour without anything particularly riveting for Bruce to put in the book he planned to write, apart from the boat's fast performance and manoeuvrability in very light winds. For me, this was a personal journey of discovery. I knew *Ellis* would be the first *Sadler* 25 to sail to foreign shores. I had read numerous accounts of people getting sponsorship before embarking on dangerous or record-breaking voyages. With this in mind, I decided to contact Martin Sadler, who owned the factory where they made *Ellis's* hull. Maybe he might be willing to sponsor me in some way.

Martin was surprised by my call. He suggested I contact him again the next day after he'd had a chance to think about it.

When I telephoned him in the morning, he asked, 'How is your sail wardrobe?'

'Basic,' I replied.

'How about a genoa.'

'It's just what I need.'

'I'll offer you the sail,' he replied, 'but in exchange, I'd like you to send me postcards and photographs of foreign places you'll be visiting on the way. I also want you to tell me how the *Sadler* is performing.'

He must have been a mind-reader to offer me a genoa, for my sail wardrobe was as sparse as *Ellis's* interior.

Martin needed a few days to organise the new sail. But genoas don't come cheap, so it was worth the wait. Besides, Poole Harbour is beautiful, so we explored it under sail, treating every aspect of the journey as a learning curve.

That particular day taught Bruce and me a valuable lesson. We had looked for somewhere to anchor for lunch, and without checking my chart beforehand, I said, 'Let's go over there, we should have ample water, judging by the number of boats anchored off.' Then as we slowly approached the anchorage, *Ellis* suddenly lurched forward, and the mud grabbed her keel. Before I got over the shock, I heard someone shout from a nearby boat, 'Why don't you lift the keel old boy!'

Then the penny dropped. These boats were shallow draft lifting-keelers. I felt embarrassed and quickly blew up my rubber dinghy and went to lay out an anchor. I couldn't very well let *Ellis* drift away between now and the rising tide. Bruce suggested we go ashore for a pub lunch which seemed like a good idea in our predicament. There were at least three hours to go until the tide turned.

It was well into the afternoon closing time when we left the pub. By now, *Ellis* would be afloat. Meanwhile, a sea fret had swept in. We could hardly see across the road, let alone *Ellis* in the anchorage. We launched the dinghy from the beach, and I explained to Bruce that I would try rowing in a straight line, roughly in the direction where I guessed *Ellis* could be. We paddled for a while and must have gone round in circles, zigzagging between boats.

I *don't remember such a long journey to the pub!*

Every time Bruce or I sighted a shadowy silhouette in the fog, we cried out, '*Ellis*,' only to realise it wasn't her. We ran across the same vessel three times. By then, Bruce and I had sobered up, and I decided we should head back to shore and book into a B & B for the night. Hopefully, the fog would have cleared by the morning. Then just as I altered course, using the sound of traffic to home in on the shore, we bumped into *Ellis*. Poole Harbour is thirty-six square kilometres. How amazing was that!

Rule number 47 for sailors, always check your chart and be aware that boats of all sizes may have a lifting keel. Rule number 48, always take a bearing of your boat with a pocket compass when rowing ashore for a pint.

As I was sipping a glass of beer the next afternoon, sitting on the foredeck in the deckchair we had found floating and used as 'man overboard' practice on our way to Poole, I noticed a *Sadler* motoring past. I recognised the designer, David Sadler, at the helm. So I raised my glass and shouted, 'Cheers Mr Sadler.'

He and his crew glared at *Ellis* as they went past. They did a big U-turn to come alongside us. Both men looked stern and agitated.

'I must congratulate you, Mr. Sadler,' I said, trying to break the ice. 'You've designed a fine boat and I'm very pleased with mine.' This compliment had the immediate effect of wiping away the disapproving look on his face.

'Did you buy her from us?' he asked as if wanting to confirm my boat wasn't counterfeit.

'Yes, your son Martin made this red one, especially for me!'

'Oh, it must have gone through the factory when I wasn't looking,' he remarked. 'I thought at first that somebody had stolen my design! Did you fit it and rig it out yourself?'

'Yes, I did.'

'You've done a lovely job.' Mr Sadler cried as he and his crew powered away, 'Enjoy your sailing.'

Meanwhile, his son, Martin, had given me a time to meet the sailmaker at the town quay to collect the genoa.

When I arrived at our rendezvous, he handed me the sail, hot off the lofting table. I was so happy; it felt as if my fledging boat had finally got its wings. I rang Martin again before casting off to thank him for his sponsorship. 'This genoa is going to be a vital piece of kit,' I told him, smiling inside. 'I'll be updating you on how well your *Sadler* is performing.'

'I look forward to that,' he answered.

Falmouth was our jumping-off point to cross Biscay, non-stop to Finisterre. The weather seemed promising for us to leave, but as we sailed within two miles of the southbound shipping lane, the wind dropped to nothing, leaving us to wallow uncomfortably in the swell. I didn't fancy motoring through the shipping lanes with my two horsepower engine. Besides, with the right wind, *Ellis* was three times faster under sail, especially with the new genoa. So we headed back and dropped anchor behind 'The Lizard' where we rolled and pitched all night long.

In the morning, apart from light rain, the wind direction and strength proved ideal to set off across the Channel, so we lifted anchor and, at nightfall, traversed the southbound shipping lane before entering the separation zone. It would be another ten miles before we reached the northbound lane. Night had fallen, and the rain had condensed into fog - one needed eyes and ears in this hectic shipping zone, especially in poor visibility. At least the self-steering wind-vane was keeping a good course, and I had taken a radio direction fix on Ushant beacon, bracing myself against the mast to counteract the bumpy motion. I could hear the sea hissing past the hull and the wind whistling in the rigging as *Ellis* cut through the mounting swell and thickening fog. To be trapped in this heavy mist was eerie. My world only extended to a few yards beyond the bows.

What a place to be caught in such conditions! The masthead navigation light cast strange shadows in the swirling fog, mimicking looming cliffs only yards away. It was hard to conceive that we were in the middle of the English Channel, which didn't feel like it at all.

There was no sound of foghorns or sign of a ship nearby, so I thought I had enough time to go below deck and plot my bearing on the chart. Besides, we were still some way off the northbound shipping lane.

I went down below to check our position on the chart. Sitting at the navigation table, I felt *Ellis* suddenly lurching violently, and I was thrown out of my seat and across the cabin floor.

What the hell is happening? I scrambled for the open cockpit hatch and leaned out to see what had caused such a savage jerk. I saw this wall of steel ploughing past us at a pace and *Ellis* crashing against it. Was her fragile hull about to be caved in?

The surge that had sent me sprawling from the chart table must have been the ship's bow wave thrusting *Ellis* to one side like a cork. I froze, clinging to the companionway frame to stop myself from being bounced about like a passenger in a stock car race without a seatbelt. Bruce had been asleep in the forward cabin when he was catapulted off his bunk. He staggered into the saloon in shock, and together, out of the cabin hatch, we stared at the floating monster grinding past while *Ellis's* starboard bow and pulpit plunged against it. If *Ellis* had been another ten feet further forward, we would have been cut in half.

Everything went into slow motion from that moment, like the day I somersaulted three times in my racing car at Mallory Park circuit. I was once again dodging the scythe of the Grim Reaper.

The torture went on and on as *Ellis* smashed against this wall of death, and there was nothing I could do to stop it. Then, in the glow of the masthead navigation light, horror switched to sheer terror when I realised the ship was in ballast. I had seen big tankers without cargo with their propellers thrashing halfway out of the water. And now the giant's load-line was looming twenty feet above our pitching deck.

Ellis is about to be chopped into bits when we reach the ship's stern.

With the violent turbulence of the vessel's wash, *Ellis* pounded against her steel plates. I heard Bruce shouting above the deafening roar, 'I'm getting the life-raft.' It was strapped on deck, forward of the mast.

'No, we've got to stay right here inside,' I yelled out to Bruce, grasping his arm firmly. 'You've no lifejacket or harness. If you go on deck, you'll be thrown overboard and never seen again. Just hang on. We've got to stay with the boat.'

The tanker acted like a giant magnet, sucking us in and pinning us against its hull. I thought the propeller would make scrambled eggs out of us any moment now.

I went numb.

As we came closer to the ship's deadly blades and the few seconds Bruce and I had left to live, something unexpected happened. With great force, *Ellis* was pitched to one side, and with the outward thrust the vessel's wash created, my little boat was sent clear of her mammoth propeller.

We only escaped with inches to spare from the lethal blades, which would have mashed us to a pulp. But, like Indiana Jones, we survived the tunnel of doom by dodging the pendulum of death and got away with the greatest treasure: our lives.

The self-steering gear took over as we sailed out of the ship's wind shadow. There was nobody on the well-illuminated bridge deck. I suspected that the captain and crew knew nothing of the collision, as we never heard a siren before or after impact. Then the noise of the throbbing engine steadily died away, and the vessel disappeared into the mist.

My heart was still racing, and the blood rushing through my veins sounded as loud as the hissing sea. It took me a while to snap out of my stupor.

I anticipated substantial damage and urged Bruce to go and check the forepeak from below. I clipped my harness to the lifeline and crawled along the deck to the bow with a torch. My legs were still shaking, and I felt far too weak to stand. What was I going to find where most of the pounding from the ship took place?

At first glance, I noticed the pulpit of the boat had been pushed over at a crazy angle. Then, as I lay on my stomach and leant over the deck rail to check the hull, expecting a gaping hole, there was only a graze of slime and red anti-fouling from the ship - what a huge relief.

Making my way back to the cockpit, I gripped the side-shroud to steady myself and almost fell onto the deck. It should have been as taut as a tightrope wire but was now waving about like a washing line without a clothes prop. When I shone my torch up the mast, I saw the starboard cross-tree hanging limply but still attached. I had a spare halyard I used when hoisting the second headsail, so I clipped it around the floppy rigging and hauled it up until it reached underneath the cross-tree. Then, with a short controlled heave, I managed to get it to stand out at a 90° angle from the mast back in its correct position, and the rigging was again in tension.

By the time I finished, dawn was breaking. Out of the fog to starboard, I saw several Russian fishing boats 'dead in the water,' with the crew hauling in their nets. Their presence confirmed to me we were still in the separation zone. I doubted this fishing fleet would be drifting in the shipping lanes in such fog. I thought of approaching one of the skippers to ask if he could try and radio the ship that had collided with us and inform the captain we had survived, although I felt sure he had no idea of the incident. If he had known about it, he would have blasted his siren or flashed spotlights on us, or at the very least, have had someone wave from the flybridge. We continued hearing other ships blowing their sirens, one long blast every two minutes, so why had this vessel not complied? Although we had a lingering kiss of death with the tanker, we didn't know her name. And if we set up the alarm, it would only lead to confusion.

My original intention before the collision was to give Ushant and the Chenal du Four a wide berth and set a course for Finisterre, allowing myself enough sea room lest I had to sail before a westerly gale in mid-Biscay. But alas, I was now left with two options: either to sail one hundred miles back to Falmouth, tacking against the wind through the shipping lanes, or head for Brest, forty miles away. Although I didn't have a detailed chart of Brittany, the latter seemed the lesser of two evils.

On our way south of Ushant, we sailed into turbulent overfalls. *Ellis* pitched and pounded through them with such savage motion that it felt as if we were on a rodeo ride. If only we had been half an hour earlier or later, we would have avoided these treacherous waters altogether, but the current and tide had propelled us into them faster than I could have sailed away. These standing waves must have been at least two or three metres high, resulting from more than six knots of current flowing over an uneven seabed, thus creating steep overfalls at a particular state of the tide. The outboard motor was no use even with the wind dropping below ten knots; the propeller would be out of the water thrashing air more often than not in the confused sea. So I continued battling through this, desperately holding on to the tiller and the lifelines. The crew's nerves were like overstretched guitar strings.

Bruce couldn't face it and retreated down below, where he wedged himself in his bunk. I remained at the tiller, coaxing *Ellis* in this boiling cauldron, hanging on for dear life, waiting for the tide to carry us through. The sails flapped about like some demented semaphore signalling system, for the motion shook any drive out of them.

Next time I plan to go whitewater rafting, I promise myself not to do it in Ellis. Sailing is supposed to be fun! As I recalled what I had just lived through, I noticed a French frigate abreast of us, less than a quarter of a mile away. The antics of *Ellis* must have looked alarming from the ship's bridge. Maybe they were concerned about our safety, for as soon as we sailed out of these raging waters, the ship disappeared over the horizon. It never dawned on me that the vessel could have been searching for a yacht which looked visibly damaged after a collision.

I sighed when we reached the mouth of Brest estuary. *Ellis* had cheated Davey Jones and the Grim Reaper. They must have been arguing with each other for our souls.

11. Déjà Vu

Moored at Moulin Blanc Marina seemed hardly credible after such a hellish toboggan ride. Time and again, I pictured *Ellis* bouncing against the tanker. I kept thinking how close we came to her thrashing propellor blades.

Maybe Bruce might decide to leave after such an ordeal? I wanted him to but couldn't bring myself to say it to his face. He would at least have a headline for a gruelling chapter in his book, 'Collision in fog with a Tanker.'

It was a consolation that *Ellis* suffered relatively minor damage. Although the bow looked like a modern sculpture gone wrong, I could remedy this, using block and tackle to straighten it without too much effort. However, the mast would need a professional repair from a shipyard.

As I started bending metal, I heard a woman's voice from the boat moored at the next pontoon. 'How come your bow railing is in such a tangled mess?' she yelled.

When I told her of the collision, she pouted her red-painted lips, and the man standing next to her raised a bushy eyebrow. Neither of them seemed convinced.

The following morning, the woman came bustling down the pontoon waving 'Le Télégramme de Brest,' shouting the headlines like a town crier. "Voilier en collision avec un paquebot." 'Do you want me to translate the article for you?' she asked.

'Would you?'

She began: *'After an unsuccessful search to find the wreckage of a small sailing yacht run down by the 68,500-ton Belgian ore carrier, The Mineral Alegria, the question has been raised: was there a collision, and if so, did the yacht sink? This would have been in the night between Thursday 31 August and 04h15 GMT, Friday 1 September 1977 (06h15 local time). The ship that had sailed from Brazil, bound for Gand, Belgium, was in the northbound shipping lane, 8½ miles west of the island of Ushant, when the crew noticed a yacht sliding down the side of their vessel before disappearing into the murk. It was identified as a 6-metre-long craft with one mast and two sails. No one was seen on deck and no radar reading was picked up before or after the collision. Turning back the 253-metre-long, 13-metre-draft vessel to look for wreckage took considerable time and effort. When no trace of the yacht was found, the captain radioed Le Conquet, the Ushant Lifeboat, and the Marine and Custom Patrol boats. French Naval ships were launched; aircraft and helicopters were also deployed, including foreign vessels which diverted their courses to assist in the massive sea search of the area.'*

Involving the rescue authorities was the last thing I wanted to happen. Some people might say that if I had had a VHF radio, the authorities wouldn't have needed to search for wreckage. Not really!

The aerial and masthead light would have been smashed to pieces when the top of *Ellis's* mast hit the ship. I believe the captain's conduct was unethical, and I still maintain today that he was in the separation zone. He never sounded his foghorn signal, blew his siren, used a searchlight or waved from the bridge deck. There was no sign of anyone before or after the collision.

Le Télégramme de Brest had also reported that a Pen Duick 600 with four crew on board was overdue on a passage from Camaret to Le Havre. A Navy spokesman believed the small craft might have been in the collision with *The Mineral Alegria.* It was unlikely that the crew would have sailed to their intended destination, if indeed they had survived!

I immediately telephoned Le Télégramme de Brest and informed them that my boat *Ellis* had collided with The *Mineral Alegria.* A journalist then contacted the French Naval Authorities and the Rescue Services to pass on this new finding.

A large black Citroen picked me up from the marina and whisked me to the Naval Dockyard the following morning. I was guided to the eighth floor of the French Naval Headquarters and ushered into a room where three officers were waiting pompously behind a highly polished mahogany table. They looked impressive in their uniforms, with sleeves decorated in gold braid from the cuff right to the armpit. I bade them *Bonjour.*

They never returned my greeting. Then one of the officers laid a chart of Ushant on the table and asked in perfect English: 'Can you show us where you think the collision took place? We need to establish whether it was your boat or not.' I showed him where I calculated the collision happened.

'You could have gained this information from the chartlet in the newspaper,' he said aggressively.

I felt as if I was under cross-examination while they tried to break my alibi, so I replied in a matching tone: 'My boat has flakes of paint on the foredeck off the side of *The Mineral Alegria*.'

The officer was unimpressed by my explanation.

'And the ship was in ballast, wasn't she?'

This evidence seemed significant enough for him to dismiss me. Without another word, he nodded at the able seaman, indicating that he should drive me back to Moulin Blanc Marina. *Has the French Navy still not forgiven the English for the Battle of Trafalgar?*

Stating the ship was in ballast confirmed that *Ellis* was the mystery yacht in the collision with *The Mineral Alegria*, the newspaper never reported this crucial information. Later, a journalist tracked me down, wanting to relay my side of the story. He had interviewed the watchman on the tanker who told him, off-the-record, that he had seen a masthead light sliding down the side of the ship. He spent half an hour trying to convince his captain of the collision, insisting he turned the vessel around and looked for survivors. By the time the captain informed the Rescue Services, another hour had passed before *The Mineral Alegria* returned to the scene of the collision. By then, we were long gone. Later, the journalist mentioned that the captain admitted to being on the edge of the shipping lane. As for the *Pen Duick 600,* reported missing, the crew had sought shelter in Jersey.

We were delayed in Brest for a few weeks, waiting for repairs and spare fittings to arrive from England. The September nights were drawing in. Bruce complained about having to read by oil lamps. We were staying up late and never got up before nine o'clock. He came up with the idea of advancing the time on our watches and the ship's clock by three hours. He thought it might trick us into believing that when we went to bed, thinking it was midnight, it would only be nine o'clock. As a result, we would gain three hours of daylight in the evening and benefit from an early night. I agreed to the time change to humour him.

As I walked to town one morning, a Frenchman stopped me and asked, *'Quelle heure est-il?'* Unable to answer him in French, I showed him my watch. He said, *'Merci'* and went on his way. Glancing over my shoulder, I saw the Frenchman's look of indignation and heard him muttering to himself: *'Quel imbécile d'Anglais!'*

What was wrong with him? Then it dawned on me when I got to town. The shops weren't open. No wonder, I was three hours adrift. Back on *Ellis,* I announced to Bruce, 'That's it! My watch and ship's clock are reverting to local time, and you can bloody please yourself what you do.'

Walking from the marina to the shops in the city centre took Bruce and me a good hour without transport. On our return to the marina that day, now using local time, we noticed a British yacht moored in the commercial dock. I was curious when I saw a wooden stump in place of a mast. A man and a woman were standing in the cockpit. I asked them what had happened and briefly mentioned our collision with *The Mineral Alegria,* which explained why we were in Brest.

'We were in a collision too,' the woman said. 'It happened when I was on watch. John had been at the wheel throughout the night in thick fog, and at daybreak I persuaded him to put his head down. He reluctantly agreed but insisted that I wake him up as soon as I heard a ship's siren.'

'You left it too bloody late,' John butted in.

'Shut up, John. I'm telling the story.'

'When I heard a faint siren I called John, and before we knew it, a ship was bearing down on us. Its bow wave pushed our boat to one side, spinning us broadside on and we rolled heavily against the vessel. Then there was a big crack. The whole mast and sails plummeted down around us, and we were buried under the mainsail. Next, we saw the ship's crew flashing their lights at us and waving from the bridge amidships as we grazed down the side of the vessel. We couldn't contact the captain on the radio as our aerial was carried away when the mast fell. While we were untangling ourselves, the ship returned to see if we needed assistance.' John took up the story from there.

'As the ship came out of the fog, I thought we were going to be run down for a second time. I couldn't start the engine for fear of getting ropes or rigging around our propeller but the captain's manoeuvre was amazing. He brought the ship close enough to give us a lee from the waves and he even managed to shout through cupped hands, asking if we needed further assistance. I told him that once we had cleared away all rigging and ropes and secured the mast from ramming a hole through our boat, we would carry on alone motoring to Brest. The captain held station until we completed our task which took a few hours of frantic work. Then he contacted Brest emergency services, and a lifeboat arrived at the scene to escort us to La Rade de Brest.'

I helped John with the jury rig before they motor-sailed back to the Solent for repairs. He and Annette frequently crossed the English Channel to visit relatives in Brest. Their experience seemed to vindicate my opinion of the captain's conduct on *The Mineral Alegria.* He must have been oblivious of our collision or didn't want to know until his second-in-command pushed him to take action. I wondered how often this happens between small yachts and big ships?

Bruce was now concerned about the bill for the mast repairs and thought our trip would be compromised. 'Shall I lend you half the amount?' he asked.

'No, Bruce, just pay me your share of the harbour dues as we agreed. I'll get the money back from the insurance company, so let's make ready for sea. We are out of here as soon as I've paid up.'

As we sailed across Biscay almost becalmed, the heavens seemed shrouded by a black cloak pierced with millions of pinpricks. Even under such a beautiful night sky, there was no respite for us after our narrow escape from the jaws of death. Bruce and I took turns watching for shipping, hand-held flares at the ready, standing in the cockpit to start the outboard if we should find ourselves in the path of another vessel. We spent a very uncomfortable night haunted by the memory of the collision.

When dawn broke, Bruce emerged to take his watch, just as I was working out our dead reckoning and plotting radio fixes at the chart table. 'Where are we now?' he asked, looking at the chart.

'This is my assumed position,' I pointed out.

'You mean you don't know where we are?'

'With a minimum of two bearings from known landmarks, you always quote your position as ASSUMED,' I stated. 'Dead reckoning isn't a precise navigational tool, and the accuracy of radio bearings generally depends on how far away the transmitter is.'

Bruce remained doubtful about our position until the cliffs of Finisterre loomed into view two days later, at precisely the time I had predicted.

The tension between us was mounting like a swell before the storm. We were two people who should never be confined to a small cabin for more than fifteen minutes! It was a pity I didn't fully realise this earlier!

To save water, neither of us washed while crossing Biscay. Bruce was paranoid about body odour. So every day, he splashed himself with deodorant. I found it off-putting whilst he thought my feet were repugnant after several watches in sailing boots. But there was much more. Bruce resented my knowledge of navigation and seamanship and deplored being in the hands of a less well-educated person. He hated the blues, which is my favourite style of music, while I cared little about his chamber music and modern jazz. I also thought he had an unfortunate habit of putting his hand over his mouth when he laughed as if adopting the persona of Queen Victoria, 'We are not amused!'

Close-hauled in a fresh offshore wind brought us the intense fragrance of pine trees, sending insects off-course and out to sea. One afternoon, a pigeon tried to land on the stern and missed. I watched him float away on the ocean with his wings outstretched. It seemed to me that he would never fly again. The bird, rapidly drifting away, must have realised that the boat was his only hope of salvation. He flapped his wings, and despite his sodden feathers, he became airborne. Then soaked and exhausted, he made an ungainly crash-landing in the cockpit next to me. The pigeon had a ring on his leg. I carefully picked him up, took him down below and sat him on the cabin floor with a few breadcrumbs.

I returned to the cockpit to enjoy a lively sail in the sunshine, leaving the wretched creature to recover in peace. A few hours later, the pigeon flapped around the cabin. He landed on my chart table and created a new island on my map of Biscay. Then the bird took off. He circled three times around *Ellis* before flying away towards Spain.

Our next visitor was a robin. I made him comfortable in the saloon, and when I checked on him later, he had disappeared. I presumed he must have flown off without me noticing him. Sadly, I found his remains weeks later, hidden away at the back of a locker.

El Ferrol was our first port of call in Spain. It is a naval base in a large natural harbour at the head of a short narrow *ria* with no facilities. So when I saw a fifty-foot classic wooden yawl moored against the only part of the pier that gave access to the shore via a steel ladder, I chugged along under motor towards the vessel. As I came close, I noticed a large red ensign and hailed someone on deck. I guessed he might be the owner. I asked his permission to tie up alongside.

The man promptly left his deckchair and put his gin and tonic and *The Times* down on a table. Then he lowered his glasses to the end of his nose, presumably to focus on us better before he said with a public school accent: 'Sorry old boy, I had to make jolly sure you weren't *Froggies*. Of course you may come alongside. You know the etiquette. Always walk on the foredeck when crossing our boat.

'Throw a rope, old bean!'

The man had a waxed moustache and wore baggy trousers and a threadbare stripy blazer. The shiny buttons and immaculate military medals on his breast pocket looked totally out of character. The much-neglected boat, built around the 1930s, mirrored the man's disposition, including his weathered straw boater. A woman with a creased white dress and a floppy hat was chatting on the foredeck with two young chaps in rugby shirts and knee-length shorts.

After Hubert had introduced himself and supervised us with the correct placing of fenders and ropes, he returned to his chair near our cockpit. Then acting like a monarch on his throne, he droned on in an endless monologue about World War II.

Meanwhile, a French boat of a similar size to *Ellis* was headed our way. They, like us, may not have wanted to face the twelve-foot scramble onto the quayside without a ladder. Hubert abandoned his monologue and without asking leave, he sprang over our cockpit, one hand grasping our rigging, the other waving his rolled-up newspaper as if it was a *bâton* to ward off peasants storming the Bastille. 'Buzz off, we don't want you *Frenchies* here,' he shouted in schoolboy French. '*Vous ne pouvez pas venir ici. Ça n'est pas possible. Allez-vous-en, allez-vous-en.*'

His bellowing startled the young couple, who swiftly altered course to go and tie up further along the harbour wall. Hubert later apologised for his outburst and for omitting to ask permission before crossing our cockpit. 'I had enough of De Gaulle and his type during the war,' he ranted. 'I'm sorry, I'm not having *Froggies* walking across my boat.'

We felt compelled to go and see the couple and apologise for our neighbour's eccentricities. They seemed sympathetic. One night, we ate on their boat, much to Hubert's disapproval, although he never made any comments.

We cast off at dawn on the third day and let *Ellis* wallow in the bay, two miles from the entrance to El Ferrol. Even though the sun was shining in a clear blue sky, a low-level mist blanketed the sea with the high cliffs just peeking above it. At sea level, visibility was a quarter of a mile or less. *No need to rush,* I thought. *The sun is bound to burn the mist away. A land breeze may soon spring up. Besides, who wants to listen to a barking outboard motor in this blissfulness.*

Skipper and crew breakfasted on the eerie flat sea. Tucking into our bacon and eggs made a pleasant change from Bruce's boring but healthy yogurt and muesli.

We had noticed a naval tugboat crossing our stern, but neither of us could make out what the vessel was towing in the haze. We were far too engrossed in our food to question what the crew were doing.

Curiosity, however, got the better of us when five minutes later, we noticed the tug was returning to El Ferrol, this time without a tow. I looked over my shoulder to retrace the tugboat's route and saw something floating in the water that resembled a giant up-ended chessboard. I immediately felt the all too familiar heaviness in my stomach, warning me that something terrible was about to happen.

I believed the object was a gunnery target less than three hundred yards from us - definitively not the place to be lingering over breakfast! 'We'd better get out of here,' I shouted to Bruce.

Knives and forks hit the deck as I sprang to the stern to start the outboard motor. I was on my third pull of the cord, expecting shells to whistle through the rigging any second when I saw through the low-lying fog a gunboat with a Spanish flag heading towards *Ellis*. It stopped within a couple of boat lengths of her. Then through a megaphone, we heard in perfect English: 'Do you mind steering 060°? There's an exercise about to happen.'

I continued pulling the cord on the *Seagull* outboard like a demented lumberjack trying to start his stubborn chainsaw. Once underway, the gunboat escorted us on a 060° bearing for a mile or so. Then the Commander hailed me again on his megaphone to hold station until the exercise had finished.

Soon after, we saw huge splashes erupting around the target, but the shells from the shore battery guns fell short of hitting their intended objective. If Bruce and I had stayed where we were having breakfast, *Ellis* would have been sunk, with the Spanish Navy reaping revenge for losing several of their ships at the *Battle of Trafalgar.*

While *Ellis* continued drifting near the gunboat, we could hear the delayed report of the guns from the shore batteries. During a lull in the firing, I hailed the Commander.

'How did you know my boat was near the target in this fog?' I asked. 'Did you pick it up on the radar?'

'Affirmative.'

'You're saying you received a good image of my boat?'

'Yes, you were clear on the screen,' he repeated impatiently. This conversation restored my confidence in the aluminium radar reflector mounted on the mast as *Ellis* had shown a good blip on the gunboat's radar.

When the gunners stopped firing, the officer allowed us to resume our journey. I wondered why *The Mineral Alegria* hadn't picked *Ellis* up on their radar screen? Was it even switched on?

I was relieved when we moored at La Coruña Marina after such a rollercoaster of events. I kept thinking of how close we came to being blown up during target practice. *I must stop making a habit of being in the wrong place at the wrong time!* Therefore it was more than a welcome distraction to find ourselves relaxing in the cockpit with a glass of wine in the evening, watching people walking along the pontoon. A young bearded man had approached *Ellis*, looking intently down at us. Then, in a heavy French accent, he asked: 'Was your yacht in a collision off Ushant some weeks ago?'

He might as well have thrown a bucket of cold water at me. I shivered with the memory of that day. I never expected such an opening line and was astounded that he had recognised *Ellis*, let alone heard about the collision with *The Mineral Alegria.*

'Yes,' I replied, still under the shock.

'Do you remember the missing *Pen Duick 600*? Here's a photograph of her in Jersey. You can keep it,' he said, handing it to me. 'The crew on the *Pen Duick* never told anyone when they sheltered in Jersey,' the man explained. 'When the accompanying yachts lost contact with her, they carried on to Le Havre before they reported her missing.'

What a remarkable coincidence! It churned me up so much that I never thought of asking the stranger where he had learned about the collision. When I looked up from the photo, he had disappeared, leaving me perplexed. Once again, my headsail had been taken aback by the wind.

After all these near-misses, I had almost forgotten the meaning of plain sailing, so it was a respite to day-hop for a week in untroubled waters from La Coruña along the Spanish and Portuguese Atlantic coast playing tourists at every harbour until we arrived in Lisbon.

12. Armadas and Dolphins

As we left Lisbon's bright lights to sail under a starless night sky in lumpy seas, I felt as if I was riding the Black Knight's snorting steed. At least my self-steering wind-vane kept an accurate course, but I was frustrated that I couldn't navigate by the stars, especially along this featureless coast towards Cape Vicente. Every hour I plotted my estimated position and speed. Then in the dead of night, I noticed lights emerging from the north. *They must be city lights, but how come when the land is to the east?* I checked the compass course and thought something was wrong, then grabbed the binoculars and looked.

What I took for city lights were ships bearing down on us from the north. At a guess, there must have been fifteen or more. Even in the congested English Channel, there wouldn't be so many vessels sailing closely together. Were we being overhauled by another naval exercise?

I didn't have time to panic. Some 'port and starboard' lights were rapidly approaching from seaward, and before I knew it, I was blinded by the searchlight of a gunboat. The crew took a good look at *Ellis* with me on deck, then shot off in a southerly direction like aliens disliking the sight of earthlings!

Have we just been checked out by one of the armada's picket boats? Is this a naval convoy, and are they friend or foe?

I had to think of a strategy to get out of the way. Tacking against headwinds in the path of a fleet of warships would be like doing a slalom on a ski slope, trying to outrun an avalanche. For a start, we were outnumbered, and I doubted that an armada would give way to sail. *Ellis* could be a collateral sinking.

There were no towns or lighthouses on this stretch of coastline to help me with my navigation. The only option left was tacking back and forth in thirty to forty metres of depth to keep out of the shipping lane. I would maintain this avoiding action unless the wind shifted. Such being the case, we could then sail parallel to the coast. Navigating by the contour lines on the seabed is a recognised strategy when there are no visual features. Looking at my chart, we were about half a mile offshore. As the depth gauge showed thirty-five metres, I realised I would soon have to tack out. Then when I heard the roaring of the Atlantic swell crashing onto the pebbled beach, I knew it was time to turn. By now, the armada was out of sight. I checked the depth sounder once more, but this time to my horror, I saw multiple bleeps flickering all around the dial.

Rocks, I thought!

I pushed the tiller hard over, pulled in the sails and when I looked over my shoulder, I saw something breaking the surface where I would have been if I hadn't turned out to sea. But then I noticed something else far more menacing.

Two foaming phosphorescent tubes were speeding towards *Ellis,* just like those seen in U-boat movies with torpedoes about to blow a ship to smithereens.

So this is it - we are being used as a target again.

The explosion, thank heavens, never happened.

These phosphorescent tubes dived under the keel before making a U-turn. I realised they were dolphins joining others on the bow wave, which explained why my depth gauge went berserk. Had they been torpedoes, they would have obliterated Bruce and me in a shower of blood, guts and fibreglass.

I felt the dolphins hadn't just come to play with *Ellis's* bow wave but to warn me of running into danger. Maybe it was a semi-submerged container lost from a ship or an unmarked wreck? Had I not tacked at that moment, we would have found ourselves with a big hole in the bow, and *Good Night Vienna* or, in our case, *Lisbon.*

I believe that the dolphins saved us, for as soon as I headed into deeper waters, they swam away. Had this been their mission? I will never know.

By then the wind had shifted, and I sailed along the coast with no further engagement with the Portuguese Armada. I covered an extra two hours on my shift to catch the dawn and give Bruce a lie-in, even though we had agreed on a six-hour watch, reduced to two if sea conditions worsened. He took over from me, oblivious of the drama that had taken place while he was asleep. Saying nothing saved me from him quoting Laurel and Hardy: 'Here's another fine mess you've gotten us into.'

Before I retreated to my bunk, I gave Bruce strict instructions to update the logbook every hour and keep a 185° course. I also reminded him to stay alert and watch out for shipping. *George*, the self-steering, would do the rest. I slept for the next six hours, and when I came on deck, I noticed we were 90° off our course to Cape Vicente. 'What's happening with the compass heading Bruce?' I asked.

'Oh, *Ellis* was sailing better on this bearing,' he replied casually.

'Fine! But when did the wind direction change?'

'Two or three hours ago,' he answered flippantly. 'I can't remember for sure. I've been making notes for my book. *Ellis* is sailing okay, isn't she?'

'Yes, if you fancy America as the next stop!' I growled.

Bruce couldn't grasp that the self-steering gear kept the boat at an angle to the wind and not necessarily on the course required. As the skipper, I had failed to ensure he understood my instructions on reading the compass and adjusting the self-steering gear accordingly. I had learned to use a sextant and taught myself celestial navigation but never enjoyed complicated mathematical theories. However, the book was simple to follow. I entered my sextant readings and time into Pro Forma pads and applied Versine and Cosine tables. I added and subtracted these figures and followed instructions which brought me to a presumed position on the chart. I had shown Bruce each stage of the process several times, from taking a sunsight to applying it to the mathematical tables in my books, but he kept insisting I explain, in minute detail, how and why I extracted my results. For me, as long as I came up with a usable fix, it was all that mattered.

My outlook on the subject infuriated him. Then one day, I lost patience and said, 'Here's the book, it should be child's play for a university graduate like yourself. Just learn as I have!' He never opened the book but complained to other people we met that his Uncle Peter had refused to teach him navigation. I thought, if Bruce was from Mars, my origin, according to him, could be lost beyond the Solar System.

Visibility had deteriorated by then. We would have been within sight of land if only Bruce had noticed the wind change and not left the boat to sail off-course for several hours. As a result, we were back into the shipping lanes. Finally, after a few hours of sailing in a south-easterly direction, we sighted land and resumed our course along the coast once again. Before dark, we rounded Cape Vicente and moored in the first bay to shelter from a force five northerly. I expected a few fishing boats to be anchored off close to the sleepy village, but the anchorage was deserted and eerie. Maybe I was paranoid after all the recent events!

Then Bruce and I settled down to another of his healthy but flavourless meals of chopped raw cabbage, dried fruit, nuts, and any other vegetable on board. Shame I didn't enjoy cooking. Sometimes Bruce added a tin of tuna as a luxury treat! He usually frowned when I drowned the wholesome mix with Heinz salad cream.

After a peaceful night's sleep, we woke up to glorious morning sunshine and breakfasted on deck. Bruce was looking down his nose at me once again. 'What a philistine to be swamping homemade muesli in condensed milk,' he must have thought. I wanted to say: 'I prefer to enjoy my food rather than be the healthiest corpse in the graveyard.'

I didn't have time to dwell upon my nephew's opinion about me as two jets suddenly came flying over our mast at such a low altitude that my immediate reaction was to duck. Two other planes followed, firing rockets in the direction of the next bay.

This military exercise felt like *déjà vu*. The air was buzzing as if thousands of giant bumblebees were swarming overhead. Dozens of helicopters filled the sky, carrying jeeps and ammunition boxes in nets. While eating our breakfast, Bruce and I were treated to a personalised military tattoo.

When the sky traffic finally quietened down, we lifted anchor, making for the Portuguese port of Lagos. We rounded the headland and sailed into the next bay, where another spectacle awaited us. The armada I had managed to avoid the night before last was anchored off the beachhead.

I thought it would be exciting to go through the middle of a mock battle. Besides, it was also the shortest route across the bay.

As we sailed through the fleet of supply ships, frigates, and landing craft, we ran the full gauntlet of the officers' indignant gaze. It felt as if we were gatecrashers at an exclusive party, waiting for the bouncers to arrive and ask us to leave!

The armada was now about a mile away when we heard the roar of a powerful engine. Then we saw a giant bow wave masking the shape of a gunboat speeding towards us. I quickly put the tiller hard to port to avoid a collision, but the boat followed my manoeuvre and proceeded towards *Ellis*. The helmsman seemed determined to run us down, and there was nothing I could do to outsmart him other than for us to jump over the side to port or starboard.

When we thought we only had a few seconds left to live, the gunboat aborted its ramming course, missing *Ellis's* stern by inches, but the enormous wake almost swept us overboard. Below deck was mayhem. Everything stored away had been turned upside down as if thieves had ransacked the place. Had we upset some admiral, only for him to send a gunboat to teach us a lesson: *'Don't mess with the Portuguese Navy.'*

All came to a head between skipper and crew when we reached Vilamoura Marina. Bruce was keen to get to the Canary Islands before Christmas. Then I met Karen, and romance was in the air. She was the niece of a Canadian couple who invited me on their boat one night for dinner. I made excuses to Bruce that *Ellis* wasn't ready to leave as casual glances between Karen and me soon bloomed into an affair.

He was peeved at this new development. Besides, we constantly irritated each other. I cringed each time he introduced me to someone with, 'This is my Uncle Peter,' and I took revenge, saying, 'My little nephew Bruce,' even though he was two inches taller than me and only twelve years younger. This petty game exacerbated our strained 'skipper and crew' relationship. It was my boat, and he had no right to begrudge my brief encounter with Karen. She was flying back to Canada in a few days, and who was he to dictate when we should leave.

I never wanted him on my boat in the first place, but his mother and grandmother had badgered me into taking him. Maybe I was naive enough to think it would improve our family bond and help his career as a writer. He must have thought he would be gathering aquatic material for his book sitting in a deckchair with a cocktail in one hand and a pen in the other! After all, I had given him multiple roller-coaster rides and now a juicy love story. What more did he want? And was it not pure madness for me to contemplate sailing across the Atlantic Ocean with him in the first place? I was more than capable of doing it alone anyway. I wondered what the odds would be after a long haul at sea of one crew instead of two reaching the Americas.

Bruce had a long face the next day. Over a late breakfast, he fired a few sarcastic remarks at me about my affairs. That was when I blew up. My pent-up frustrations were like the incoming tide, and I was no King Canute to hold back the flood. 'I won't be told about when and where *Ellis* should go!' I yelled. 'If you don't like it, I suggest you leave right now.'

Bruce's know-it-all attitude was getting to me. He constantly put me down in front of other people because he went to university while I didn't. Why should I swallow a bloody dictionary for breakfast every day with my muesli? How I wanted to bash him over the head with his *Collins* and make him permanently impotent at playing scrabble.

My outburst must have caught him off-guard. He was lost for words. When he regained his composure, he asked if I could take him at least as far as the Canary Islands.

I had said my piece and consented to his plea but insisted that I would only take him as far as the agreed destination and no further. Karen then flew back to Canada a few days later, and Bruce and I set off for the Canary Islands via Cadiz.

It was night when we sailed into the Bay of Cadiz. I was surprised to see what seemed like a large island with many houses and streetlights in the middle of it. I looked at my chart; there wasn't an island there. How bizarre! I noticed helicopters landing and taking off, so I proceeded with caution. Then, finally, the penny dropped. The island was a US Nimitz class aircraft carrier, one of the largest warships of its kind ever built, with a 100,000-ton displacement and a flight deck the length of three football pitches.

The following morning, I left *Ellis* early to visit the town. Bruce was still in bed. I thought the less time we spent together, the better. I stopped at an art gallery in the city centre where I saw an unusual painting of a black Madonna carrying her infant. I hadn't seen one before and was rather engrossed when I sensed the presence of someone standing behind me.

'I hear there's a statue of a black Madonna in a church nearby,' a male voice announced with an American accent.

I turned my head and saw a black sailor in a US Navy uniform. We started a conversation, and I expressed my surprise to see a sailor in a gallery. 'My shipmates are probably touring all the bars and brothels in town,' he said with a grin. 'I'm considered an oddball for choosing to experience Spanish culture instead.'

We chatted like good old friends. Then, he asked me if I would join him in his search for the statue of the Black Madonna.

'Why not,' I said.

We visited several churches, each as elaborate as the other, but without success. Then, in a small chapel on a back street, we came across a life-sized statue of a black Madonna holding her infant. It was an unsophisticated carving that seemed to be what Jack had been searching for, judging by the bright expression on his face. I wondered if he would tell his shipmates that he had found a black Madonna in Cadiz. Would they ask him if she had big boobies like Herr Otto Flick in the television comedy *Allo Allo!*

After leaving the church, I invited Jack for afternoon tea on *Ellis*. He thought the invitation rather quaint, coming from an English guy.

Bruce was sitting in the cockpit reading when we arrived. He had the look of a puritanical mother disapproving of her wayward son, bringing a stranger across the threshold.

Over tea, I asked Jack about his role on the carrier. 'I'm an egg-fryer first class,' he said proudly.

'You mean your only job is to fry eggs?' Bruce asked over the rim of his teacup. He was holding it with his little finger in the air.

'Have you any idea how many eggs I fry each day for six thousand crew - even with a large team of egg-friers under my command?' Jack remarked.

I thought Bruce always complained about how I cooked his egg, boiled or fried. What did he expect with a paraffin-wicked stove?

Jack described the crew's quarters, deep in the bowels of the carrier. They were ghettos where officers seldom ventured for fear of being attacked and mugged. Ratings had more to worry about from the underworld quarters than the raging seas.

We sailed to Casablanca in fair winds. When we rounded Cape Trafalgar, I could almost hear the echoes of cannons, picture broken spars on the sea and feel the presence of tortured souls from foregone battles. But the vision soon dissipated when I heard over the ship's radio of an imminent gale that sent us scurrying to Barbate de Franco. Luckily, the place was only four miles away.

The wind blew hard for the next three days. Bruce and I kept out of each other's way, which proved hard to do. After all, we weren't the Nimitz!

On what was likely to be the last night in Barbate de Franco, I decided to go ashore for a drink. There wasn't much in this fishing village to see, judging by the main street, but I came across a dingy-looking bar at the end of a back alley. I heard people laughing loudly inside, which prompted me to try the place out. When I walked in, all went quiet. I felt four pairs of eyes glaring at me. Two men in executive suits, the barman and a local fisherman in a smock and wellingtons, were standing by the bar. Everyone seemed to sense my awkwardness.

'Hey Amigo, quiere una cerveza?' the businessman nearest to me asked. Before I could answer, the man had already ordered a beer.

I don't know how many beers we drank that evening. It was all on Sebastian and Alejandro's tab. Although their English was limited and I only knew a few Spanish words, we still managed to tell jokes and laugh a great deal. They were curious as to what I was doing in Barbate de Franco? I explained I came in a *barca pequeña con vellas.* Sebastian seemed particularly interested in boats and wanted to visit *Ellis.*

When Alejandro announced he had to go, it was only nine o'clock, and the party broke up. We left the bar together. Both men had parked their cars near the harbour, so I walked down with them. I heard them exchange a few words among themselves, then Alejandro shook my hand, bid me goodnight, and took off in his Mercedes.

Sebastian still wanted to see my boat, and I thought at least I should offer him a cup of coffee after all their generosity and the fun we had that night.

How out of place he looked in his pinstripe suit, stumbling across the decks between the fishing gear and winches. Unfortunately for him, I had moored *Ellis* on the outside of three trawlers, but he made it without spoiling his suit.

As I slid back the hatch, I saw that Bruce had retreated into the fore-cabin and closed the door, leaving one of the oil lamps burning. I invited Sebastian to sit down in the main cabin and asked if he wanted a coffee. He immediately made himself at home, took his jacket off, loosened his tie, and undid the collar button of his starched white shirt. I lit the paraffin stove to boil the water. As I turned, I was taken aback when I saw he had removed his shirt and was undoing his trousers. Had I given him the impression I could be that way inclined? It seemed that drinking a few beers with his friend must have meant something different to him.

Confronting a man lusting for me was the last thing I wanted to happen and in such close quarters. Sebastian looked like a regular visitor to the gym. I thought he could flatten me like a Dover sole if he got frustrated and angry.

I had to think fast to get him off the boat. I pointed to the forward cabin door and rested my head on my hands, indicating my nephew was aboard and asleep and his place might be better. Sebastian seemed happy at that. He got dressed, then we clambered once again over the fishing boats, onto the quayside, and walked briskly back to his BMW. He unlocked the vehicle, got into the driver's seat, and leaned over to open the passenger door from inside.

'No, no, not tonight, maybe another time!' I said as I slammed the passenger door and quickly walked away. I dared not look back as I could sense Sebastian's anger. I heard the engine start and the squeal of tyres as he drove off.

I was still shaking when I returned to *Ellis*. I locked the hatch from the inside, which I hadn't done before. God knows what Bruce was thinking!

Over breakfast, I asked him if he was aware of what had happened the evening before. He blushed but insisted he heard nothing - which seemed unlikely. Was he now feeling unsafe in his bunk at night after this episode? I doubted he believed my story about Sebastian pretending he was interested in seeing *Ellis* and trying to force himself on me. Then there was the American sailor I had invited for afternoon tea. I noticed the way Bruce frowned when he saw him.

The gale abated by late morning and many fishing boats were now setting out to sea. We cast off too. The wind, however, was still funnelling force 5 to 6, gusting 7 out of the Straits of Gibraltar.

Ellis was racing through the water at maximum hull speed with only one small headsail. Now and then, splashes of spray landed on our backs as we braced ourselves against the windward rail, enjoying an exhilarating sail. It was mesmerising to watch the sun's reflections, with the waves turning pale turquoise below the foaming crests, then deepening to dark Atlantic blue in the troughs. I was lost in thought when I heard a rumbling roar that jolted me out of my reverie. Realising that trains don't run through the Straits of Gibraltar, I only just had time to yell out, 'For God's sake, Bruce hang on!' before a rogue wave that sounded like the Orient Express on steroids savagely threw *Ellis* on her beam-ends. The top of the mast hit the water, and within a split second, we went from reclining to standing position on the cockpit wall-locker, clinging for dear life to the guardrail.

Ellis was sluggish when she righted herself. No wonder. The cockpit had filled up when the hatch washboards were washed away during her near-capsize. It was a godsend that the cockpit drained quickly, but the cabin was still awash with a foot of water. One of the spray dodgers and the lifebuoy had also floated off. All this equipment was rapidly disappearing astern. Without the washboards, I had no means of closing the hatch securely, putting us in a dangerous predicament. Fortunately, I had a spare sail in the cockpit seat locker. I scrambled to get it, then draped and lashed it over the open hatch in case of another knockdown. Next, we tried to retrieve the washboards and lifebuoy. If the lifebuoy was left floating out on the sea and found, it might trigger an unwanted search for a missing yacht with *Ellis of Tamar, Scarborough*, painted on it.

While we retraced our course, we came upon *Ellis's* vital equipment, but I had to abort the attempt to recover anything back on board. In such heavy seas, it would have risked the crew's lives.

I quickly resumed my intended course before another wave could flatten us again. Next, we bailed out the water from inside the cabin.

The sea subsided as we reached the lee of the Moroccan coast. I would have to make new washboards in Morocco before setting a course for the Canary Islands, and it seemed unlikely that we would get there before Christmas after all. Life is what gets in the way of plans!

13. Christmas in Morocco

Dark, ominous clouds began to form as dusk fell, and it seemed as if they were about to engulf us. I could faintly make out the beam of Casablanca lighthouse from a distance. At least there were no vessels nearby for me to worry about. If only I could see stars. Our near-capsize through the

Straits of Gibraltar hours ago still haunted me. I am not generally anxious, but something was wrong. Was I being paranoid?

As I stood in the cockpit, I could sense an overwhelming presence around me, yet I couldn't see anything through the darkness. All I could hear was the gentle gurgling of our wake and the whisper in the rigging. But when the hairs on the back of my neck suddenly stood on end, I knew something was amiss.

I turned hard to port, dived through the hatchway and switched all my navigation lights on. Then came the shock when I cast an eye over to starboard and saw a sailing yacht just a few yards from me. The crew immediately switched their lights on too and turned to starboard. Like me, they must have been saving the ship's battery and only using theirs when sighting another vessel. I would have to rig an oil lamp from now on.

Luckily, my instinct saved us from becoming two warring galleons with splintering spars and crashing masts! I dared not imagine the consequences if we were to have collided.

After the excitement, I hailed the crew. Thankful that our yachts were still afloat, both skippers agreed to meet again in better circumstances. The Swiss sloop was heading for Casablanca too. By then, Bruce had emerged on deck. The clamour and shouting must have woken him up.

I was relieved when we sailed into the port. I dropped anchor, away from the heavy traffic. I was far too tired to think any further. I took my sailing boots off and removed my jacket.

Then, just as I was about to step below deck, I saw two men in a rowing boat approaching. One was bald, wearing a dirty white tank top, with a suitcase on his lap. I thought by the way he was clutching it, it was more likely to be stuffed with banknotes than a dinner jacket and Bermuda shorts. The other man looked like a fisherman with his yellow dungarees. The straps over his shoulders made his trousers hoop around his stomach, just like those of a circus clown. The men seemed an odd pair.

The rowing boat's gunnel bumped into *Ellis's* hull. Then the fisherman asked in pigeon English: 'Would you take my passenger to Spain? He has no passport but is willing to pay you well.'

Where have I heard this line before! It would have made the perfect opening scene for a gangster movie.

I looked at him, stern-faced, and replied sharply, 'NO.' Had I been desperate for money, the answer would have been the same.

The fisherman didn't insist; maybe I wasn't the first person he'd approached. I watched him row away with his suspicious cargo and then Bruce and I turned in.

There was only one foreign yacht in the marina where we berthed the next day. Bruce and I got up early. I made a fresh pot of coffee to go with our breakfast. I noticed Bruce seemed in a hurry to eat his muesli and head off to town. He was in charge of the boat's kitty and would be buying a courtesy flag. I stayed behind to swab the decks before going out.

Later, as I was relaxing in the cockpit reading Reginald Perrin, Bruce returned. He looked pleased with himself and couldn't wait to tell me about his happy adventure.

After visiting the chandler who wanted too much for a courtesy flag, Bruce walked to the Casbah. When he found a stall that sold fabric, he asked the young trader for half a square metre of red material. Bruce explained he wanted to make a Moroccan flag. The youth felt flattered and cut him a small piece off a big roll, then invited him to his house, leaving his father to mind the stall.

Together, they wound their way through a labyrinth of narrow alleys until they eventually came to a pale blue building with a heavy studded wooden front door. It led them straight into a room serving as a kitchen and living space, where the whole family were sitting at a table. First, young Ahmed introduced Bruce to his two sisters, his uncle, and three small nephews, then he asked his mother to serve them tea before making the flag.

They hadn't even finished their tea when Ahmed's mother returned with the flag. When Bruce asked, 'How much?' Ahmed said: 'It's been a pleasure to arrange it for you, knowing it'll be flying from your boat. So accept it as a gift, and may *Allah* be with you.'

The flag was flying from the cross-tree. It looked crudely sewn together, but Bruce seemed happy with himself. After all, he hadn't taken any money out of his precious kitty.

My experience in town proved far from pleasant in comparison. I was hassled by a young Arab in a café while eating couscous. At first, he claimed he wanted to improve his English, and I bought him a soft drink. We chatted for a while and then he insisted on taking me to a party.

'There'll be drugs and sex with English girls for a very cheap price,' the youth said.

'I'm not interested,' I barked.

'You've been wasting my time. At least you should buy some drugs,' he yelled.

I couldn't get rid of the Moroccan, so I deliberately walked into a busy street - with him on my coat-tails. When I saw two police officers on the other side of the road, I grabbed the whining scoundrel by the lapels and threatened to punch him on the nose if he didn't clear off. Although I had no intention of hitting him, I knew this pretence would arouse the officers' attention. The villain then broke loose as they crossed the road, and he shot off down a side street like a greyhound out of the starting trap. After the youth had gone, the officers lost interest and walked away in the opposite direction.

The Swiss sloop was now berthed near us - thankfully not on a collision course! Bruce felt he had met his tribe as the crew were all university graduates. He visited them on the first night for a drink. One of the crew, Guido, popped round to *Ellis* later in the evening to ask why I hadn't accepted their invitation. 'Oh, I didn't know about it,' I said. 'Bruce must have forgotten to tell me.'

The four youths were all expert skiers. One of them also hang-glided off mountains. During a lively conversation, Bruce suggested we spend Christmas together in Safi. I welcomed the idea. Unfortunately, the crew couldn't leave the next day. They had surrendered their revolver at the police station while in port and needed to retrieve it. As the sloop had an inboard engine and would be twice our speed, I decided to leave one day earlier, giving us enough leeway to arrive before them, or hopefully at the same time for Christmas.

The wind was light when we set off. Safi is one hundred and twelve miles from Casablanca. We motored for fourteen hours, thirteen hours more than my poor *Seagull* engine had been running since leaving Scarborough.

When we arrived in Safi, there was no sign of the sloop. The only foreign vessel in the port was a

French sailing yacht. Bruce was angry with me for setting off before the Swiss did. I thought they must have changed their minds about Safi. It would mean that Bruce and I were now stuck together for Christmas Day. Neither of us relished that prospect, plus we had no food aboard. But in the spirit of Yuletide, the solution for us was right there. A vendor had turned a forty-five-gallon drum into a barbecue on the nearby quayside and was grilling sardines fresh from a fishing boat. We ate some with large chunks of bread for our Christmas lunch, washed down with a bottle of Coca-Cola.

Later, we met the crew on the French vessel, which was moored next to a fishing boat. The couple invited us to tie up alongside. They offered to look after *Ellis* while we shopped, and in return, we agreed to keep an eye on *Arc-en-Ciel* while they went to the cinema later that evening.

Bruce hoped to meet someone on the way to town who knew about the Norwegian ethnographer Thor Heyerdahl. He had read about the adventurer who built his papyrus reed raft *Kon-Tiki* in Safi and sailed it across the Atlantic in 1970. Bruce wanted to see the very place. Was he expecting to stumble across some papyrus reed remains scattered on a beach after all that time?

As we walked through the Casbah, a teenager with his little brother offered to be our guide. The youth didn't want any money, only the chance to speak English. He promised to keep away the hasslers and buy food at the market cheaper than we could. He knew how to bargain, being the eldest son who did all the shopping for the family. He bought fruit and vegetables at a price my frugal nephew couldn't have believed possible. We thanked our two young guides and had to insist they take our loose change.

We could hear music blaring out when Bruce and I walked across the marina to *Ellis*. I recognised my favourite song by *Fleetwood Mac*. I suddenly remembered I had left the cabin hatch unlocked. But the French couple had promised they would look after my boat while we went shopping.

They were nowhere to be seen.

As we stepped into the cockpit, I peeped through the open hatch and saw a young Arab, feet up on the settee, nodding in time to the tune. He looked up, then said with a big smile, 'How lucky you are. There'd be nothing left on your boat if I hadn't been here on guard.' Was he a genuine Samaritan, or had we returned too early? I wanted to believe he had saved the day, so I offered the youth some tea.

After he left, I heard someone hailing us in Arabic and left Bruce to sort it out. There was a good-hearted bargaining exchange, even though I only got one side of the conversation. When Bruce peeked through the hatch, he was bare-chested, wearing a triumphant grin on his face.

'I've just bartered my old T-shirt full of holes for this beauty,' he announced, dangling an enormous spider crab in my face.

'Has the fisherman given you a dustbin to cook it in?' I said sarcastically. I took the beast from him and squeezed the long-legged creature into my pressure cooker, turning the crab into one of the world's first crustacean contortionists. Then, the Moroccan hailed us again just as we had finished eating this delicacy, which contained little meat for the effort it took to prepare. When I came on deck, I saw a skinny old chap wearing Bruce's T-shirt as a turban. He wanted to sell it back. Bruce gave him a handful of small change, and when the 'wheeler-dealer' returned it, Bruce carefully took the item between finger and thumb as if it was contaminated. 'He's been sweating in this,' he protested, wrinkling his nose as if the T-shirt smelled like a Turkish wrestler's jockstrap. Finally, he deposited the offending item in a plastic bag and planned to dispose of it later.

Bruce and I buried our differences for the sake of Christmas. We cooked steak and potatoes, not forgetting cabbage which was now coming out of my ears. To accompany our meal, I found the bottle of vodka that two cash-strapped boat owners gave me as payment for the primitive self-steering gear I had used on *Ellis*. Vodka and lemonade instead of wine seemed better than nothing to celebrate with. Moreover, it might lighten the mood between us.

As I was about to refill Bruce's glass, there was a sudden thump of heavy steps on deck, followed by a knock. Who could be visiting us at this late hour? I drew back the hatch and saw three Moroccans standing in the cockpit. They gave me such a stern glare that I felt uneasy. *Are they the three 'not-so-wise' men bearing gifts?*

'I'm the Port Health Officer,' the taller one announced in perfect English. 'May we step inside?'

How odd they should call at ten o'clock at night when we had arrived early that morning. The men entered the cabin and sat on the settee like three parrots on a perch. The one claiming to be the Health Officer would have been more credible if he had declared he was the local mafia godfather with his two henchmen. My mind flashed back to my workshop when the axeman had asked Del Cooper, 'Shall I break his arms now, boss?'

Despite my growing apprehension, I offered the Moroccans a shot of vodka to share the spirit of Christmas.

'No, we don't drink,' the officer said with a hint of reproach. 'We're Muslims.'

He asked to see our passports and vaccination certificates. I handed him the documents. He flicked through the pages casually and returned them, looking satisfied.

Still eager to pursue his Thor Heyerdahl search, Bruce asked the officer if he had heard of the raft. He shrugged his shoulders and shook his head in reply. The other two never spoke, and when he addressed them in Arabic, they nodded and climbed out of the hatch onto the boat next to us. The officer started to make a move to follow them, and as he passed the bottle of vodka on the chart table, he grabbed it.

Quick as a flash, I snatched it out of his hand.

'Don't you want to offer me this as a present?' he barked.

'You know that today is our Christmas celebration and the most celebrated day for Christians,' I explained.

He nodded with a grunt.

'If you take this bottle, we'll have nothing else to celebrate with.'

By then, his two sidekicks were already back on the quayside. The officer followed, and before he left, he said, choking on his words, 'Have a nice Christmas.'

The following day, an old Moroccan tried to sell me some diesel off the trawler he was guarding. The vessel was moored in front of *Ellis*. I explained to the man that I had a *Seagull* outboard petrol motor, so diesel was no use. He must have thought I was bartering and immediately lowered his price. I tried hard to get through to him. The man finally left in a huff. I presumed he had cut his price so much that stealing the diesel from the vessel he was guarding wasn't worth his while anymore.

We were getting ready to leave. I had gone to town for some bread while Bruce was busy stowing *Ellis* for sea. When I returned, I asked: 'Are we all done?' He looked sheepishly at me, then said: 'Two policemen have taken our passports away to be stamped. They said we must pay and collect them before we leave.'

'Bruce, why did you let the officers take them?' I asked in disbelief. 'You could have found an excuse that the documents were with the skipper who was in town shopping. You'll just have to go back and retrieve them.'

The office was a minute away, outside the port gates. Bruce went off in a huff. When he returned, he said: 'The policemen insist we pay for the stamps before they'll give our passports back.'

This demand was a scam! We never got charged stamp duty in Casablanca. I marched off to the office, leaving Bruce with strict instructions to be ready to cast off the second I returned.

When I walked in, I asked the officer for our passports, but he repeated what he'd said to Bruce.

'We've got no Dirhams,' I pleaded. 'We need our documents to change our money.'

He checked the photos on the passports and handed me mine. I insisted I must have them both and said, 'I'm not paying for his stamp,' pointing at Bruce's passport. 'He'll have to go to the bank as well.'

The officer reluctantly handed it over and ordered us to return as soon as we'd been to the bank. I left him and rushed back to *Ellis*.

'Okay, cast off, I've got the passports,' I shouted to Bruce. I freed the ropes from the bollards, jumped back aboard, and while Bruce hoisted the sails, I started the outboard. Then we motor-sailed as fast as we could out of Safi, expecting to see several policemen running along the quay like keystone cops waving their pistols in the air, shouting, 'Stop, Stop or we'll shoot,' but, once more, I got away with it!

It was getting dark when I sighted the northern tip of the island of Lanzarote. We had another eighteen miles to go to Arrecife, hugging the coast. The wind had shifted to the south, and we tacked for hours against it. I could see the narrow shafts of car headlights moving along the coastal road. Judging by the size of their beams, we must have been about a mile offshore and well out of danger. I was still being economical with my navigation lights. However, after our close encounter with the Swiss boat off Casablanca, I now hung an oil lamp off the backstay.

When I checked the depth sounder, it was still out of range. It didn't record below sixty metres. I had to be watchful because the seabed off this volcanic coast can alter from deep water to rocks breaking the surface within a boat's length. So when I noticed headlights pointing out to sea and flashing on and off, I immediately took this as a warning. I turned the tiller hard to port. Then, I quickly glanced over my shoulder amidst the clamour of loosening the starboard sheet and simultaneously pulling in the one on the port side. My heart jumped when I saw, by the clear starlit night, rocks jutting out just above the water where *Ellis* would have been if I hadn't altered course. *Guardian angels must be looking over me once again.*

As we headed into deeper water, I questioned why the driver had flashed his headlights out to sea. Was he a smuggler expecting a delivery or someone trying to warn me? Yet how could he have seen the dim glow of my oil lamp from my estimated one mile offshore? Could it have been a coincidence? The mystery remains unresolved.

Long after the event, propped up at various bars, retelling the story to other sailors, I put forward a third possibility. Was the driver's gyrating bottom causing the flashing headlights to go on and off when he caught the dashboard while making love to his girlfriend? Joking apart, I started to believe that two forces were at play: one ready to destroy me, the other coming to rescue me.

14. The Woman in a Black Dress

I saw Bruce wincing at me as I drowned my muesli mix with condensed milk. I was about to say something to him when I noticed someone shaking the rigging and peering down at us from the trawler we had tied up to. 'Hi! I waved to you from *Morning Glory* when we came in,' the young man explained.

I had seen a blue motor-yacht with a rakish funnel and counter-stern, making her stately entrance into Arrecife Harbour earlier in the afternoon. The man introduced himself as Alex, the chief engineer. He was tall, good-looking, red-haired, twenty-something, and certainly a Scot, judging by his heavy accent.

'The crew and I are going out to celebrate Hogmanay this evening,' Alex announced in a cheerful voice. 'Would you like to join us?'

'Yes,' I said. After all, it was well on cue for my birthday. So we rendezvoused at a bar early in the evening.

When we arrived, the place was buzzing, but it wasn't hard to spot Alex in his tartan kilt, fitted jacket, and frilly shirt with a white cravat. He even had a sporran hanging from his belt and a sterling silver dirk thrust down his sock, a proud Scot if ever I saw one. Simon, the steward, also slim, wore a smart dark suit and tie whilst Lionel, the chef, was in brown trousers with a knitted blue cardigan that hid a bit of a tummy. Bruce and I had thrown on wrinkled shirts and slacks. Sir Mark, owner and skipper of *Morning Glory,* had lent the crew his hire car for the evening.

We drank one or two beers each, then the five of us set off like *Musketeers* on our way to rescue a few maidens. First, we visited some bars in town, then Simon drove us to Jameo Del Agua nightclub. The place was like a cave in the Amazon forest but with multi-coloured lighting and loud music. The large dance floor was packed. We ordered our drinks at the bar and then plucked up the courage to invite some señoritas to dance.

At midnight, the musicians began to play *Auld Lang Syne,* and everyone joined in. The five of us tried to find as many señoritas as possible to hug and kiss, and the crew wished me a 'Happy Birthday.'

The dancing resumed, and as Alex was doing his stuff on the dance floor with a pretty damsel, I saw a chap tapping on his shoulder and heard him say in a drunken stupor, 'You shouldn't be wearing this kilt because you are not a true Scot like me.'

Alex ignored him and continued dancing.'If you were a true Scot,' the drunk insisted, 'you'd have hit me by now!'

That was it! Alex spun on his heels and floored the sod with one punch to the jaw. He was out for the count. People stopped dancing, startled by the body lying spread-eagled across the dance floor.

That night, everyone witnessed the 'Clashing of the Clans.'

Shortly after, three burly bouncers marched in. They grabbed Alex by the arms and escorted him out of the club. We were hot on their heels. Alex retrieved the dagger he had surrendered at the reception, and then we all strode away.

Simon, our driver, had remained sober throughout the evening. He was now keen to make up for it. So we dropped the car at the harbour in Arrecife and visited more bars.

The five *Musketeers* decided to call it a night at three in the morning. Sadly, no maidens had needed rescuing. On our way back to the harbour, we passed a restaurant and noticed some teenage girls sitting at a table by the window. As they saw Alex in his kilt, they started to bang on the glass, waving and shouting something in Spanish that required no translation. Alex knew what they wanted and had no wish to disappoint them. Happy with the charade, he took a combat pose as if he was 'Robert the Bruce' in front of his army.

The girls became hysterical, making suggestive gestures. All this female attention was spurring Alex on.

Keen to make his game of seduction last, he waited like a stripper gyrating and teasing his audience, and when he thought the girls' arousal had reached its climax, he slowly and deliberately raised his kilt to his chin. The screams and laughter soared. Customers hurried to the window to look at what was happening. We had to drag Alex away before the police could arrest him for indecent exposure.

The following day, deep in my intoxicated slumber, I could hear an elephant dancing on the cabin roof above my bunk. I sat up, vowing never to drink again, staggered to my feet in a haze and drew back the hatch. What was happening around me soon cleared my head!

The large trawler in front of us, second from a row of five, had just set off to sea, leaving the end boat adrift with only one stern line attached to the remaining vessels in the trot. A near gale-force wind was now blowing the steel trawler onto *Ellis* like a giant nutcracker about to open a delicate peanut shell. As for the elephant I had heard earlier on deck, he was a skinny old fisherman in big boots, doing a good impersonation of *Charles Atlas* holding up the world. The man had as much chance of fending off the three-hundred-ton vessel from crushing *Ellis* in a pincer movement as plaiting fog. Within the chaos, I could hear *Ellis's* hull creaking under the pressure of the towering trawlers.

Despite my nudity, I grabbed a knife and rushed on deck. There was no time to untie the straining ropes, so I hacked away at them. Then Bruce emerged in his pyjama bottoms, and the three of us pushed *Ellis* away from the deadly scissor grip. She started to move, but the rigging caught some fish boxes protruding from the trawler's deck. Knife in hand, I ran across the deck like a crazy pirate and cut the lines that held the boxes, then quickly sprang back to avoid the inevitable avalanche. Once the rigging broke free from the snagging boxes, *Ellis* was spat out like a pip squeezed between two fingers.

It was a close shave, for had I not moved away fast enough, the falling boxes could have knocked me overboard, and then I might have drowned or been crushed to death between *Ellis* and the steel fishing boats.

I quickly tied *Ellis* to the next row of trawlers before modesty overtook me, and I dashed below to put some trousers on, leaving Bruce to tidy up on deck. I had had it up to the *Plimsoll line* with these trawlers, including the stench of rotting fish. Then Sir Mark invited us to moor alongside his *Morning Glory*.

A few days later, Alex announced they were sailing to Puerto Rico in Gran Canaria, and if we needed to earn cash, we could do some painting on the decks.

Bruce and I caught up with *Morning Glory* in Puerto Rico and started work on the motor yacht to top up the kitty.

One evening, Alex and I went out to town, leaving Bruce to his chamber music. Over a few drinks, Alex told me about Sir Mark's volatile character. He had dismissed the last engineer without repatriating him to his country of origin. Alex's insurance against an unwarranted dismissal was a secret switch on the fuel system that immobilised the ship's engine. He was adamant Sir Mark would never find it. In the event of a dispute, Alex would only disclose its existence after his boss had paid his wages and bought him an air ticket home.

What a canny Scot!

In a bar that night, we met two attractive Norwegian girls who offered to buy our tickets to a disco. Having little money on us, we went along with it. During a dance, Ida, the petite five-foot-two blonde, asked me to guess what she did for a living After numerous suggestions, I gave up.

Ida was the humane gun operator in a slaughterhouse. It was hard to picture her as an executioner. She had such a sweet-looking face and soft blue eyes. *But I suppose somebody has to pull the trigger.*

Alex and I spent the night in the girls' chalet. We returned to our boats at ten the following day, singing the Beatles song, *Isn't It Good, Norwegian Wood* - but we didn't sleep in the bath!

Bruce was eating his rolled oats and raisins when I boarded *Ellis*. He had the look of Mother Superior learning that one of her nuns had fallen pregnant!

After finishing work on *Morning Glory* that day, Alex invited us to the crew's quarters for a beer. We caught Simon with a girl in his bunk. When they drew back the curtains, they looked flushed and embarrassed.

Finding the couple in such an untimely way prompted another of Bruce's impersonations of Mother Superior while Alex and I exchanged some mild banter.

Wendy was crew on a forty-foot French wooden ketch. She had answered an advertisement on the hostel notice board back in Nice. *'Berth available on a sailing yacht heading for the Caribbean.'* She and two American students from the hostel decided they would go and check the boat out. They fell in love with the romance of sailing across an ocean to the Caribbean, so they signed and paid for their passage as crew. But, when they brought their belongings aboard the yacht before departure, they were miffed to find a New Zealander and a French couple there too, which meant they were eight altogether with only six berths to share between them. The skipper told them not to fret, as there would be enough bunks with two people always on watch.

After they cast off, Wendy discovered there was no loo aboard - not even a bucket. So she had to deal with the humiliation of being held over the side rail while she fulfilled the call of nature. On top of that, when the yacht reached Puerto Rico, the French captain ran out of money and asked the crew for further funds. He and his first mate were delivering the vessel for the lady owner without pay, so they rented out berths to finance the trip.

One afternoon Wendy and the two Americans were sitting in the main saloon while the French couple slept in a hammock rigged above the table. The trio were chatting quietly, when suddenly they noticed the hammock gyrating to the rhythm of the couple's lovemaking. It was the final straw. Wendy was now as desperate as the Americans to get off the good ship *No-loo*.

'Do you think I could stay on *Morning Glory* until I sort myself out,' Wendy pleaded with Simon after we had finished drinking our beers.

'No way!' he retorted. 'If Sir Mark finds out you're here, I'll be walking the plank. What about you Peter, could you put Wendy up?'

'Sure, Wendy. If you don't mind sleeping on a bunk cushion on the cabin floor, then it's fine by me.'

She brought her belongings aboard *Ellis* later that evening. Bruce's puritanical views of my wayward lifestyle hastened his plans to leave the boat. After all, I had agreed to take him as far as the Canary Islands and no further.

Two days later, he announced he had found a loft apartment up the coast in Arguineguin, where he planned on settling for a while. Maybe he had a vision of becoming another *Ernest Hemingway*.

The next thing I knew, *Ellis's* main cabin looked like a corner shop. Bruce had pulled everything bought with the kitty out of the food lockers, including half a jar of coffee, half a bag of rice, sachets of custard powder, and the remains of his muesli-making kit. He added up their cash value in British pounds sterling after he had converted the items purchased in various currencies. I wondered how long this all took for him to do? And he had included seventy-five pounds for the mast repairs. The final invoice he produced looked more like a bailiff's demand.

'Come on Bruce,' I said, shocked at his cheek. 'I remember saying NO to you when you offered to lend me money towards the repairs as I would recover the amount later from the insurance company.'

'Oh but you did borrow the money,' Bruce insisted.

'Bruce, Stop! I'm certain I didn't. What you gave me in Brest was half of the harbour dues. Remember, we had agreed before leaving England to split the cost of food and moorings between us. However, I'm going to pay you what you're asking for because I'm keen to raise *Ellis's* waterline by getting you off the boat.'

'You ought to be pleased that I gave you such a healthy diet all these weeks and I saved you money on victuals,' Bruce replied.

I wrote him a cheque, tossed it on the chart table, and went ashore for a walk before being tempted to keelhaul him. *At least I'll get him out of my hair, and he won't be able to complain to his mother and grandmother that I left him marooned on an island like Robinson Crusoe.*

Later, I heard 'through the grapevine' that Bruce had shipped out to the Caribbean on an American yacht. *Hemingway* must have been too tough an act for him to follow.

My work on *Morning Glory* came to an end and Wendy decided to return to England. To thank me, she bought chocolates with what little money she had left after purchasing her return flight. Her gesture touched me. But, she wasn't to know that I have an aversion to coffee-flavoured chocolate. The distaste stems from when I was four years old.

As a boy, I loved fishing off Scarborough Pier. With the 'get out from under my feet' money from my mother, I often bought a halfpenny's worth of mussels as bait to use with my twopenny handheld fishing line wrapped around a wooden frame. When I stood on the pier, looking down at boats leaving the harbour, I was the same height as their masts. It was a fun game when the skippers shouted, 'Pull your line in.' They didn't want their propellors fouled. I would always pull mine in at the last minute. As a result, I spent more time untangling my line than fishing. Then one day, I swung it too high before letting go. The lead sinker dropped from above my head, and the hook pierced my forearm. The pain felt like the dentist extracting a tooth without gas. In shock, I grabbed the lead weight and remainder of the fishing line to ease the pressure off the hook and rushed over to a grown-up fishing a few yards away. 'Please, mister,' I pleaded. 'Can you take this hook out?'

'No, son but I know someone who can.'

He quickly cut my line to thc hook and walked me to the fish dock, half a mile away. Blood was dripping from my arm, and I saw people staring at me.

Finally, the fisherman brought me to the St John Ambulance below the Harbour Master's Office. Inside were a man and a nurse in black and white uniforms sitting at a desk.

'Can you sort this little boy out?' my rescuer asked them. He patted me on the shoulder and said, 'You'll be all right now son.' Then he went.

'We'd better take you to hospital,' the nurse said as she examined my arm. She and the man helped me into the white ambulance with a black and white cross on its side. As I sat in the front seat between the nurse and the driver, I thought: *I'll be in trouble with my mother again.*

Two nurses and a doctor attended to me at the hospital. They sat me down. Then the doctor explained he'd be putting my arm to sleep and, with a pair of pliers, would cut the eye off the hook that the line was still attached to. But he couldn't pull it out the same way it had entered because the barb needed pushing further in to enable it to be curled out of my arm, point first.

His convoluted explanation made me even more nervous!"

He asked me to be brave, keep my arm still, and if I were a good little boy, I would get some chocolate. He pointed at the box of Black Magic on a table the other side of the room.

I braced myself for the needle, winced at it, and turned my head away. I didn't cry. The doctor and nurse held my arm firmly and then extracted the hook all in one go.

They praised me for my courage. As a reward, the nurse showed me the box of chocolates. She asked me to choose one, which was a real treat as sweets were still on ration in 1947. I picked one at random. Alas, it was a coffee cream. I thanked the doctor and the nurse. When I put it in my mouth, it tasted as horrible as cod liver oil. I forced a smile, too polite to spit it out, and swallowed it whole.

Meanwhile, a policeman had been despatched on his bicycle to inform my mother I was at the hospital. When she arrived, I could read on her face, 'What a nuisance you are. I'll have to pay the usual two and sixpence to the police. Lunch will be late and my prized Yorkshire puddings might be like pancakes by the time we get back, all because of you.'

After Wendy left Las Palmas, I sailed to Los Cristianos and found a sheltered spot inside a small harbour. There were two other yachts and a few open fishing boats moored up. I dropped an anchor to keep *Ellis* off the shelving rocks and tied two long lines ashore. I intended to use the dinghy as a ferry.

One afternoon, sitting in the cockpit sunbathing, I noticed a young couple standing on the quayside. 'Nice boat you have there!' the man shouted. He had curly black hair and looked athletic. A tall blonde woman was standing beside him.

'Thank you,' I replied. 'Would you like to come aboard for a cup of tea?'

They said yes, enthusiastically, and I ferried them across to *Ellis*.

Steve and Julie were Canadians backpacking around Europe. They had just arrived from Malaga on the ferry. We talked for hours. Steve had sailed in the Florida Keys and loved boats, and Julie enjoyed being a traveller.

It was getting late when they mentioned going to look for a camping site.

'You can sleep in the forepeak,' I offered. 'You are welcome to stay for a while if you want.'

A few days later, they were still aboard, so I asked if they fancied sailing to an uninhabited island south of Madeira. I suggested we could chill out like the mutineers of HMS Bounty on Pitcairn Island.

'Let's sail there and check it out,' adventurous Steve said. 'First, we ought to find you a girlfriend.'

Meeting the right woman to join us on this epic journey could be a lot more challenging.

I was hopeful when the three of us checked out a few bars that evening. We met up with five other Canadians in one of them - all chaps, unfortunately. The place was busy, but we found a table in the upstairs restaurant for all of us to sit together. As we studied the menu, a tall, slender, dark-haired woman in a tight-fitting black dress walked up the stairs. She was balancing a jug of wine on her shoulder, holding it with one hand, the other resting on her hip. Without a word, she placed it on our table and looked at us, half-smiling like *Mona Lisa* - only she was a lot prettier.

The Canadians were falling over themselves, their libidos running out of control as their eyes remained fixed on the woman's generous cleavage. The boldest chap amongst us shuffled up on the bench and invited this stunning woman to join us. He offered her a drink and then asked her name and whether she worked at the bar. She never replied but kept her elusive smile.

Her lack of response wore thin. After a while, we resumed our conversation, and the mysterious dark beauty walked away. We looked at each other, shrugging our shoulders, thinking, 'What was all that about?' When we finished our meal, we went to the downstairs bar. It was buzzing with backpackers, boat crew, and campervan travellers. I talked to a few Australian girls, but they all had boyfriends.

The following lunchtime, I returned to La Paloma bar and met one of the Australian girls from the night before. We were both perched on high stools at the counter when I suddenly felt a tap on the shoulder. When I swivelled around, I saw the mysterious dark-haired woman from last night sitting behind me.

'Aren't you going to buy me a drink?' she said in a heavy Marlene Dietrich accent.

I nearly fell off my perch. I couldn't believe that this stunning woman who had held such an inscrutable countenance the night before was sitting next to me. I managed to answer, 'Yes, sure! What would you like?' The Australian girl must have felt upstaged by this low-neck-lined seductress. She quickly drank up and left.

Gertrude was from Berlin. She spoke slowly and deliberately. After she had finished her wine, I asked if she wanted to have lunch aboard *Ellis*. 'My friends, Steve and Julie, are cooking spaghetti,' I said. 'I'm sure there'll be enough for four.'

'Ja Gerne,' she answered. I felt as if I had won the lottery. We walked with linked arms down to the harbour, and I hailed Steve to pick us up in the dinghy. His jaw dropped when he saw this goddess in a black dress standing next to me. I wore some old jean shorts and a working T-shirt, contrasting starkly with the dazzling Gertrude.

Over lunch, Steve asked her, 'How would you like to sail to a deserted island?'

She was excited and said she would bring her *'Sachen'* - 'things' the following day. Then she asked, 'When are you leaving?' Her keenness took the wind out of my sails. Steve explained we would need a few days to provision the boat. But, before we embarked on this expedition, I suggested that we sail the fifty-mile round trip to La Gomera Island to see how we got on. We were all excited.

Gertrude arrived with her luggage the following day: a handbag and a large earthenware salad bowl. Julie had gone shopping, so it was just Steve and myself aboard. I ferried Gertrude over in the dinghy and asked her if she had any other belongings.

'Nein,' she replied as if it was customary to go on a long trip with just a handbag and a salad bowl! Steve and I looked at each other, puzzled. We chatted enthusiastically about the upcoming adventure and then Gertrude asked if she could have a bath.

'Yes,' I replied, unfazed. 'We have a plastic container with holes in the lid. I hang it upside-down from the rigging and shower in the cockpit in my swimming trunks. I can also put warm water in a bucket for you to have a sponge bath, here in the cabin if you prefer?'

'A sponge bath is *gut*,' she answered.

I filled the kettle and lit the paraffin stove, and as I turned around, Gertrude was naked. Steve popped his head through the hatch, blinked a few times, and returned to the cockpit. I prepared the bucket and sponge and left Gertrude.

'You're a fast mover,' Steve said when I joined him on deck. 'She's got a beautiful pair of tits!' he whispered leeringly.

Gertrude's bizarre behaviour didn't stop there. After her ablutions, she asked for a pencil and paper. 'I'd like to draw Steve,' she said. Thinking we had the female version of *Michelangelo* with us, I imagined Gertrude painting the underside of *Ellis's* cabin like the Sistine Chapel! Excited at such a prospect, I rushed to get my large sketchpad and a B 2 pencil from one of the lockers. Steve, meanwhile, had taken a pose on the stern with his chest expanded like a Greek statue. He wore a bright yellow T-shirt with *The Workshop* written across it in big letters. Only he knew what it meant. As for Gertrude, she was sitting in the cockpit with her back resting against the side of the cabin. I watched her wielding the pencil boldly as she drew Steve. She looked so immersed that my anticipation grew by the minute, expecting a masterpiece.

When she presented her work, I could hardly contain myself from laughing.

The drawing bore no resemblance to Steve and was a rather pitiful, childish scrawl. Steve was deflated and said to Gertrude mockingly: 'You've missed the words on the front of my T-shirt!'

With a blank look on her face, she picked up her drawing and quickly scribbled some letters without hesitation. Steve and I couldn't make sense of them, but something told me to get my shaving mirror.

The Workshop read perfectly as a reverse image! Steve gasped when he realised what Gertrude had done. She had written it instinctively - something I couldn't do without careful forethought.

Over dinner, I explained to Gertrude that we needed provisions before sailing to this deserted island. The crew would put money into the boat's kitty, and I asked her if she could do the same. 'It's usually me who asks for money!' Gertrude replied awkwardly. 'Why do you need money?'

'For the food,' I explained. 'We need a lot of it,'

'*Ach so*, I shall bring some food tomorrow,' she promised.

Later, I made the double bed up. Gertrude didn't seem the least perturbed when I got into it naked. I watched her dress slide down slowly, revealing her perfect figure, then she came and laid next to me. Her long black hair flowing over her voluptuous bosom and delicate pale skin reminded me of the *Rokeby Venus*. Neither of us felt awkward or hesitant in our embrace. We were just two lovers reunited after a proverbial absence.

Gertrude woke up early the following day and asked if she could borrow my jean shorts and a T-shirt. 'I've things to do before we leave,' she explained. So after breakfast, I ferried her ashore, and she sat awkwardly, clutching her handbag as if it were a baby she needed to protect. Once I got her there, I returned to *Ellis*. The three of us made lunch and waited for her to come back.

Afternoon, evening, and night went by, and still no sign of Gertrude. After two days, I almost believed she had been an apparition. Feeling like a jilted bridegroom, I had lost interest in the deserted island. Steve and Julie didn't know how to react or console me.

Then I suggested we sail to Hierro Island, seventy miles away from Los Cristianos. It would be the perfect place to get away from the crowds. Hierro wasn't a popular destination for tourists or even yachtsmen as there was no airport.

When we sailed into the harbour, we were the only boat to tie up against the wall. We had a quick cup of tea, then set off, keen to explore.

We walked up a steep hill that led us to the main road, where we tried to hitch a lift around the island. I thought it might prove challenging for the three of us, but it wasn't long before a woman van driver stopped - only to apologise for not having room in her vehicle. After a short wait, a Land Rover picked us up. On the way, the lively driver spoke incessantly, mainly in Spanish, while chewing a toothpick and looking at Julie in the back seat.

If only he'd concentrate on the twisting mountain road rather than the pretty Julie! Is there life after the next bend?

When I couldn't take it anymore, I told the driver we had reached our destination even though we were in the middle of nowhere. In my mind, he was *The Horseman of Death* in the *Apocalypse.* The Spaniard looked puzzled and disappointed when he halted his steed. From there, we walked along the majestic road flanked by mountains and waterfalls cascading down into lush valleys. In the bliss of this unspoilt landscape, we could hear the haunting sound of bagpipes blowing in the wind. The music made me feel even more melancholic. I kept asking myself why Gertrude hadn't returned. We continued walking along the mountain road for a mile when a car drew up. The driver was German. He lived on the island and spoke of an eccentric Scot playing the bagpipes from a cave in the mountains.

The atmosphere was intense on the way back to Los Cristianos. Julie confessed that long-distance sailing wasn't for her. She flew back to Canada a few days later, and Steve found a boat bound for the Caribbean.

I had cast adrift my dream of sailing to an uninhabited island by then, but Gertrude continued to prey on my mind, and I couldn't help hoping to hear her hail me from the quayside.

I was still grieving my loss when I came across Klaus and Anneli a few days later. They were a young Danish couple living in their Volkswagen campervan on some waste ground near the harbour. I mentioned Gertrude to them and described her in detail, just in case they had seen her.

I couldn't believe it when they said they had met her and her boyfriend on their way to Tenerife on the ferry. What a coincidence!

'They were an odd couple,' Klaus remarked. 'We were travelling tourist class, using the communal showers and toilets. One time, I was having a shave when Gertrude's boyfriend walked in. I took a shower and left my clean socks and underpants outside the cubicle. When I came out, I found a smelly old pair of underpants and socks with holes in them instead. I was fuming. In the afternoon, Anneli left her sweater and towel on a deck-chair while she got a drink from the bar. When she returned, her top was gone. Two hours later, Gertrude walked past, wearing it over a black dress.'

Anneli chipped in. 'I tapped Gertrude on the shoulder and said, excuse me but this is my sweater. Without a hint of embarrassment or a single word, she pulled it off over her head and handed it back to me. I was stunned when she walked away without shame.'

'And that's not all,' Klaus resumed.

'The following day, before we disembarked in Tenerife, I saw the boyfriend on deck with a portable typewriter on his lap, tapping away. So I went straight up to him and said, "Hey, was it you who took my socks and pants from the shower yesterday?"

"Yes, man, I needed them," he replied. "You can't just take people's things. How would you react if I took your typewriter now?" His response was: "If you need it, have it." Then he handed it over to me.'

'I think you're better off without Gertrude,' Anneli remarked, 'but if you'd like to know what happened to her, you can ask her boyfriend Ernst. He sits at his typewriter in the piazza, most days, just outside La Paloma Bar.'

I wasted no time looking for Gertrude's boyfriend and found Ernst, where Anneli told me he would be. I said, 'hello,' then sat down opposite him at the table. Ernst was the stereotypical German, blond, blue-eyed, and self-assured. 'Do you have anything to contribute to my island news magazine?' he asked with hardly any accent.

'No, I'd like to talk to you about Gertrude,' I said straight out.

He peered over his round metal-rimmed spectacles and asked sarcastically: 'Are you another one of Gertrude's boyfriends?'

He didn't wait for my answer and continued typing. Then he stopped to remove his glasses and laid them carefully on the table. 'I suppose you want me to tell you about Gertrude. Do you know she's been deported?'

I stared at him in disbelief.

You must be aware of her habit of drinking in bars and walking out without paying. Everybody knows. She did it too many times, and Pepe's Bar owner called the police. Having no money on her, she was treated as a vagrant and sent back to Germany.

I felt numb.

'I heard about it too late to bail her out,' Ernst continued. By then, I had had enough. We fell out weeks ago after we arrived in Los Cristianos.'

What could I say? I wasn't even sure I wanted to hear more about Gertrude, but Ernst went on.

'Gertrude's mother wanted to put her daughter through college. When her husband deserted them, to earn money she became a prostitute. It was too much for her, and she committed suicide. It was just after Gertrude and I broke up. She dropped out of college and went on the game herself. Then she had a nervous breakdown and ended up in an asylum. When I visited her, I couldn't believe it - she was like a vegetable, somebody so beautiful. I don't have to tell you that, do I! I couldn't bear seeing her wasting away so I made up a story that we wanted to get married. I signed for her release on the understanding that I would take her away from Germany for a long holiday. And this is how she treated me after I rescued her from the loony bin.'

I fought hard to hold back the tears and didn't know what to say. It was all too tragic.

'By the way, has something funny been happening to your "downstairs" lately?' Ernst asked scoldingly. Was he saying this out of spite?

'Don't worry. I had it myself. Just go to the doctor. He'll prescribe you some antibiotics and you'll be all right after ten days or so.'

Ernst picked up his glasses and resumed his typing. I remained sitting opposite him, feeling gutted. Then he asked again, keen to break the awkward silence between us, 'Do you have any interesting stories about the island for my travellers' magazine? I'd be happy to include them in the next week's issue.'

It was clear that my private audience with him had drawn to a close. Without a word, I got up and walked away.

Over a glass of wine at La Paloma bar, I reflected on Gertrude's comment: 'It's me who usually asks for money.' Then I recalled her writing that we deciphered through a mirror, the black dress, and the salad bowl she left behind. At least she didn't pass on the gift that required antibiotics.

Sadly, I never knew Gertrude needed help. The beautiful woman had been trampled like a flower. Then, as I wallowed in grief, two of the five Swedish nurses I had taken for a sail earlier in the season walked in. When they saw me at the bar, they came and sat next to me. They worked at a clinic run by the Swedish Health Service, giving people with multiple sclerosis the chance to live their last days in the winter sunshine.

Heidi was a nurse, and Emily an occupational therapist. I mentioned Gertrude to them. The two women believed that destiny played a big part in people's lives and suggested I light a white candle and offer a prayer for her.

'The girls are throwing a party for Emily, she's going back to Sweden, Heidi later announced. Why don't you come along? This might help cheer you up.'

I arrived at Emily's address early that evening. The apartment was on the first floor of an elegant holiday complex. I felt intimidated when I entered the large living room full of women of all ages. Although I was the only man, it didn't take long before I felt like a chocoholic in a sweet shop. It was a lively party, and after the drinking and dancing had quietened down, one of the nurses, a tall, middle-aged blonde, sat down at a table with some playing cards. I guessed what was coming next.

'Come on Peter,' Heidi said. 'Let Birgitta read your cards.'

How could I refuse when everyone was egging me on!

Birgitta asked me to shuffle the cards, pick seven at random, and hand them back to her. I waited, feeling anxious as she spread the cards across the table and psyched herself up to see into the future. 'You'll be going on a long journey,' she began.

I thought it didn't take much to predict this, being on an island and aboard a sailing boat. Then she said, 'I can see a disaster but you'll survive and reach your destination.'

I couldn't remember much from the reading apart from 'disaster' and 'you'll survive.' I had come to the party to be cheered up before sailing single-handedly the one thousand seven hundred miles back to England. This prediction was the last thing I wanted to hear. Had I not suffered enough disasters for a lifetime already?

15. Two Waves that Meet

Florence was the skipper on a sixty-five-foot schooner, *Spirit of Labrador.* He was short with curly hair and a frizzy beard. He and his first mate John had sailed the yacht from Ireland to the Canary Islands on behalf of an English doctor who was a friend. Florence and I chatted at the bar as sailors do, swapping stories of storms, sea monsters, and mermaids. When I mentioned someone had turned the tap off on the fishing pier, and I was out of drinking water on my boat, Florence said in a heavy Irish accent, 'If it's only drinking water you want, bring a jerrycan along. We've got plenty in our tanks.' *Everything seems to happen at La Paloma Bar!*

The following day, I walked over to the far end of the fishing pier where *Spirit of Labrador* was tied up. I hesitated before calling out when I saw the skipper adjusting the mooring lines on deck. I had forgotten his name but knew it had something to do with a children's TV programme, "The Magic Roundabout." Word association is how I remember people's names, so I yelled: 'Hi, Zebedee.' The skipper turned his head towards me, and it was evident by the puzzled look on his face that I had the wrong character. I tried Florence next, and he responded with a grin and a gesture to come aboard.

Once on deck, he took my jerrycans and invited me into the saloon. There was a galley on the port side where I saw a petite brunette in a green dress checking the oven. I could smell oregano and fresh dough. The young woman had a pretty face. When she caught my gaze, she asked, with a heavy French accent, 'Would you like a coffee?'

'Yes, please,' I replied, struck by her dazzling green eyes. By that time, Florence had returned with my jerrycans. 'Here's your water,' he said. 'I can see that Monique has been taking care of you. Why don't you pop round tonight? We'll probably be going out to a few bars before we get the new charterers tomorrow.' I drank my coffee and left, keen to return later.

When I climbed back aboard *Spirit of Labrador* and popped my head through the saloon door that evening, I saw Monique in the galley washing up. I called out, 'Hi.' She looked over her shoulder and said, 'Florence and John have already gone. You'll probably find them in La Paloma Bar. I shall be coming along when I finish here.'

'I'll wait and give you a hand,' I offered enthusiastically.

'Okay, maybe you can dry some dishes.'

After clearing up in the galley, Monique and I walked into town, chatting like two old friends. We passed a few bars, peeked in to see if Florence and John were there, then gave up and sat on a terrace, drinking wine and talking about life. Monique explained she had found the position as cook and purser on *Spirit of Labrador* through a friend who owned a property agency in Lanzarote. The yacht hopped between sun-soaked islands, taking German and English charter guests on luxurious two-week vacations.

Through the course of the evening, we began to speak more intimately. The power of wine has a way of loosening tongues.

'I was the unwanted child, the third in a line of girls, this kind of messed me up,' Monique confided. 'My mother worked all hours in a hotel. My sisters and I never saw much of her and when we did, she just shouted at us.'

'What about your father?' I asked, trying to diffuse the sadness on her face.

'Whatever ambitions I had, wanting to go to university, my father would say, "You aren't intelligent enough." And when I mentioned a singing career, he told me I had delusions of grandeur.'

It was my turn to tell her about my life, and with the recent events still hanging heavy on my mind, the floodgates suddenly opened, and I talked about the bankruptcy. I described how an old school friend, John, who I hadn't seen in years paid me an impromptu visit one day. He had heard I was involved in welding and engineering, modifying steel wheels for racing cars, and knew I was renting reasonably-sized premises. He asked me if I wanted to go into partnership with him, making amusement machines. He assured me he had ample experience in the field. I felt the days in my line of business were numbered, as aluminium wheels were becoming more prominent and affordable, so I accepted his offer.

The next day we made a gentleman's agreement, and I became a penny slot machine manufacturer whilst I still carried on my other engineering business.

Our new venture rapidly expanded, our order books were full for the coming season, and we used all our credit to buy the necessary materials to cover the massive orders. We even turned down a takeover bid from Phonographic Amusement Machine Distributors. Meanwhile, I had handed my wheel-modifying business over to my employee-friend Jeff for him to carry it on. Then came the big crunch.

The Chancellor of the Exchequer decided to put a high tax on gaming machines. As a result, arcade owners stopped buying our slot machines because they were no longer profitable. It was the death of the business, and I filed for bankruptcy. The process wasn't straightforward. One of my debtors was a rich man eager to profit from our situation. He lied in court, which resulted in John and me being held personally responsible for the company's debts, despite being the owners of a limited company. I even had the man's signature on the invoice he gave me. Yet, he denied it was his when I presented it to the court. I was defending myself and lost the case. It took me five years to pay the debts off.'

I took another sip of wine and laid back in my seat when I finished telling Monique what had happened. I noticed the sad look on her face and began to regret burdening her with my baggage. 'I'm sorry,' I said. 'I got carried away with the past.'

'Who hasn't got one?' she replied thoughtfully.

That evening she and I parted with a gentle kiss on the cheek. I wondered if she was as keen as me for us to meet again?

The following day, *Spirit of Labrador* left Los Cristianos with new charterers. Unfortunately, I would have to wait until the yacht returned to see Monique again. Was she free or in a relationship with the skipper or the first mate John? He was a tall, handsome blond fellow who wouldn't have looked out of place in a rugby scrum. I was yet to find out.

When the schooner returned to Los Cristianos, I called to see the crew, determined to spend more time with Monique. The skipper and John welcomed me. They opened a few beers, and the conversation turned to politics and Ireland. It soon appeared that Florence held radical views. I should have kept in mind that diplomacy is the art of remembering what to forget! But I made the mistake of asking him how he would solve the Northern Ireland issue.

'Just give it back to us,' Florence said.

'Would this be the end of the conflict?'

'Yes, for sure - then we'd kick the *shite* out of the Protestants.'

His comment wasn't at all what I expected!

When *Spirit of Labrador* sailed to one of their stop-offs in Lanzarote, I followed Monique for another chance to see her. Was I too eager to think I had met my soulmate? Then fate played a hand in my life once more. Monique fell ill and needed a wisdom tooth extraction. She couldn't get a dentist appointment straight away in Lanzarote, and the schooner had to continue her itinerary.

Before Monique joined the yacht, she lived in an apartment on the island. But, as the rent hadn't expired, she invited her friend Felicity to use it until then. The two had met when they worked in a skiing resort in France and had kept in touch. Monique suggested Felicity could stand-in for her, and she jumped at the opportunity for a new adventure.

Felicity had the allure of a Bohemian free spirit, always dressed in jeans and a long blue shirt worn on the outside. The daughter of a general, she loved cooking and was a qualified cordon bleu chef. She seemed ideal to replace Monique in the galley, and she enjoyed sailing.

When we caught up with *Spirit of Labrador* after Monique's ordeal with the dentist, she received a frosty welcome. Then I learned that she and John were in a relationship. 'We were thrown together in the same cabin and things just happened,' she said. Was John jealous of us? If he suspected Monique of being unfaithful, then he was wrong! She had spent four days with me on *Ellis*: the first day waiting for her extraction, the second nursing her discomfort before we sailed hard on the wind for the two remaining days until we caught up with *Spirit of Labrador*.

Romance, meanwhile, had blossomed between Florence and Felicity, making it awkward for Monique to take over the reins. Then, Chay Blyth Agency in England went overboard with the bookings, and the yacht was short of berths.

The first new charterers to arrive for a reunion were three German couples. The men introduced themselves as ex-U-Boat Commanders. Two chaps from England followed, one of whom had flown as a navigator for the RAF Bomber Command, while the other served as a Naval Commander on an anti-submarine frigate during WWII. Oddly enough, they were both called Nobby Clarke and had never met before. Florence and the crew feared a re-enactment of the Second World War with this ominous turnout!

It appeared the Germans were stuck-up, particularly the women. They expected gourmet food and a hot bath every day. They didn't appreciate how lucky they were to have a full-size bath on a sailing yacht in the late1970s.

In contrast, the two "Nobbies" had no airs or graces. One of them even brought his can opener, thinking it would all be tins and hardtack on the *Good Ship Labrador*! Yet, despite their differences and the overcrowding, tension seemed to be largely contained.

Over a meal one evening, the naval Nobby said to the Germans: 'It must have been pretty scary for you down below with me exploding depth-charges all over the Atlantic!'

'Surely, it was pretty spine-chilling stuff for the convoys being sitting ducks on the surface,' Hans responded.

'Did I give you a fright when I was bombing the submarine pen in Brest?' RAF Nobby asked.

'*Nein,*' the other German Commander retorted. 'You had no chance with five metres of concrete above our heads.

The submarine pens were bombproof.'

Hearing the story from Monique, I remembered the catchphrase in the comedy *Faulty Towers*: 'Don't talk about the war to Germans.' But these people exchanged good-hearted banter and seemed to share a respect for each other's role during the heat of conflict.

After the schooner arrived in Los Cristianos, Felicity left the boat and moved into the forward guest cabin on *Ellis*. Florence had a girlfriend coming over for a holiday. Then Felicity took up with a handsome dark-haired traveller called Mike, whom we met in a bar one night. Mike was driving around Europe in his converted old English Bedford single-decker bus, earning his living as a street artist. To pay his respects to a fellow Yorkshireman, he had turned the destination board on the front of his bus to Scarborough. I was flattered!

When *Spirit of Labrador's* charter season ended, Florence offered me a few weeks of work if I met the boat in Tenerife or Gran Canaria. I was pleased with the offer as I would be seeing Monique again. After lifting anchor in Los Cristianos, I checked out Puerto Rico in Gran Canaria, but the schooner must have sailed to Las Palmas. I had been there three months earlier when I had an unfortunate encounter with the Port Captain.

Puerto Rico had two marinas owned by separate companies. One of them was still under construction, although the company had gone bankrupt. Boats would berth there for free with no water or electricity. The harbour master, who ran the other marina, saw an opportunity and decided to ask for harbour dues, so the boat owners, including myself, told him to take a long walk off a short pier, knowing he had no jurisdiction to enforce the charges. We guessed they would go straight into his back pocket.

That day, I had motored to his marina to get fuel and had temporarily tied *Ellis* to a ladder. I climbed the ten feet up to the top with a petrol can in hand, then found the attendant asking me to wait for the harbour master. I guessed he would blackmail me into paying harbour dues I didn't owe and refuse to sell me fuel if I didn't cough up.

I didn't wait for him and returned to *Ellis* with my empty petrol can. I quickly released the ropes from the quay, expecting the boat to drift away but it felt as if we were still attached.

When I looked up, I saw the harbour master hanging onto the rigging. He yelled something about *dinero* and *Policía.* Instead of listening to his protestations, I gave a mighty heave with my legs against the pier and pushed *Ellis* away. The harbour master didn't anticipate my move and was forced to let go. Within seconds, I had raised the genoa. Luckily, a good breeze blew *Ellis* out of the harbour, leaving the angry man to his tantrum, shouting and waving furiously.

Three months on, I was in the free marina again, and there was no sign of *Spirit of Labrador*. I decided to check *poste restante* for mail. *Surely, after all this time and with so many holidaymakers, the harbour master won't remember me if we pass each other and what is the likelihood of such an encounter anyway?*

As chance would have it, I saw him on his scooter heading towards me on my way back from the post office. Fortunately, he didn't seem to recognise me.

I returned to *Ellis* only to find him standing on the quayside, looking down at my boat. Throwing caution to the wind, I casually walked towards him and said, *'Buenos Dias.'*

I heard him babbling away angrily in Spanish. I answered: *'No entiendo.'* He pointed his finger at his head and repeated, *'loco, loco,'* then strode back down the quayside, shouting, *'Aqui, Policía.'*

I wasn't going to wait for his return and made another hasty getaway, deliberately sailing in the opposite direction from where I intended to go. Once out of sight of land, I doubled back on myself in case the harbour master had contacted other marinas he thought I might be heading for on the way. It was another lucky escape.

I arrived in Las Palmas two days before Monique was due to fly back to Switzerland, just in time for a farewell night out with the rest of the crew.

In the first bar we visited that evening, we stood at the counter next to two police officers carrying machine guns over their shoulders. Halfway through our drinks, we suddenly heard shouting and screaming outside. The officers swigged down their whiskies and ran off to go and investigate.

At the next place, we sat opposite a line of prostitutes who gave Monique some dirty looks that intimated, 'What are you doing in our territory with three potential customers?'

Monique and I grew tired of Florence's choice of bars, trailing behind him and John. Then Florence announced, 'Oh look at all those classy-looking women. Let's go in there.'

'Don't bother following them,' I said to Monique, holding on to her arm. 'They'll be out like a shot when they get close enough to see the stubble on their chins!' Within seconds, they were rushing out of the bar, red-faced.

'Mother of Mary, they're all bloody men,' Florence shouted, looking sheepish.

I had fallen behind the party when a young Spanish man tried to pick me up. 'Hang on,' I shouted to the others, feeling put out.

All evening, John acted like a bachelor, encouraged by Florence. He seemed resigned to seeing Monique and me getting on so well. He had said to her, 'You two would make a terrific couple. I could never be as nice a guy as Peter.'

The following day, Monique was leaving *Spirit of Labrador*. I waited with her on the harbour wall for the taxi to take her to the airport. I had asked her to sail to England with me, but she had her career as a singer-songwriter to follow. She mentioned a friend in Germany who might help her with an agent he knew - singing to charterers after a hard day's night wasn't doing it for her. She felt she had more to offer to the music industry.

We exchanged addresses, and I held her hand tenderly. Sadly, the cab arrived far too soon; we only had time for a quick kiss on the lips before Monique was gone.

Two weeks later, the work on the schooner finished. It was nearly May. I had earned enough money to load up the supermarket trolley with 22 tins of fruit, 5 of soups, 7 of carrots, 2 of mixed vegetables, 6 of stew, 2 of corn beef, 2 of ham, 5 of hot dogs, 9 of tuna, 5 of baked beans, 30 large bars of milk chocolate, six tubes of condensed milk and one box of teabags. The young woman cashier at the checkout looked at me strangely. I shrugged my shoulders and smiled!

On top of my provisions, *Ellis* carried fifteen gallons of water in the tank. I added four jerry cans of extra water and had a gallon of petrol for the outboard.

12 May 1978, was departure day from Los Cristianos to sail the one thousand seven hundred miles back to England non-stop.

As I slipped the umbilical cord of the mooring, my excitement suddenly turned to panic. Had I become too familiar with caution? Maybe this was a bad case of harbour fever? I had buried the prediction somewhere in my mind, but it kept roaring to the fore like a crashing wave. In the swirling foam, I could hear the woman's words. "I can see a disaster, but you'll survive and reach your destination." Was I taking too much on, pitting myself alone against the mighty Atlantic Ocean?

16. Mid-Ocean Epiphany

I checked the crude instruments on the dashboard and marvelled at how the aeroplane's wings held together with just a few wooden struts and wires.

As I flew amongst dense clouds, I scanned through the whirling propeller and wiped the mist off my goggles with the back of my leather gloves. Clutching the joystick of my flying machine was empowering, and I couldn't help stroking the open leather-padded cockpit like a much-loved pet. Despite poor visibility, I was confident in myself, savouring this moment of oneness with my WWI fighter plane.

Time seemed to stop ticking. Then, without warning, the aircraft suddenly took a nosedive.

What the hell is happening?

I felt a bump on my head and found myself flopping about on the floor of a ship's cabin.

What am I doing here? I must hallucinating. If I don't snap out of it, I'll crash the plane.

I struggled to fathom what was taking place. Then reality dawned upon me. I was aboard my yacht and the WWI fighter aircraft was just an illusion.

I must have been asleep in a sitting-up position, with my back against the bulkhead, as *Ellis* plunged into a trough, and I was thrown off the saloon seat and hit my forehead on the cabin sole. This was when I thought the plane had taken a nosedive.

Feeling shocked and disorientated, it was a while before I could move. I checked my aching forehead. Fortunately, there was no blood. I dragged myself up into the cockpit for fresh air. A weak heart might have finished me off! This traumatic sequence of events felt like being in a horror movie where the editor had got the clips mixed up.

I sat in *Ellis's* cockpit, wondering how the vision of a WWI fighter plane had materialised. What it a flashback from a previous life?

Lack of sleep, diminished appetite and dehydration probably contributed to my altered state of consciousness. My mind was too hazy to come up with a straight-forward explanation. I needed to get a grip on myself and keep alert if I wanted to make it home to Blighty. There were vessels out there far larger than the 253-metre ore carrier, *The Mineral Alegria,* which little *Ellis* had nudged in the English Channel. I had no wish for such a close encounter with another ship.

Settling into a routine between watches had proven difficult though I can fall asleep anywhere, anytime. Solo navigators hold various theories on converging courses. For example, some say it would take twenty-five minutes for a ship out of sight, below the horizon, to run a small vessel down. With this in mind, I adopted a regime where I would sleep for twenty minutes at a time, leaving me five to get out of the way in the event of a ship bearing down on me.

That said, I slept through two alarm clocks and the radio alarm at full blast on the second day. Why is single-handed sailing promoted so widely? It's exhausting. Whenever I cross a shipping lane, I force myself to stay awake the whole time as these bodies of water are congested highways. In a fibreglass boat, one is playing chicken with steel monsters.

My fate was in the hands of providence, but it was up to me how I dealt with challenging situations. As the expression goes: *'Worse things happen at sea.' I must stop saying that.* After all, I could only blame myself for choosing to sail back to England alone with just a compass, a sextant and a radio direction finder. I had no safety net like a 999 phone number or a device to pinpoint my position, not even a VHF radio. I knew I couldn't rely on ships keeping a good lookout but hoped they would at least have their radar switched on. When a vessel spotted the tiny red dot of *Ellis*, I couldn't be sure either that the captain would comply with the rule of 'power gives way to sail.'

On the third day, I sighted the Selvegen Islands at 030° off the starboard bow. The main island is locally known as 'Pirate Treasure Island.' History books mention that sailors brought goats to the island as a living food supply in the fifteenth century. It's just as well I wasn't starving, seeing that some hungry buggers managed to eat them all by the early nineteenth century!

The following day, I noted 'light zephyr' in my logbook. Later, two swallows landed on *Ellis*. They rested for a while before taking off again. Next, a house-martin flopped on the stern. He made no effort to fly off when I approached him. I left him some crumbs and water where he crouched, looking thoroughly exhausted. Sadly, he was dead the following morning. I wrapped him up in a rag with a ten-millimetre nut and bolt to weigh him down, parcelled together with string, then recited the Lord's Prayer before committing him to the deep.

There was no sign of life for days after the house-martin. All I could see was the glassy ocean stretched out to infinity. Then one morning, a turtle floated past my starboard bow. I altered course to come alongside. She lazily swam away, leaving only six feet between us, and then she stopped paddling to watch me gliding past. I met her large inquiring eyes that seemed to say, 'Fancy meeting you here!' I felt a pang in my heart, for a sea creature had acknowledged me in the vastness of an ocean. I still wonder, if I had run out of food, whether I would have had the heart to kill her.

Although I was alone, just me and my boat, I didn't feel lonely. People have pointed out that I often use 'WE' instead of 'I' - which I do instinctively. I've always sensed the presence of guides looking after me, although I wonder why they let me get into such harrowing situations! While I pondered upon my narrow escapes, a dolphin suddenly appeared only feet away from me. He jumped out of the water at such a height that I managed to look straight into his eye. I felt as though he was asking, 'Are you okay?' Dolphins usually play around the bows of a boat. How strange he chose the stern where I was sitting. Could he be one of the dolphins that I had mistaken for torpedoes the night I avoided an armada on the Portuguese coast?

The dolphin came again to play the next day. I couldn't tell whether he was the same one I had seen earlier. Then in the afternoon, I sensed his presence once more and got my camera ready. A few minutes later, I caught him clean out of the water. I never saw him again after that.

The lack of progress was getting to me. I became melancholic and began to talk aloud to the ocean and *Ellis*. As a distraction from this endless monologue, I decided to learn the words from *The Grey Funnel Line*, one of my favourite sea shanties. I like the *acapella* version most of all, and as I don't play an instrument, I tried to emulate the singers. The lyrics matched my mood:

'Here's one more day
on the Grey Funnel Line,
the finest ship that sailed the sea
is still a prison fort he likes of me,
but give me wings like Noah's dove,
and I'll fly above her to the one I love.'

Where was my Swiss miss, I wondered? What wouldn't I give to be close to her now? We had only exchanged one tender kiss on the lips, but that moment still lingered with me. Monique had often sung on *Spirit of Labrador*. I remembered her singing *Dis Quand Reviendras-Tu?* by her favourite French singer Barbara. It tells the story of a heroine longing for her lover to return, but she warns him that she doesn't have the virtue of a sailor's wife and won't wait forever - the last few words resonated with me.

Before dusk, the sea turned into a bloom of white jellyfish spreading beyond the horizon. They were so packed together that *Ellis*'s bow pushed them aside as if she was ploughing through pack ice. I imagined ancient galleons, becalmed for days, stranded amongst giant rafts of weed in the Sargasso Sea, and wondered if I would find my mermaid-bride amongst Neptune's myriad jellyfish, strewn upon the ocean like rose petals at a wedding. I didn't want 'Captain Nemo' throwing the reception twenty thousand leagues beneath the sea!

Although mesmerised by such magnitude of jellyfish, I couldn't help feeling uneasy. However, curiosity got the better of me. I scooped one of the creatures up into a bucket to look closer. The jellyfish was semi-transparent, with a hint of the rainbow spectrum reflecting in the sunlight. It was shaped like a large coin with a half-moon membrane on top acting as a sail. I grabbed my winch handle and tipped it upside down, and saw that its underbelly was like a miniature version of Medusa's head covered in waving tentacles instead of snakes. I identified it as a *Velella* or 'by-the-wind-sailor' and wondered if these jellyfish sailed closer to windward than *Ellis*? When I slid the creature back into the sea, it landed upside down but soon righted itself before I lost sight of it. The jellyfish seemed to occupy their own space, keeping themselves ten to twenty centimetres apart, their membranes all presenting the same angle to the breeze.

I regretted losing sight of these ethereal beauties, which for a time had become my companions in the desolate ocean. Apart from my slow progress, my concern was my reserve of chocolate running out before I reached England. *I am a chocoholic.* Keeping well-hydrated also proved challenging. The water I had taken on board in Los Cristianos was heavily chlorinated. Even in strong tea, I couldn't disguise the taste, so I replaced my liquid intake with the syrupy juice from the various tins of fruit I had in store. For fresh fruit, I only had one banana left. As I peeled it, discarding the skin, then breaking it up into mouth-sized chunks, I reminded myself why I was eating it in such a fashion. I reflected back to the day that changed it all.

I was working as an electrician's mate on a multi-million-pound smokeless fuel plant outside Doncaster. One morning at break time, sitting with a gang involved in cable-laying, I noticed Harry, a short, stocky, red-haired electrician, was staring at me, eating my banana. I couldn't understand why. Then he stood up, leant across the table, and shouted in my face: 'You aren't bloody eating that banana, you are sexually assaulting it.' There was a brief silence before two hundred 'rough and tough' workers burst out laughing. They jeered and banged on the tables. I turned so red that my face would have outshone the brightest crimson on an artist's pallet. I was twenty-two years old at the time, and it was a long while before I could bring myself to eat a banana in public again.

My frustration at *Ellis's* lack of progress began to worry me after eight and a half days at sea. It was a good thing I never told people which June I intended to be back in England! Tenerife was still only five hundred miles astern, leaving me one thousand two hundred left to go. At least it was warm. The only thing I wore was a bright orange life-harness. I never removed it, even when sleeping, lest I had to rush on deck. If I fell overboard, nobody would be there to rescue me. As I scanned the empty horizon, I said to myself: 'I see no ships, only hardship,' like Nelson lifting his telescope to his blind eye.

A lazy swell began to build up from the north despite the gentle zephyrs. In the afternoon, I went inside to keep out of the sun. By then, the motion had increased. I wedged myself in a corner to avoid being thrown about in the cabin. Why such a swell with so little wind? I glanced at the speedometer, flickering between two and three knots. My progress was a tad better than that of a water boatman bug on a pond.

I tried to bury my feeling of foreboding by reading Spike Milligan's *Puckoon,* but the Tarot reader's words, 'You'll be in a disaster,' kept echoing in my head. Was a storm brewing? Maybe I should reduce sail, but the precaution seemed pointless with hardly any wind.

I didn't have time to consider my next move, for suddenly without warning, *Ellis* reared up like a horse, then crashed with a shudder, and I was pushed against the bulkhead with great force.

She won't take much of this, and neither will I! I must do something fast, at least try and get Ellis to approach the waves at a different angle rather than face them head-on and thud into the troughs.

I made for the hatchway and was flung across the full length of the cabin. After *Ellis* mounted the second wave, she dropped from a greater height and shook more violently. Then came a thunderous banging on the coach roof just as she smashed into the trough. I clambered on deck, dreading what I would find.

The crash I heard was the mast that had broken in half before collapsing on deck. At the sight of the chaos, the Tarot reader's prediction ran through me yet again. In a state of shock, I searched the horizon but couldn't see any evidence of the two rogue waves that had caused the mast to collapse. There wasn't a ship in sight either. Maybe, I had run into a sleeping whale. I had read about navigators on small boats, leaving their depth sounder switched on the whole time so that the sonic signal would warn the slumbering giants of their approach. I didn't have mine on. As for *Ellis's* deck, it was mayhem and looked as if the big top tent had collapsed on Fred Karno's Circus. I thought of the Commodore at the Scarborough Yacht Club, who had asked me with a smirk which circus I belonged to. He was referring to the red and yellow colour scheme on *Ellis*.

There was no time to waste if I wanted to survive this. The mast had broken in two, and half of it was now in the water. It could smash against the hull in the heavy swell and put a big hole in *Ellis*. The rigging and sails were in a haphazard tangle and mostly over the side. Luckily, the mainsail had remained attached to the two halves of the mast, which was one small consolation. By now, *Ellis* was wallowing in a three-metre swell. I enjoy a bit of fun but 'bugger a pantomime!' I did say to people that if I got into trouble at sea, I would sort myself out on my own. So here I was - *get out of this one, Peter!*

I clipped two lifelines onto my harness and went on deck to sort out the mess. My first task was to quickly retrieve everything that had fallen overboard. I've read various dismasting accounts, which suggest chopping the rigging away with a big axe. I didn't have one as I disagree with this theory. My small outboard motor was no use in the situation either. I only had enough fuel for forty miles, and the nearest landfall was three hundred miles away. So, I needed to regain the ability to sail as soon as possible. My survival depended solely on it, so I told the Grim Reaper, *'Thee can put scythe back on shoulder!'*

While I dragged the two halves of the mast out of the water, I was tossed about like a drunken sailor on a merry-go-round. It was a gruelling effort to lift such considerable weight with a heaving deck threatening to throw me overboard. I was running out of strength, though I still managed to lash the two pieces of the broken mast to the side rails before collapsing, thoroughly exhausted. I lay there for some time before regaining strength. With *Ellis* pitching and tumbling alarmingly, I had to move around the deck with two lines securing me to the boat at all times, leaving one hooked on while I clipped the other to my next working station. This manoeuvre restricted my movement when undoing each shackle and coiling every piece of rigging and halyard that could be useful to prepare the jury rig. Unscrambling all that felt as painful as trying to untangle my fishing line the day I caught a hook in my arm.

The sun was setting as I continued labouring, only stopping once to put some clothes on and check the chart to assess my next strategy. I estimated that I was five hundred miles north of the Canaries, one thousand two hundred miles from England and two hundred and forty miles north of Madeira. Although Madeira would be my nearest landfall, I immediately ruled it out because I needed a new mast. Having it shipped to the island would be too complicated, so my best option was to make for Vilamoura in Portugal, three hundred and thirty miles to the east. I knew the place. Besides, this passage would put me on a 'beam reach' to the gathering storm. I needed to prepare myself for the assault of the sea like a soldier ready to do battle, ignoring the thought that he could die that day.

It was well past midnight when I finished rigging two booming-out poles as a crutch to hang an oil lamp on, then set up my trusty self-steering wind-vane so that the port quarter faced the weather. Next, I devoured a cold tin of beans and a bar of chocolate, then wedged myself into my narrow quarter-berth. *Ellis* was now bouncing about like a barrel going over the Victoria Falls. I was far too exhausted to worry about it and soon fell asleep.

I woke up to the wind-driven rain hammering on the deck above me. As I lay on my bunk, water was trickling down my face. It must have found its way through the hatch. I pulled out a towel I had been using as a wedge to stop myself from rolling about and covered my head with it. I didn't have the strength to get up and do anything else. I had to trust *Ellis* and *George*, my self-steering wind-vane, to keep me safe. Then the cradle of hell rocked me back to sleep.

I had no idea how long I was out of it. By then, the motion had worsened, so much so that it felt too dangerous to venture on deck. At least the rain had stopped, which was one small consolation in this hellish nightmare. But I had to carry on. My survival depended on my next move. For once, food had to come first. I needed to build up my strength. So I ate a cold tin of stew and another bar of chocolate, wedging myself in the navigation seat to avoid being bounced around in the cabin like a lottery ball in its dispenser.

I slid back the hatch and saw the sun piercing through the clouds, illuminating mountainous waves with foaming crests ready to devour me while *Ellis* reared heavily broadside to the breaking seas. She shuddered on impact as the waves slapped hard against her beam before rolling underneath her with the force of an avalanche, leaving her decks awash with wind-driven spray. *I won't survive this much longer if I do nothing!*

I donned my foul-weather gear and harness with two clipped lines and crawled on deck. When I looked towards the bow, I was stunned at the sight of *Ellis* without a mast. Although I had faced the devastation the day before and had lashed everything down, I didn't fully realise the gravity of my situation. I thought again of the Commodore at the Scarborough Yacht Club. What would he make of my predicament? At a guess, he might say, 'What circus act are you going to perform now to get out of this?' I laughed, then struggled on all fours while *Ellis* tobogganed down the face of the waves with just the windage of her bare hull. A capsize was imminent if I didn't reduce her speed immediately.

After adjusting the self-steering gear to keep her running downwind, I fought my way to the forward locker, pulled out every piece of rope, halyard, and sheeting, and fastened them across the aft toe-rail, then streamed them out from the stern. Next, I attached the two longest ropes onto the tack and clew of an old storm sail and secured them to the port and starboard aft mooring cleats. Finally, I draped everything astern. The ropes and sail created a long blanket on the water, which reduced my speed to one and a half knots. This process lessened the broaching effect of the waves and eased the foaming crests from smashing with great force into the cockpit.

With *Ellis* more stable, I could now start making a 'jury rig,' using the lower part of the mast, cobbling together the rigging I had salvaged to erect a forestay, backstay, and two side-shrouds. I planned to assemble it all on deck with some bulldog clips and then haul up the fifteen-foot broken mast section with the anchor winch. But, this would only be achievable when the angle of the mast to the deck reached over the horizontal plane. Lifting the top of the mast onto the two-metre-high crutch I had constructed out of the two booming-out poles would be like crossing a fairground cakewalk while threading a needle.

To attempt this mammoth task, I took up a combat pose to steady myself, then started to raise the mast. It was excruciating, even though I only managed to lift it as far as my waist before being forced to drop it down to avoid injuring myself. It had already taken me ages to get to this stage. By then, I had lost my strength. But I knew I had to persevere. If I didn't, it would be like lying down, waiting to die.

The second time I tried, I got the mast to my shoulder but instantly lost my footing. I thought I'd cracked a rib. After that, I lost count of how many more times I attempted to raise the mast. With each go, I became weaker and weaker. I was now panicking, for if I failed to get it in place, I could be lost at sea.

I pleadingly stretched my arms to the heavens, then bellowed out, 'Please God grant me the strength to raise the mast.' My scream was so loud that I thought my lungs would burst. I heard a voice inside me saying: *This has to be the Herculean lift.* I bent down, and with a sudden mighty rush of adrenaline, I picked up the mast and raised it just high enough to sit on top of the crutch - all in one snatch like a true gold medallist weightlifter. Then I sank to my knees, overcome by exhaustion.

I couldn't say how long I remained holding on to the mast. I must have passed out. By the time I came to, the sun had broken through the clouds, but the wind had increased. I went to fetch my camera to record my first step in erecting the jury rig before the weather got worse. Then I secured two side-shrouds and a backstay on the half-mast and sat down at the bow with the anchor winch between my outstretched legs.

From this position, I monitored the reaction of the mast with each stroke of the winch handle. I stopped when the wires came under tension.

Relief rippled through me when I finished. With half a mast, I could now hoist some canvas. I had two storm sails, one I laced to the mast like a loose-footed mainsail; the other fitted perfectly as a headsail in the forward triangle of the jury rig. Finally, I stored away every rope trailing from the stern and set course more or less due east.

At midday, I took a noon sight from a hazy sun. *Ellis* was in a trough one minute, surfing down a crest the next. My sextant reading could be a long way out with this yo-yo motion. However, after my dismasting, I estimated that I had drifted fifty miles south, so I adjusted my course accordingly.

The following day, the squally winds and heavy rain stopped me from taking another sight. Finally, the day after, the sun peeped through for a short spell, and I managed a noon sight, which at least gave me a latitude. But I had to tie myself to the mast to avoid being thrown across the deck; this also freed both hands to operate the sextant.

In the afternoon, the clouds parted long enough for me to take a further sun sight and make a running fix. I untied myself from the mast, and when I looked over to the port side, I was horrified to see a large tanker ploughing past. The monster must have been less than a quarter of a mile from *Ellis*. How come I hadn't noticed the vessel before? Then I understood why, for I instantly lost sight of her in the trough of these enormous waves. I only saw the tanker once more when *Ellis* was on the pinnacle of a gigantic crest.

When I plotted the last fix, I was surprised that my *25-footer* had averaged over a hundred miles a day under jury rig. At this speed, I could be off Cape Vicente in less than twenty-four hours. I then applied Sir Francis Chichester's navigational theory to make landfall safely.

During his record-breaking solo flight over the Pacific Ocean, Sir Francis Chichester used his theory of 'deliberate error.' Locating a remote island for refuelling on the way was vital. To do so, he navigated 10° south, and after running his distance on dead-reckoning, he knew that if the island wasn't in sight by then, he needed to turn north to find it.

The ocean swell eased as I sailed closer to land. Then, when I saw a large vessel approaching out of the murk, it confirmed I was now in the shipping lane that rounded Cape Vicente. The ship was about a mile away, heading for the English Channel. Although we were on a collision course, I intended to hold my position until she came closer. I could then bear off to starboard, resuming my initial heading once I passed her stern.

However, before I could follow this strategy, the ship bore to starboard and did a complete 360°

turn which must have been the distance of a mile across. By the time the captain had completed the manoeuvre, I had safely sailed past the vessel's original track. How incredible that the captain had granted little *Ellis* such mighty respect.

Shortly after, a Russian cargo ship came into view, but the captain didn't offer me the same courtesy. Being so close, I could see the crew lined up on the port side. Were they betting on who would be the first vessel to chicken out? I didn't want to take the chance, so I turned my little 25-footer to starboard and ran down their port side, well within a safe distance of the waving crew.

When I saw the Portuguese coast looming out of the mist, I wanted to trumpet my triumph as loudly as Angel Gabriel blowing his horn, but tears overwhelmed me. I had been alone at sea for twelve days, becalmed, dismasted, and then caught in the storm. I would have been lost at sea if I hadn't been able to raise part of the broken mast and rigged some temporary sails.

After the dismasting, I was driven in a southerly direction for fifty miles in twenty-four hours before sailing the three hundred miles to Cape Vicente. With two sun sights and dead-reckoning, I was just one and a half miles north of my target. I can only thank Sir Francis Chichester for his life-saving tip of deliberate error. I still believe it was a miracle that I survived.

It was early afternoon when I approached the Portuguese port of Lagos. I dropped anchor just off the Ribeira de Bensafrim River. I was glad to remove my heavy weather clothing and harness, which had adopted my body shape. What I needed more than anything now was to talk to someone. I knew Monique's friend Felicity and Mike, her travelling companion intended to drive to Lagos. Maybe they were there already.

After a quick shower, which was a makeshift affair in the cockpit, I inflated the dinghy, then rowed ashore against the out-going tide.,It was exhausting. My struggle to survive must have sucked everything out of me. I felt weak and out of breath when I reached the outer mole of the river entrance. I found some steps by the harbour wall, fastened the dinghy to a rail, and climbed onto the mole. I saw a Portuguese Customs Officer leaning against the parapet, staring out to sea and suddenly remembered I hadn't taken my passport. *I'll pretend to be a tourist on an evening stroll along the pier.*

I was fifty yards past the officer, chuffed at my ruse, when I heard his voice calling: *'Señor, Passaporte e documentos do navio, por favor.'* The officer was pointing at *Ellis*, then looking back at me. I wasn't so lucky after all!

I felt shattered by the time I had rowed to *Ellis* and returned ashore with my passport. My legs were like jelly when I got to the quayside. The officer was still there waiting. The ground seemed to heave like the ocean swell as I followed him to the Customs Office. The place was officially closed, so he took me straight into the officer's mess while another colleague processed my papers. Two other officers were taking a break from duty. One spoke English and offered me a brandy while I waited. 'What a wonderful welcome to Portugal,' I said, raising my glass.

When all the formalities were complete, I asked the officer if he had seen a green bus, and to my surprise, he told me it was parked on some waste ground in the town and gave me directions. I then left the Customs Office to go and look for my friends, Felicity and Mike.

It was almost dark when I found the wasteland the officer had mentioned, and 'lo and behold,' parked in the corner was the green charabanc. I knocked on the side of the vehicle, and Felicity appeared at the passenger door. She looked startled and didn't recognise me at first in the fading light. I must have been the last person she had expected to see in Lagos, knowing that I was sailing back to England non-stop. They both welcomed the weary sailor with wine and homemade cooking. I babbled away to them, making up for my days of confinement. I doubted they were ready for that!

After an uninterrupted night's sleep, I woke up to a sunny morning. The sky was a deep ocean blue, and the air felt warm. I went ashore to ring my mother to tell her I was okay. I didn't call her often, being so expensive. Besides, she usually talked about Mrs X, who had shingles and the people at number 11 buying a new carpet for their lounge. So I would send her postcards instead.

When I arrived in Vilamoura, the marina wasn't busy, and *Ellis* was high and dry in the boatyard within twenty-four hours. Then I caught an overnight bus to Lisbon. Once there, I checked the flights to London, found one for the following morning, and headed for the bank to draw enough money for my ticket, food, and accommodation for the night. I presented my credit card to the cashier, and to my surprise, the pretty young woman returned it straight away and declared in perfect English, 'Your card expired yesterday.'

I stared at it in disbelief. Surely this was a mistake. Then, seeing the distress on my face, the cashier said: 'One moment, I'll see if the Bank Manager can help you.'

He came, looked at my card and saw my pitiful expression. I told him my story in a few words, stressing my urgent need to fly back to England. He was sympathetic and allowed me to draw out a limited amount, back-dating the transaction to the day before. It was just enough to cover my flight and some food. I was unable to bargain for more cash and thanked him for his understanding.

After leaving the bank, I rushed to the travel agency to buy my plane ticket. The English money

I had left would get me from Heathrow Airport back to Scarborough. But where was I going to sleep that night - maybe on a park bench! Surely a June night in Portugal wouldn't be that cold.

I felt people's stare, walking through the streets of Lisbon in my yellow sailing jacket, carrying a sail bag over my shoulder. I bought a sandwich at a kiosk and wandered around town until dark. Then I found a suitable out-of-the-way park bench. I was about to fall asleep when I noticed strange men in raincoats eyeing me suspiciously as they walked past. *I must be in the wrong area of town.* Feeling increasingly nervous, I left and headed for the city centre. *I'll be safer amongst people and street lights,* I thought.

I settled on a bench under a glaring street lamp in one of the main Piazzas. Sleep eluded me. I took out my book *Puckoon* and started to read. I laughed out so loudly that passers-by kept staring at me. Spike Milligan's humour calmed me down, and I fell asleep, sitting up with my chin on my chest. Then I suddenly became aware of people standing nearby. Through half-opened eyes, I saw faces peering down at me. I noticed the men were wearing make-up and funny hats. They gabbled away in Portuguese, and then one of the revellers made a grab for my sail bag. 'No, please don't take this, it's all I have,' I begged my attacker while I tried to hang on to it. Next, I heard someone saying in Portuguese about *Ingles* and motioning to my aggressor to let go. The man was holding the gang back with outstretched arms, like a policeman restraining a baying mob. What had prompted the ringleader to order the others to leave me alone? My few English words must have stirred some compassion in him, saving me from being robbed, beaten up, or even raped. The men stared at me strangely as they walked away. My heart was still racing when I picked up my book again, but I had no stomach to laugh at *Spike* anymore.

On the flight to London, I reflected on my voyage. The most frightening experience, apart from the dismasting and the storm, had been my hallucination, flying a WWI plane. I could never forget such a chilling episode. *If a cat has nine lives, how many do I have left?* I wondered whether I would ever see Monique again. If she became famous, she might forget about me. Finally, my thoughts turned to my next project of building a steel boat I would call *Capricorn*. I had no idea where or when, but I was sure I would find a way to make it happen.

17. Desert and Cuckoo Clocks

James parked his new, silver metallic E-type Jaguar behind my old yellow van. How could I not be envious? The last time I saw him, he was driving a flashy Porsche during his leave from Saudi Arabia. I had worked with James there. He was the one who told everybody he used to have brown hair but left the grey stage out to go straight into pink!

'What are you up to?' he asked.

'I'm looking for work.'

'How about a six months contract in Iraq with the company I work for? They're looking for an engineer on a chicken farm. It's very good money.'

The opportunity seemed perfect. I was in dispute with my insurance company, who had offered me five hundred pounds for my damaged mast. Ironically, the damage happened precisely in the same place where the shipyard in Brest had made the repairs.

While I had no intention of profiting from the disaster, I wanted a fair settlement of a new mast shipped to Vilamoura Marina. Working in Iraq would enable me to earn enough money to go cruising or at least sail *Ellis* from Portugal back to England. Then I would sell her and start building a steel yacht - strong enough to face what fate might throw at me. I wanted to end my relationship with *Miss Fortune.*

James arranged an interview for me with his company based in Wolverhampton. It was difficult to get there on public transport, so I decided to risk the old van I had bought as a run around from my ex-boss Gary at the Renault Garage. It played up on the way, and I was late for my interview.

The secretary called me in after I'd waited half an hour. Mr Adams was sitting behind his desk and was off-hand when he asked me to take a seat. I apologised and explained why I was late. In hindsight, it was a mistake to mention the fuel lock on the old van. I must have hammered it too hard on the motorway.

'It doesn't look good applying for this post in charge of maintenance when you can't even manage your own vehicle,' he snapped.

I couldn't argue with that, and while he chastised me, I noticed a photograph of some sailing boats on the wall behind him.'Are you interested in sailing?' I asked. I wasn't sure if the question sprang out of desperation or cunning trickery.

'As a matter of fact, I am. Why do you ask?' He was looking puzzled.

'I noticed the photograph behind your desk. I've just sailed solo from the Canaries on my 25-foot yacht.' I dared not tell him that I was dismasted and only managed to get as far as Portugal, in case he thought it was due to my poor seamanship.

'Have you really sailed all that way?' he said, visibly impressed. He paused, then announced, 'You've got the job because you're going to be single-handed out there, in the desert!'

I landed at Baghdad Airport two weeks later and looked for a sign, 'Newby - Big Dutchman,' as I walked out of the arrival gate. It was a while before I found Mustafa amongst the crowd, casually holding a board waist-high. Mustafa was the appointed taxi driver working for 'Big Dutchman' and thankfully spoke English.

After clearing a police checkpoint on the outskirts of Baghdad, Mustafa drove me to a large farm complex in the desert, just thirty miles north of the city. Although it seemed like the middle of nowhere, the River Tigris was only a mile away and provided all the water for the farm. While the Tigris conjured up many biblical stories, from the Hanging Gardens of Babylon to the Battle of Jericho and numerous wars fought over for its control, my romantic visions were soon shattered when we approached the complex. A guard with a rifle stopped us at the barrier.

This high-security compound seems more like a penitentiary than a chicken farm. Am I going to be released for good behaviour at the end of my six-month contract or incarcerated here forever?

The complex accommodated six farms, divided into four large chicken-houses, with a twenty-four-hour live-in guard allocated to each building. The hens had free range within the houses. They laid their eggs in nesting boxes that ran down the centre and were collected on a conveyor belt before being transported to an incubation building - the very area I was forbidden open access to. My boss Henry, the regional manager in Baghdad, had warned me: 'Don't ask the Iraqis for anything and remember there are places on the farm which are out of bounds but never ever question why.'

I shared a villa with another Englishman, Gary, a tall, fair-haired, thirty-something from Lincolnshire. He was the farm manager on the site. The accommodation was luxurious compared with that of the guards, whose only facilities were a mattress on the floor, a one-ring gas cooker, and a washbasin. In comparison, we had two bedrooms and a large lounge furnished with a table and chairs, a dartboard and a television. The kitchen, which was big enough to eat in, had a full-size cooker, large refrigerator, chest freezer and a washing machine. All the floors were tiled throughout the property, and I swore to myself I would maintain a permanent vigil for scorpions. I suspected they would favour the shower tray. I stood the legs of my single iron-framed bed in large empty bean cans half-filled with water and oil to deter these deadly creatures from joining me in my bed. Thankfully, I slept undisturbed on my first night.

Next to us was a villa occupied by a Korean chick-sexer and her Iraqi female chaperone. Koreans held the reputation of being the fastest chick-sexers in the world, able to identify males from females, separating a thousand chicks an hour. They sent the females off in truckloads while the poor males were discarded and scattered in the desert. They became prey to wild animals or vultures or died of thirst or starvation.

My work as an engineer was to assist the Iraqi workers with maintenance and repairs, but they seemed reluctant to approach me. Were they too proud to ask for help, or did they believe they knew better? I had to remind myself that I had been brought in as an advisor and representative and should only become involved when someone requested assistance. However, with warranty work, I was obliged to carry out all the repairs myself.

A few days into my assignment, an Iraqi maintenance man, desperate for a waste-trap, borrowed one from the guardhouse sink. Later on, the guard complained that each time he washed his hands, his feet got wet. He was pleased when I gave him a bucket to put under the sink. But when the bucket was full, he poured the contents back into the sink - nearly flushing himself out of the door! Such was the logic of some of the people I was dealing with.

At least I wasn't covered in chicken shit! A little grease behind my fingernails was my only affliction apart from boredom and the heat. It did have its advantage though, for when I hung my washing outside on the line, my clothes were dry by the time I finished pegging out the last items. Jeans took the longest, a mere ten minutes.

Driving to Baghdad to get to the shops was a nightmare, especially with my limited knowledge of the language. The few road signs were all in Arabic. Iraq was once pro-British and what seemed to remain of its influence were the old cars still being driven around the city. They were all rust-free, including the Vauxhall Victors with their winged rear lights. In England, they called them rust-buckets. One night, I got desperately lost in a suburb. Fortunately, my navigation skills came to my rescue. The farm was due north of Baghdad, so I followed the North Star, which guided me safely through a labyrinth of streets, then over the desert roads back to the farm.

Drivers in the city were aggressive, always cutting others off, partly through no sense of speed or distance. To survive such assaults on wheels, I developed a driving technique of doing it to them before they did it to me. During my racing days, I had learned to anticipate, judge speed and distance, analyse the traffic ahead, and see gaps in-between, although one race in the past almost claimed another of my nine lives when I did three somersaults in my car.

My racing days started when I drove my one-year-old Vauxhall Victor to the Crystal Garage to fuel up, and a blond chap in a suit with glasses approached me in his 'salesman's fashion,' to ask if I was ready to trade the Vauxhall in for a new Ford. I had done twenty-thousand miles in one year driving across the Yorkshire moors, working as an electrician's mate at the RAF Early Warning Radar Station.

I told the salesman I wanted to sell the Vauxhall, get an older vehicle, and buy a Mallock U2 racing car with the money left.

'This is incredible,' he said. 'I've been dreaming of building such a car. But, I cannot envisage being able to afford it on my salary and with a wife, a two-year-old child and another on the way!'

I thought we must be the only two people in Scarborough who had ever heard of a Mallock U2 and wanted to race one!

'Maybe, we could build a new Mallock U2 together,' the salesman declared.

This chance meeting took me on a different track from qualifying as an electrician. We discussed the project over a few cups of tea, then signed the partnership where I agreed to provide most of the funds while Barry dealt with the nuts and bolts of the construction.

I sold my Vauxhall privately and bought a second-hand Ford Anglia at trade price from Barry. With the money left, I purchased the chassis and components to build our racing car.

A few days later, I saw a TVR advertised in Hull and bought it on a whim, knowing that I had good equity against the Ford. It was too pedestrian for me anyway and didn't match my image of a 'would be' racing driver! When I introduced my TVR to Barry, he was less than impressed.

'I've put my job on the line, knocking that Ford Anglia down below trade price for you,' he said, red-faced. 'This is how you thank me, exchanging it for a lump of fibreglass! And there's nowhere to fit a tow bar on that thing.'

I upset him again a few weeks later when he saw my picture in the local newspaper, posing next to my TVR with the caption:

'Twenty-one-year-old Scarborough man wins his first ever race at Mallory Park in his TVR sports car.'

It was in 1965.

Despite my success, I sold the TVR after losing a wheel on a corner one time. Luckily, I was only doing a few miles an hour.

Racing and the need to work long hours to finance this expensive hobby took over everything. I had just finished another contract as an electrician's mate when Rob, one of the rally drivers who shared some garage premises where I kept my racing car, asked me if I wanted a welding job at his factory. He worked as an engineering draughtsman for Ward Brothers, making steel structures for skyscrapers and hangars for Jumbo jets. Rob was keen for me to get the job because he received a £5 bonus for every worker he introduced to the firm. There was a snag, though. I wasn't a welder. 'Don't worry, Pete,' another friend chipped in. 'I'll show you how to weld before you go for the interview.'

Eddie gave me a half-hour crash course. The next day, I applied as a professional welder. A couple of white lies and some exaggeration got me accepted.

Ward Brothers were expanding, and overtime was available. I needed the money to continue racing as I was self-sponsored.

Becoming involved in widening wheels also happened by chance while Barry and I were building the Mallock U2 together. When I mentioned we needed wide-rim wheels for the racing tyres, my rally friend Rob suggested I make my own. He showed me how to bend the strip metal around an acetylene bottle before welding it onto a split steel wheel. Later, I designed and made a purpose-built roller.

Drivers at the circuits and local rally lads often asked me where we bought our wide-rim wheels. That was when I thought of starting a business.

Barry and I burnt a lot of midnight oil during the construction of the Mallock U2, trying to re-invent the wheel. We ought to have gone for Webber carburettors instead of four Amal motorbike carburettors. Before long, I bought him out and we parted company. I regretted not buying the Mallock U2 in the first place, which won the Clubmen's trophy.

One of my favourite racing circuits was Ingliston. During practice, one day, I was braking heavily for a right-hand hairpin bend when I suddenly saw a wheel overtaking me. I slithered to a stop on the grass verge, only to realise that it was my runaway rear left-hand wheel. Before climbing out of the car to retrieve it, I noticed a kilted 'Robert the Bruce' type marshal running towards me, his sporran swinging from side to side. He was shouting, 'idiot Sassenach,' as he held my wheel above his head, threatening to use it as a claymore and smash my skull in. I was lucky that two other marshals stopped him in time, but I still had to convince him that my wheel missing him by a fraction of an inch was neither personal nor deliberate.

Mallory Park was also a favourite circuit. Like Ingliston, it had no long straights. It was one corner after another, so the racing relied more on driving skills than horsepower. I came third in a race and was entered for another one the following weekend. So I arranged with the organisers to leave my Mallock U2 in the paddock to save trailing it the three hundred and sixty miles return trip to Scarborough and back. I covered it with a tarpaulin and removed the rotor arm from the distributor to stop anyone wanting to borrow my racing machine for joy-riding.

It was close to practice time when I arrived at the circuit on my next race day. I tucked my silk necktie into the top of my striped shirt, my trouser bottoms inside my socks, donned my motorcycle helmet and rushed to prepare the car. I would often use soft spark plugs to warm the engine up before changing them to hard ones for racing, which proved the easiest way to start the car from cold. To gain time, for once, I tried the hard plugs first, but they soon flattened the battery. Fortunately, help was at hand. Some of my fellow competitors and mechanics tried to push start the car, but nothing happened. I thanked them enthusiastically, although I felt guilty seeing them looking so deflated. I had to do something quickly, or else I would miss the race.

As I raised the aluminium engine cover, I felt a bulge in my pocket. No, sorry, lifting the bonnet doesn't do it for me! What a fool! I had forgotten to put the rotor back in the distributor! I hoped no one noticed when I quickly re-installed it. Luckily, my car was on top of a slope. I free-wheeled down, letting the clutch out in second gear, and my racing machine burst into life with a roar. I heard a raucous cheer from the guys who had tried to help me. If they had known about the missing rotor, I would have been dodging flying spanners and ballistic oil cans!

I drove straight to the gate leading to the circuit. Cars were fast approaching, having completed two warm-up laps already. I knew Mallory Park so well that I could drive flat out without prior practice. Amateur racers didn't have many laps in the main race, so they used the practice as an unofficial one to qualify for pole position on the starting grid.

When the race marshal waved me onto the track, I put my foot to the boards through first, second, and third gear, tyres screeching before the other cars could bear down on me. I rounded 'Gerard's bend' on the limit without warming up first. I saw the rest of the field pursuing me close behind through my rear-view mirror. I went for it as I was now in the lead, holding off more powerful cars than mine for three laps. Then, when my brakes started to overheat, I compromised by braking earlier into the corners. The fastest three cars soon overtook me but I was up to their exhaust pipes for another two laps. Then at 'Gerard's,' an 80/90 mph bend, the leading car lost it and began to spin. The second car took to the grass to avoid a collision; as for the third, because the driver had been relatively slow around 'Gerard's' during the previous lap, I knew I could re-overtake him again there. If I got myself through this fracas, I should be back in the lead. So, I overtook him on his left-hand side, in third, flat out at 6000 revs (90 mph), but instead of going for the same gap as myself, the driver suddenly braked heavily, his car swerved and the wheels of our two vehicles interlocked - then total blackout!

I became aware of my back on the tarmac and could see the upside-down rear doors of an ambulance and a worried face looking down at me from under a peaked cap. I screamed out: 'My back is killing me!' Grazed and soaked in petrol, it was burning like hell.

'Don't move and stay calm,' the ambulance man cautioned me. 'We'll get you to the hospital in no time.' Someone counted one, two, three before they lifted me, just high enough to shuffle a stretcher under me. Unable to move a muscle, I stared straight up at the sky with one eye, looking for solace. I could feel myself levitating until my gaze focused on the ceiling of the ambulance. Every bump was excruciating as the vehicle lurched forward over the grassy emergency exit. At this point, I passed out.

When I regained consciousness, I found myself in a hospital bed with the mother of all headaches, aware that I was looking at the world through one eye. Panic set in. I could hardly move my arms. Was I in one piece?

I wiggled my toes, which seemed unhurt, but the throbbing in my head was unbearable, especially with the slightest movement. I touched it gently - no bandages. I felt my stubbled chin.

Everything seemed in place until I came across the heavy swelling. My right cheek had become level with my eyebrow, closing my right eye completely. Then, out of the corner of my good eye, I saw nurses dashing to and fro, but no one was attending me. I continued calling out, complaining of unbearable pain. I pleaded for what seemed a long time. Why were they ignoring me? Maybe my voice was too faint? Finally, a nurse came to my bedside.

'We cannot administer anything for your pain until the consultant has seen you in case he needs to operate,' she explained. 'He'll be able to assess your eye and see what to do with that heavy swelling.' If only I could sleep until then.

'Your girlfriend must have a hell of a right hand,' the nurse added with a mischievous smile. 'What did you do to upset her!'

I never knew the true meaning of 'It only hurts when I laugh,' until then. Despite the pain, I eventually fell asleep through exhaustion.

When I woke up the following morning, my heart skipped a beat. I could see the world with both eyes, although my vision through the right eye was still blurred. Thankfully, I felt less pain eating my porridge. Until then, I hadn't thought of Elisabeth. At the time, we were still courting on and off. Did she know where I was? At a guess, she would have been lapping up the attention, being the girlfriend of a racing driver involved in a crash. She was used to hospital procedures and must have known what to do in the circumstances.

I was pleased when she walked down the ward later on that day. She held my hand, but we were too overwhelmed to speak for a while. Then, she told me what had occurred.

'I thought something was wrong when I heard the crowd gasping around the circuit just after the screaming engines stopped. I rushed up to a marshal and asked him what had happened. He told me this was the most spectacular crash he had seen in years. The car did three somersaults in the air before landing in a ditch. I asked him whether the driver was hurt, but he didn't know.

He said the ambulance took him away, and with a crash like that, he doubted the man would survive. He noticed the look on my face and asked if I knew any of the drivers. I told him my boyfriend was out there.

He was so embarrassed that he tried back-peddling on what he had said. "It's probably not your boyfriend," he kept repeating, choking on the words. Then he took me to the Chief Marshal at the control tower.

He confirmed that a white and orange Mallock No 11 was in the crash. I nearly fainted. The marshal put his arms around my shoulders and reassured me that you were conscious on the way to the hospital. He promised he would ring later to check on you. Then the marshal first on the scene told me that your car did three somersaults before you were ejected from the vehicle. You landed in a ditch and what saved you from being crushed to death was the car straddling the ditch above you.'

'I can't remember the somersaults or anything else until I felt my back burning,' I replied, bewildered. Elisabeth was looking through me, seemingly reliving the nightmare.

'The crash bar protecting your head was ripped off,' she continued. 'If you hadn't been pitched out of the car, you would have been decapitated. The engine was still running when the marshal crawled under your car to reach for the emergency stop button on the dashboard. Petrol was pouring out from the rear tank. He said he started praying to God that the whole f**ing thing wouldn't blow up before he could pull you out from underneath. Then he and another marshal dragged you out of the ditch.'

'I owe my life to those two volunteers who risked theirs to save mine,' I said with lips quivering. 'If a seatbelt had been mandatory I would have been decapitated, from what you told me.' She squeezed my hand firmly.

'When the breakdown truck brought your car back, they loaded it onto the trailer, tied it down, and covered it with a tarpaulin. Apart from the smashed up fibreglass nose-cone, the torn-away roll-over bar, and the missing petrol cap, the car seemed relatively intact.'

Elisabeth knew her stuff! We chatted away until the consultant arrived. After a thorough examination, he discharged me. However, I wasn't to drive and should take to my bed for at least a week in case I experienced a delayed concussion.

Two days later, I returned to work. After all, I was self-employed. My eye still looked as if I had been in a fight. When the jokes finally stopped, I knew that the swelling had gone without looking in the mirror. I fixed the car and only raced once more. If thrown off your horse, you need to get back on again. Then I swapped the Mallock for a Mark II Jaguar, thinking I would live longer if I gave up the motor-racing game.

The wind-driven sand swirling in from the Iraqi desert jolted me back to the present. Gary and I had gone to collect parts from another Big Dutchman's farm in the company Nissan pickup. It was a three-hundred-mile round trip. The last leg was through the centre of Baghdad.

As we approached a roundabout, a mini-bus full of Iraqis overtook us. Usually, I would have cut the driver off before he could do it to me, but I felt benevolent this time and let him go.

Misjudging the length of his vehicle, he pulled over to my lane too quickly, allowing me no room to manoeuvre. With the roundabout curb being three feet high, he forced me to make an emergency stop. The mini-bus swerved so sharply that his rear bumper and my front one interlocked with a bang. The driver halted, and passengers poured out of the mini-bus and ran towards my pickup. The only visible damage to the bus was the partially twisted back bumper. Although I wasn't responsible for the accident, I could be thrown in jail regardless.

Not wanting to risk such an ordeal, I put the accelerator to the boards and left the passengers behind, shouting and waving. My action seemed cowardly, but I had heard so many stories of ex-patriots involved in accidents through no fault of their own being thrown behind bars. They could remain there for weeks before appearing in front of a magistrate, providing that the company had noticed their absence in the first place and could bail them out. My boss, Henry, only visited the farm once a month. I didn't even have his telephone number with me.

When I thought I had lost the mini-bus, I drove at the maximum speed limit and headed out of Baghdad on a dual carriageway.

What a relief - but it was short-lived. A woman driver had caught up with me. She tried to wave me down. I ignored her as we drove parallel to each other. Eventually, she sped away. Then as I approached the next roundabout, I saw the woman standing beside a traffic cop, pointing directly at me. The policeman started to blow his whistle, trying to wave me down. I quickly tailgated the car in front to shield mine from his view.

Luckily, the officer didn't have the presence of mind to halt the vehicle in front, which would have forced me to stop.

I asked Gary if the policeman had a gun. As he didn't seem to have one, I screeched around him and the woman driver as if I were James Bond in his Aston Martin. The back end of the pickup swung out in a sideways drift with tyres smoking. In the rear-view mirror, I saw the policeman running after me, still blowing hard on his whistle. Feeling very nervous, I ducked down a few backstreets before heading to the checkpoint out of the city.

Had the officer reported my description and car registration number? It was a relief when the control barriers lifted and someone waved us through.

Back at the farm, I set about repairing the pickup. I lodged a piece of wood between a wall and the bent bumper, let the clutch out gently, and then drove towards the concrete wall to straighten the bumper. There was no sign of damage to the vehicle by the time I finished. Later, I told my boss Henry about the saga. He laughed and said, 'We would have brought you food parcels.' It was two weeks before I dared drive to Baghdad again. In the meantime, Gary did all the shopping.

The farm plumber, Fadi, was a Christian and spoke good English. One Friday, being a day of rest, he invited me to his home to meet his family. They lived in a third-floor flat near the centre of Baghdad. His home had basic 'mod cons' but lacked comfort. Over the meal, Fadi spoke warmly about the days of the Shah when life was freer, better, and food more plentiful. 'If I want to buy a television now,' he said, 'I have to fill in a form and wait months before I get delivery.'

I wasn't too surprised to hear his complaint. Shopping in supermarkets was such a bizarre affair. On some occasions, I would find shelves bare or overfilled with washing powder as if a ship had arrived to prepare the country for a big clean-up. Then it would be a glut of honey, and when that had all run out, some other product or food would appear on the shelves. I soon learned to stock up because there was no telling when certain items would become available again.

Jabir was a young Iraqi in his mid-twenties, working in middle management. One day, he took me to a park in Baghdad. As we walked through the impressive ornate gates, I expected to see tall, lush trees and manicured lawns, but instead there was bare earth and sand, with dead scrub and leafless stunted trees.

We came across a rundown brick building with two exhibits behind glass. One was an open-top four-seater Mercedes that the German Kaiser had gifted to the Shah during WWI. Sadly, all the tyres were flat, and the leather upholstery cracked with the stuffing protruding.

A seaplane close to it originated from the same era. The fabric of its wings was moth-eaten and torn, half the under-carriage had collapsed, and one of the wings was drooping on the ground. Both displays would have been magnificent original museum pieces, but they mirrored the unkempt appearance of the surroundings, which failed to pay homage to the city of Baghdad.

After the park, Jabir took me to his home. We sat on hard chairs in a large walled garden. The herbaceous borders were just sand and rubble.

When his mother brought cups, saucers and a teapot, the only thing I saw of her was her wrist when she passed the tray through the back door.

Jabir had mentioned how oppressed he felt by the Iraqi police. One time, he drove his girlfriend into the desert in his Lada. They parked in a lonely place near the River Tigris, where they hoped to enjoy some quiet time together. They kissed under the palm trees, far from prying eyes, or so they thought, but it wasn't long before a patrol car pulled up alongside. They were arrested and escorted to the police station. A doctor examined his girlfriend to check for signs of sexual intercourse.

This regime of persecution was hard for young Iraqis to bear, especially Christians. The onsite electrician, a Muslim, had only just been released from prison for stabbing his sister to death. Because she was pregnant out of wedlock, he murdered her to defend the family honour.

Had this happened in the past, the brother wouldn't have been prosecuted but praised for his action. At least justice for women was slowly reaching Iraq.

One night, as I was engrossed in designing my next boat *Capricorn,* named after my horoscope sign - a goat with a fishtail, I heard a commotion and went to investigate. One of the guards was banging on the door of the Korean woman with the butt of his revolver.

Moments later, he returned to his post. Then I heard a car speeding off over the desert through a seldom-used back entrance. A friendly Iraqi manager told me that a guard had spotted a taxi driver entering the villa. When he noticed the vehicle still there the following morning, he suspected it belonged to the chaperone's boyfriend. He knocked at the door, but the woman refused to answer. He gave her an ultimatum that if the boyfriend didn't leave by the time he returned, he would shoot the lock off and the man too. Fortunately, it never came to that.

With plenty of free time from my work, I often wrote to Monique. However, composing a letter would involve two full evenings or more, covering up for my dyslexia. How debilitating it was for me.

I remembered the humiliation all those years ago when I was about to sit my 11 plus exams and our teacher asked us to read the story of 'Joseph and his coat of many colours' from the Bible.

'I don't think you're reading the story, Peter,' the teacher suddenly blurted out.

'But, Miss, I am,' I answered, blushing.

'All right. Stand up and tell the class about it.'

I had heard the same passage at Sunday school the previous week and managed to give the teacher an outline. 'Very good, Peter,' she remarked, almost choking on her words before summoning me to sit down.

As an experienced teacher, she must have noticed I hadn't been reading the story to myself. My parents were informed I lagged in English. They believed my progress had been hampered by time off school with mastoiditis, and although they had paid for me to have private tuition, it was too little too late. I consistently covered up for my inability to read and spell correctly. People were unaware of dyslexia in the 1950s, so it was no surprise when I failed my 11 plus, and the school transferred me to a B class.

To help me with my dyslexia, I developed the ability to identify complete words as shapes. Meanwhile, I excelled in every subject but English, which put me at the top of the B class for two years. Despite my poor reading and writing, the school was then obliged to move me to the A-class.

At the end of my last term at school, I shocked my schoolmates when I came second in class by being top in Art, Metal Work, Woodwork, Technical Drawing, History and Religious Studies (the latter, only God knows why). However, before prize-giving, the headmaster, Mr Stoddard, took me to one side.

'I'm sorry Peter. We can't have you claiming six book prizes. You'll have to give the other boys a chance to come up on stage so I've decided to award you three prizes instead.'

It felt as if I had just completed a four-minute mile run, and someone forgot to start the stopwatch. How could I argue the point and defy authority when my parents showed no interest in my education? Sadly, for me, they could only see my future as a labourer or preferably a full-time barman in the hotel they ran. I learned the meaning of life's unfairness with Mr Stoddard's decision that day. So I grinned at him and thought, smile and be happy; things could get worse. So I smiled and was happy, and 'lo and behold,' things got a lot worse.

After winning a scholarship to Art School, my teacher tried hard to convince my parents that I had a natural talent for drawing and painting, but he couldn't alter their attitude. 'We're not keeping you till you're twenty-odd years old,' my parents told me categorically. 'You'll need to get a job or an apprenticeship.'

Why couldn't they be more sympathetic? They had both left school at fourteen; my father to work at a cotton mill in Skipton and my mother at the family greengrocer in Featherstone. Then at sixteen, she had run away to Scarborough to go and work as a live-in barmaid in a men-only bar.

My parents couldn't imagine a future for me after Art School, and I failed to convince them that having a degree could lead to other opportunities. I felt gutted as children who failed their 11 plus had no future in the academic world. I was a fifteen-year-old about to leave school at the end of the term, June time, with no idea of what I wanted to do apart from Art.

Mr Stoddard redeemed himself when he acted as my career adviser. He arranged two interviews on my behalf, the first one at a Chartered

Accountant, given my excellent results in mental arithmetic.

That day, I pressed creases into my grey school trousers, donned my herringbone sports jacket and my most conservative tie and then set off for my interview. I knew Scarborough as if I had swallowed an A to Z map. We had lived near the address Mr Stoddard had given me. However, I couldn't remember seeing a Chartered Accountant in the high street.

Looking for the number, I noticed a door between a shoe shop and a man's outfitters with 'Hoggard Chartered Accountant' engraved on the unpolished brass plaque. I knocked, hurting my knuckles on the stout door and waited a while, but no one answered. I tried the handle. It was unlocked and opened onto a long, narrow, steep flight of stairs. It was so dark inside that I left the front door ajar. As I strode up the worn linoleum-covered steps, my spirit sank. I knocked on the large glass-panelled door on the landing, which displayed the company name in imitation gold-leaf letters, then heard a high-pitched male voice.'Come in,' the man shouted.

I walked timidly into a small room that looked disproportionate with its lofty ceiling. Dark walls supported shelves with hundreds of ledgers. The two desks and stools facing each other reminded me of the ones my school teachers used. A tall, thin, elderly gentleman stood up from his seat.

With it being so high, he was the same height when standing or sitting.

'Ah, you must be Master Newby,' he chirped, offering his handshake.

Mr Hoggard had an inquisitive frown and piercing eyes. I stared at his hands, almost expecting to see woolly gloves with fingers cut out like Scrooge's, and it seemed to me as if I had come to replace 'Tiny Tim's father' as the ledger clerk.

Mr Hoggard ushered me over to a desk with a high stool. I was tall for my age, but I didn't find it easy to climb up onto it. He opened a ledger on the sloping desk where I saw words and figures which looked as if they had been handwritten in ink with a feather quill pen. Mr Hoggard explained what my duties would be and I thanked him for his time.'I'll be in touch,' I said as I left his office.

Later, I reported to Mr Stoddard and told him that accountancy was not for me.

'Okay,' he replied dismissively.

He had also arranged another interview for me as a junior draughtsman with a firm of architects.

GW Alderson Architects were on the first floor of what used to be a grand townhouse at 41 Pavilion Square. Originally a bedroom with a high ceiling and prominent architraves, the drawing office was divided by a wooden partition that finished three feet short of the ceiling. One third was the reception area which included a counter, a desk, and a telephone switchboard with plug-in lines connecting to other offices. The rest accommodated two draughtsmen, a printing machine that copied full-size architectural drawings and large cabinets to store them in.

Mr Alderson addressed everybody as 'young man,' even when the person was older than himself. He told me I would attend a Technical College two afternoons a week and shouldn't expect wages apart from £1 a week as a token because he provided a great deal more than just an ordinary apprenticeship. Both the headmaster and my parents were delighted when I accepted the offer. Sadly, I left the apprenticeship after a year. What old Alderson wanted was cheap labour. The draughtsmen and secretary could have warned me. It was common practice to take on an aspiring school leaver each year, promising to teach him the profession under false pretences. But my experience hadn't been in vain, as I had learned to read and draft technical drawings.

When my mandatory ten-day leave from Iraq arrived, my boss, Henry, gave me a plane ticket back to England. With a scheduled flight, I could divert ten per cent of my journey and make a stopover anywhere I chose. So I told Monique in a letter that I wanted to visit her in Switzerland on my way to England. 'It would be great,' she wrote back. Although we had only shared a kiss in Las Palmas before she left, I felt love was on the cards.

When we met at Geneva Airport, I thought she looked prettier than I remembered her from the photograph I had kept by my bedside. We embraced like old friends, and I saw the excitement on her face. I certainly felt my pulse quickening. From Geneva, we caught the train to where her parents lived. We took little notice of the mountains and lakes whizzing past on the way. We only had eyes for each other and far too much to say. Thankfully, we were alone in a compartment. I gently put my hand on her thigh, and she placed hers on mine. I felt a rushing flow of energy passing through my body. It was just like an electric current. I hoped she felt it too.

'Would you enjoy walking up mountains while you're here?' she asked, looking animated.

'I'll climb a mountain anytime to be with you.' I answered.

She giggled and blushed.

'I can't wait to take you to the Gorges of l'Areuse,' she said in her irresistible French accent. 'It is the most magical place in the world to me.'

Picture postcard Switzerland became the backdrop of a fast-growing romance. But, alas, the honeymoon ended far too soon. A few days later, I flew back to England to tackle the broker, the claims agent, and the insurance company. Then I returned to Iraq to finish my contract.

During the next three months, our passion crossed continents with our letters flying back and forth between cuckoo clock country and the

Arabian desert. Our feelings grew stronger through the written word. Then when I asked Monique in one of my letters if she would sail back to England from Portugal with me, she said YES. Just as well she hadn't agreed the first time I invited her. She wouldn't have enjoyed the luxury cruise in a storm across the Atlantic under jury rig!

Later, Monique received the offer of a well-paid job as 'cook' on a large motor yacht near Cannes and asked me if I would be interested in being the deckhand. I was game and suggested that we sail *Ellis* from Portugal as near as possible to Sète before joining the gin palace in Cannes. Then, when the season ended, we would head back to England via the Canal du Midi. We had it all planned.

18. Whitewater Sailing

I could read Monique's face, 'A man with baggage,' as I exited the arrival hall at Geneva airport.

'I've got a lot to bring to *Ellis*,' I explained as I put my three suitcases and a seven-foot canvas bag down.

'We all have baggage!' she said, smiling. We kissed tenderly to make up for lost time. The next day, we boarded the train from Boudry, carrying breakfast, lunch, and dinner for our three-day journey to Lisbon. Monique must have chosen the smelliest cheeses guaranteed to keep the carriage all to ourselves. She overheard a snooty couple of Swiss Germans say, *'Diese Leute smeck wie alte Käse'* - *'These people smell like old cheese,'* as they slid back the compartment door.

We were immune.

With the changing landscapes of four countries, we held our gourmet party on the way, lunch in Switzerland, dinner in France, and breakfast in Spain. On approaching Lisbon, an officer came to check our passports. No one had been since we left Switzerland. He looked at Monique's passport and said in perfect French, *'Votre passeport n'est plus valide.'* He was pointing at the expiry date.

'Ah, Mon Dieu, je suis désolée, Monsieur,' she replied, blushing. 'I never looked at it before I left.' Was Monique going to be refused entry to Portugal?

Fortunately, the officer returned her passport, suggesting she had it renewed at the Swiss Embassy in Lisbon, and wished us both a happy holiday. We sorted it out at the Embassy later that morning, then headed for Lisbon railway station.

The hall was impressive, with its walls and ceilings covered in ceramic tiles depicting epic scenes of Portugal's glorious past. We presented our tickets to the controller at the barrier. Surprisingly, there was no platform or train, just a ferryboat next to a jetty. Was I hallucinating again, thinking our train was a boat? Monique couldn't fathom it out either.

It turned out the railway station was on the river's north bank, and as the train was on the south side with no bridge to cross over, we needed to take the ferry to get to it. I had made the two and a half hour journey from the Algarve to Lisbon by bus before. It would be a lot quicker by rail, so I thought!

The train left the station at the stroke of midnight. The compartments were stuffy and packed to capacity, with many passengers standing in the corridor. There were soldiers in uniform with their rifles and kit-bags and country folk carrying live chickens in cages. We were fortunate to find room in an eight-seater compartment.

On the way, the train stopped at every village, with or without a platform or a station. We saw mail picked up and dropped at the side of the track. No one seemed in a hurry. It was snail-pace at its slowest. After two hours, Monique and I gathered our bags, ready to disembark, but it was three hours later before we finally reached Faro. The journey took us over five hours as we had caught the mail train. No wonder it was cheap and popular with soldiers and country folk. We managed a quick breakfast in a café before boarding the early bus to Vilamoura in the pouring rain.

Welcome to sunny Algarve!

I expected the new mast for *Ellis* to have been delivered to Vilamoura Marina by the time we arrived. It wasn't there. After several telephone calls to the agent, I learned that it had got lost between Southampton and Lisbon! How do you lose a thirty-foot mast? It surely wasn't put through the wrong letterbox!

Two weeks later, I found out that a lorry had waited for a full load before leaving England. When the mast arrived in Lisbon, customs became suspicious after they opened the container and saw a thirty-foot package encased in a cardboard tube and plastic wrapping. They allocated an officer to accompany the load by train to its destination. Then it took two more days to load sufficient cargo in the goods yard to leave Lisbon. Meanwhile, the customs officer was obliged to wait at the passenger railway station all that time until the goods train picked him up from the platform. He could have taken up a new hobby - train spotting!

It only took a short while to unload the mast onto a truck when it arrived at Faro, and on the same day, the officer was overseeing its delivery in Vilamoura.

Before checking the package for contraband, he asked me for a torch to peep down the thirty-foot long mast. He examined the contents thoroughly, and once satisfied, his mission was thankfully complete. This had been the sole purpose of the customs officer's three-day journey! Poor man. He looked unshaven and travel-weary.

The harbour master had been our interpreter during the whole rigmarole. His English was almost native. When I asked him what to pay the officer, he said: 'Nothing,' though he suggested I tip him generously. So I did.

Next, I needed to hire a crane to hoist the new mast. Waiting for it might hold me up. In the end, I decided to do it myself. I'm a Yorkshireman, after all. Health and safety didn't cross my mind either. I once walked across an eighteen-inch-wide girder, fifty-foot above the ground, carrying an oxyacetylene cutter in my hand to help dismantle Scarborough gasworks. It was just as well I didn't suffer from vertigo.

Lifting the mast would be more straightforward, and Christian, a fellow boat owner, offered to help. With the foot of the mast attached to the boat's deck-fitting, it protruded 15-feet horizontally past the stern. I climbed on stepladders and raised the top of the mast over my head, then Christian winched it up the rest of the way just like that! Monique didn't enjoy watching my ladder balancing act!

She was my muse, my cordon bleu cook, and so much more, keeping me well-fed on mussels, the size of a spectacle case, which she picked up from the beach at low tide and served in white wine with garlic, tomato sauce, or homemade mayonnaise. I mentioned she could try serving them with custard. '*With Sauce Anglaise* you mean? How revolting,' she retorted.

She must have known I was joking. I thought Monique had the patience of a saint, making elaborate meals on a two-ring paraffin cooker with the thermal temperature of a tea candle.

With March upon us, the air felt warm. Skipper and crew were almost ready to set sail. However, we still needed to buy provisions, which usually involved walking to the shops or catching a bus. Luckily, there was one going to Faro which had a good selection of supermarkets.

Monique and I returned to Vilamoura laden with shopping late in the afternoon. By then, we were more than ready for a sit-down.

We walked along the floating pontoon, doing a balancing act with our shopping bags, and were about to step aboard *Ellis* when Monique suddenly gave out a blood-curdling scream. I looked down at the water to determine what had caused her to react so fiercely and saw a black coffin emerging from under one of the floating piers. Inside was a man staring at the sky with his arms crossed over his chest. Was somebody playing a prank on us? Maybe Dracula had decided to use his coffin as a boat instead of leaping ashore like the black dog from the doomed ship on the Yorkshire coast.

Once clear of the pontoon, the apparition sat up and paddled towards the adjacent one before he resumed his corpse-like pose. We were relieved to realise that it wasn't a dead body but a man, very much alive, taking a shortcut under the marina pontoons in his specially adapted homemade canoe.

Hans was German. We had seen him before with a pack of dogs tagging along. He often rummaged for scraps from the large waste containers at the backs of hotels to feed them. Apart from building his coffin-like canoe, he made his own clothes. He looked like the Pied Piper of Hamelin with his floppy linen hat. In his case, the young children were dogs.

Hans had converted a wooden sailing dinghy, grafting three feet onto the stern and adding a cabin. He intended to cross the Atlantic Ocean with the boat but needed to decide whether to take a female crew or six crates of St. Miguel. Finally, he opted for a liquid companion, given his limited carrying capacity. Anyway, he thought women would have too much luggage.

One day, he needed to haul himself up the mast. Neither of us wanted to miss this comedy act. When we saw him hoisting himself up the flimsy aluminium pole, it was like watching a clown at the circus. Even though Hans was slim, his body weighed more than the keel itself, and when he reached the top of the mast, the inevitable happened. The boat heeled onto its side, then rolled over completely, dunking him into the sea like the ancient trial by water dished out to suspected witches.

When he let go of the mast, it seemed as if the boat righted itself somewhat mockingly. We laughed so much that it hurt, seeing Hans breach the surface, blowing air and water out like a whale.

He wasn't amused.

Before we left Vilamoura, he purchased the two halves of *Ellis's* broken mast. He didn't believe in lightning striking twice! He paid me with a twenty Gibraltarian pound note he couldn't exchange anywhere. We were heading for *The Rock* and felt sure we could spend that money easily there.

I envisaged some gentle passages, day-hopping from Vilamoura along the coast to ease Monique back into sailing. It didn't happen. We had strong offshore winds the whole way to Vila Real de Santo Antònio. Although the seas were relatively flat, *Ellis* spent most of her time heeled over at 45.° It didn't deter Monique from preparing lunch on the way, but she said: 'I'd find it easier cooking on the side of the Jungfrau Mountain than at that angle!' Her experience on *Spirit of Labrador* had been more sedate by comparison. Hopefully, a nice sail up the quiet Rio Guadiana might make up for it.

Skipper and mate left Vila Real in the early morning and motored upriver with the incoming tide. Every mile along the Portuguese side, there were lookout posts, which appeared more like menacing concrete gun emplacements. Each time we pointed our binoculars at these observation posts, the guards had theirs on us. Did they take us for smugglers? Maybe it was rare for a sailing boat to venture this far upstream.

The Rio Guadiana marks the border between Portugal and Spain. On the eastern bank were vineyards and pretty villages with terracotta-tiled roofs. The atmosphere seemed more relaxed. We saw the Spanish Customs Land Rover following a dusty track along the river, but the driver didn't show interest in the little red boat sailing upstream. Further on, we passed an imposing castle looming over the river, which narrowed from there into a gorge with towering cliffs. There was debris caught on bushes, thirty feet above the current water level - definitely not a place to be if the river flooded! Then the scenery softened to a flat plain of lush pasture, giving way to rolling hills. These were primeval landscapes, far from the sea.

The river was only a stone's throw wide where we tied up for the night. We watched a salmon leaping up and landing back in the water with a big plop, leaving ever-expanding rings on the surface. The symphony of birdsong added to the joyful ambience. What a sharp contrast from *Ellis* sailing at a dizzy angle with the wind howling in the rigging!

In the morning, I noticed the water level had dropped by almost two feet. I wasn't unduly concerned as we had found plenty of depth on the way up. However, with no navigational information on the river, I had no idea how the tide would affect the levels ten miles up from the sea. Why worry on such a glorious sunny day, which promised us a gentle passage downstream, back to salty water. I hoisted the sails, and we made a brief series of tacks from one side of the river to the other, enjoying the thrill of split-second timing. While Monique was at the helm, I trimmed the sails on each tack. It was very much like training for a race, slaloming downstream. Our teamwork and precision were faultless, and *Ellis* was the type of sailing yacht that could turn on a sixpence. Monique was enjoying it all until she shouted: 'What are those waves in front of us?'

'Oh, hell, they're rapids! Hard to port,' I yelled out.

Monique swiftly swung the tiller hard over to starboard, but it was too late. The current had swept *Ellis* into the tumbling water, and her keel soon bounced over the boulders like a tractor over stony ground. Slamming against rocks was the last thing we expected in these quiet backwaters. It was excruciating.

The keel hammered over the riverbed for a few more yards, and then the current carried us into deeper water.

Monique might believe plain sailing is just a myth!

To comfort her, I expressed my surprise at the sudden changes in the river depth from yesterday. 'Perhaps it was just a freak moment,' I said.

She didn't comment, but I could see she was thinking: 'Does he know what he's doing?'

Then as we approached a large sweeping right-hand bend, I noticed the shallow water to starboard. I told Monique: 'Keep our port side close to the bank,' but at the last minute, I chickened out and instructed her to steer towards the middle of the river. Again, our keel struck a bottom. This time the water was shallower, and there were more boulders. *Ellis* pivoted sideways on her keel, pushed by the current, her mast pointing dangerously downstream at a 45° angle. I was now the captain going down with the ship. In my mind's eye, I saw flashing before me all that *Ellis* and I had gone through. With each rigging-rattling bump on the riverbed, I feared rocks would pierce a hole through the hull. *Am I going to lose Ellis, nine miles up a river under blue skies in this magnificent landscape?*

'Hang on tight to the tiller,' I told Monique before I crawled over the tilted deck to get to the mast. The boom was in the river, and the mainsail had filled with water. If it touched the riverbed, I could lose the new mast. At that awkward angle, and with the extra weight of the water-logged sail, I struggled to secure the boom. By the time I finished, *Ellis* was slithering into deeper water. She righted herself and headed downstream. Below decks everything was in complete disarray like our jangling nerves. The kettle had fallen off the stove, teabags and biscuits were scattered on the cabin floor, and so was the fruit bowl. We certainly didn't expect to stow away for rough conditions!

It all proved too much for Monique. She demanded I use the depth gauge to navigate the river from then on. I tried to explain that monitoring the depth under the keel was all very well but wouldn't help ten-foot in front of us or around the next bend. I promised her we had experienced the worst and that navigating downstream would be easier through the flat plains ahead of us.

She took no notice of me and remained glued to the depth-gauge as if life depended on it. Maybe it was her way to calm herself down! Later, I convinced Monique that hoisting the sails again would be perfectly safe.

As we tacked downstream, I shouted: 'Lee helm.' Then Monique pushed the tiller hard over while I handled winches and sails. Each tack lasted only seconds, with *Ellis* almost grazing the banks. Adrenaline spun through me, Monique too, no doubt.

Then she yelled: 'Have you seen the fisherman on his boat anchored in the middle of the river?' I said, 'YES. We'll clear the boat on the next tack.'

Next, I instructed her to head downwind of him and across his stern.

As we passed the fisherman for the second time, Monique asked, 'Have you noticed the look on his face?' I couldn't make out whether his expression was one of terror, incomprehension, or maybe both. I doubted he could appreciate how exciting navigating the river was under sail. The wind would have been strong enough to blow us back upstream against the current had we not been tacking.

The following five miles were plain sailing, but Monique maintained vigil over the depth gauge, which showed a healthy distance between keel and riverbed. She rounded *Ellis* into the wind as we approached Vila Real, and I downed the sails before engaging the outboard engine.

At this state of the tide, we couldn't make it back to the pontoon where we had moored the day before. Another fisherman was watching us from the entrance of the harbour. He indicated the way in, where the deeper water was. We confidently followed his instructions, but he couldn't have been aware we had a deep keel. Next thing, we ran aground.

He looked embarrassed and explained with a gesture that he was going to get help. I dissuaded him with hand signals. What could he do with a falling tide? There wasn't even time for me to inflate the dinghy to lay an anchor and pull ourselves out. I quickly probed the seabed with a pole to ensure *Ellis* wouldn't rest on anything sharp. There were six hours to wait, leaning at a crazy angle until the next tide.

I thought, *what a pity to be stuck on mud instead of hard sand. I could get the scrubbing brush out and pretend we've gone aground on purpose to clean Ellis's bottom!*

Meanwhile, Monique made pancakes, undeterred. She was a Swiss mountaineer, after all!

Before dark, we headed for the riverside jetty and then sat in the cockpit with a much-needed glass of wine. It was a welcome change, watching people strolling along the quayside, enjoying the warm evening. This whitewater rafting had almost depleted all our reserves.

While we watched the world go by, I noticed a middle-aged couple, smartly dressed, walking along the jetty. As the pair approached *Ellis,* the man said: 'We saw you sailing upriver yesterday. How far did you get?'

'About ten miles,' I replied with a grin. 'It wasn't the plain sailing we'd hoped for.'

'Why is that?'

'We were surprised after an easy sail upriver to hit boulders on the way down,' I said. 'The mast ended up at a jaunty angle with our sails in the water.'

'You were lucky the dam had released water allowing you to sail that far up,' he stated. 'They must have shut the water off today and that's why you found the rapids. If you like rivers so much, why don't you go up to Seville?'

'Are there any rapids?' Monique said, half-jokingly.

'Large cargo ships sail up the river but they don't shoot rapids,' he answered with a chuckle. 'You would be sailing past one of Europe's biggest Nature Reserves, the *Doñana,* on your way.'

The following day, I cast off alone for Bonanza, which is at the mouth of the Guadalquivir River, leading to Seville. Monique had jumped ship for this leg of the journey. She had made friends with a French couple on a yacht also sailing to Seville. I set off the night before as their vessel was larger and faster. There was little wind 'en route,' but *Ellis* could sail in a strong fart! I caught a fish, which was a big deal for me. My catch was a garfish with a long snout and luminous green bones. It didn't look very appetising, but I felt obliged to eat it. Surprisingly, it didn't taste that bad.

In Bonanza, Monique stowed back on board. I was more than relieved. She told me the journey was very uncomfortable. The yacht did not perform well in light winds. The sails flapped and banged, and they were thrown about in a cross swell. She was upset when she had to do a wee over the side and nearly fell overboard.

'It wasn't easy,' she said. 'I had to hang on tight to the side-rails with the boat bouncing about.

The chemical loo aboard was only for number twos.'

Over dinner, Monique asked: 'Aren't you curious as to why I jumped ship?'

'I presumed you had lost faith in my seamanship with our whitewater escapade!'

'I wanted you to think that as I thought it would hurt your ego. Actually, I was punishing you for writing love letters to your old flame back in Scarborough. I saw the letter. You left it on the chart table in an unsealed envelope. Did you expect me to resist reading it? You wrote, "Ice cream, wine, and sailing in the sunshine." When are you planning to do this with Olga?'

I didn't reply. Neither of us had promised the other anything when we embarked on this adventure. What about Monique's intention to pursue fame in the music business? Even if she decided that sailing wasn't for her anymore, I certainly wouldn't give it up.

19. Butterfly with a Sting

I promised Monique we wouldn't be shooting rapids on The Guadalquivir River or running aground unless we strayed out of the shipping channel, which was signposted with buoys to port and starboard all the way to Seville. Therefore it really would be 'plain sailing.'

The wind was fluky when we motored upstream, and Monique and I endured the monotonous putt-putt of the Seagull engine during our three-hour journey. It was low tide when we entered the cavernous lock. *Ellis* looked like a Lilliputian boat from Gulliver's travels.

We tied up to a floating bollard let into the concrete wall and heard the giant lock-gate close with the clang of a jailer's door. Then torrents of water gushed through the open sluices. *Ellis* jostled at her mooring lines like an impatient filly pulling at her reins. As the lock filled, she was raised to the inner harbour level. It was then that we caught a glimpse of the impressive golden dome looming above the skyline.

After exiting the lock, we moored *Ellis* up to a multi-national raft of other sailing yacht and were dwarfed under a dockyard crane. With no wind, the air felt heavy, but it wasn't long before a breeze picked up, and all the tightly-packed boats moved like an ill-squeezed accordion. If the wind increased anymore, we would need to find another mooring, or else, with the weight of other yachts leaning against *Ellis*, she might be crushed like a ping pong ball. I put some extra ropes out to the quay and the boat next to us. We had a bite to eat before setting off to visit the port authority's office to pay our mooring dues.

The young, overweight clerk greeted us cheerfully when we walked in. He asked me for the ship's tonnage and what cargo we carried. 'We weigh two and a half tons, and my cargo is a fifty-two-kilo Swiss miss,' I said, nodding towards Monique.

He laughed.

'We only deal with ships carrying thousands of tons of cargo,' the clerk explained. 'The fee for your fifty-two kilo Swiss miss wouldn't cover the cost of the paperwork. So I suggest you go and enjoy Seville.'

We returned to *Ellis* to check the moorings. By then, the wind had eased. The skipper of the sloop next to us was working on deck. *Schmetterling - butterfly* in English, was a sixty-foot classic steel yacht with fine woodwork begging for a new coat of varnish. We chatted, and then Gunter invited us over for a drink in the afternoon.

When we boarded the yacht, he welcomed us into a large, well-lived-in saloon, where we sat comfortably around a battered mahogany table that spoke of many lively parties. He poured us a glass of white wine, and his Dutch partner Ingrid served us a piece of her homemade apple strudel. She was a petite blonde, soft-spoken with sad blue eyes. Gunter was tall with a chiselled face and a complexion that betrayed his love for liquor. They had two guests aboard, Fritz and Oscar, both tall, blond, and blue-eyed. I thought they almost looked like twins.

The conversation between us was animated, and after another glass of wine, Gunter asked us if we liked flamenco. Monique and I nodded.

He fetched his guitar from the aft cabin and started to play, plucking the strings and drumming on the instrument. I thought it might cave in with such exuberance. The music was stirring and foot-stomping, which far exceeded our expectations. Then, as the afternoon turned into evening, we all agreed to visit The Doñana Nature Reserve together. We had sailed past it on our way upstream. As *Schmetterling* had a powerful engine, Gunter proposed to tow *Ellis* downriver.

Two days later, both yachts left the lock side by side. I had fastened a long rope to our bow and gave Gunter the other end to tie up to his stern. Within seconds, he opened the throttle, and we powered downstream at a great rate of knots. *Ellis* reared up like a rodeo horse with a bow wave nearly as high as the foredeck. We could feel our speed through the quivering tiller. It was no wonder, being towed by a 100 hp engine at full blast. *Ellis* was never designed to do nine knots.

People might say this was impossible, but the speedometer clocked it. It was unnerving as well as thrilling. Monique looked more nervous than excited.

'We'd better get used to *Ellis* behaving like a powerboat,' I told her. 'We could be in this predicament for an hour or so before we reach the anchorage.'

She didn't comment. Seemingly, *Ellis* was coping better than the crew.

I tried to keep *Ellis's* bow pointing directly at Gunter's stern to ease the motion. It helped a little. Monique started to relax; she even picked up her guitar, singing and playing her unique rendering of *'La Vie en Rose,' 'Bobby McGee,'* and her own compositions. Then she came to an abrupt stop when we heard the sound of gunshots from *Schmetterling*.

What was happening?

In shock, we watched Gunter standing on the starboard side, holding a bottle in one hand and a handgun in the other, shooting at some imaginary targets on the bankside.

What a lethal combination! Was this another toboggan ride to hell? I thought of the Spanish shore battery almost blowing *Ellis* out of the water during a naval exercise. And now, a crazy German was firing a weapon under the influence. What if he got tired of this game and turned the gun on us?

Thankfully, his bullets ran out, and the inebriated Gunter retired below deck. Had he passed out, or did the gentle Ingrid manage to calm him down?

We didn't see Gunter again until we approached the *Doñana Reserve,* where he resumed his position at the helm. He never gave us any prior warning before he reduced speed. A boat doesn't have brakes like a car! He must have forgotten about that.

So to stop *Ellis* from smashing into *Schmetterling's* stern, I ran forward to the bow, let the tow rope go, and while Monique steered away from the yacht, I rushed to the stern to start the outboard engine. By then, Gunter had already dropped the hook.

'How about tying up alongside us?' he shouted as we held station. 'It would be easier to party together.'

Gunter had dropped a large anchor, and as our two boats couldn't swing separately in this part of the river, I agreed. Close by was a beach where we set up a barbecue, and it was well after midnight when we returned to our yachts, full of wine and merriment.

I woke up with the first light of dawn, startled by the sound of creaking ropes. I rushed on deck, feeling disorientated until I realised what was happening. The night before, we had rafted up on an incoming tide. By morning the ebb tide had turned the two yachts, and there wasn't enough depth to keep them afloat. *Ellis* was now between *Schmetterling* and the beach. With her deeper keel and already aground, the German sloop was heeling alarmingly towards mid-river, pulling *Ellis* over with her.

Quick as a flash, I released the ropes, woke Gunter up, and explained our situation. Next, I lashed two booming-out poles to port and starboard and used them as crutches to keep *Ellis* upright. Then I rowed ashore with the rope I had tied to the top of my mast and made it fast to a tree, two hundred yards away. The rope would keep *Ellis* from toppling onto *Schmetterling* and worsening Gunter's predicament. By the time I finished, the sloop was well and truly heeled over, while *Elli*s stood on her keel like some giant red flamingo.

'We need to get off the boat,' I told Monique. 'We mustn't walk to the bow or the stern as it could compromise her balance, and we might fall over onto *Schmetterling*.'

She grabbed some food, water, and a camera while I threw a rope ladder over the side, and we quickly climbed off the boat onto the beach. *It isn't often you hear the captain shout 'Abandon ship,' when the vessel is high and dry!*

Soon after, Gunter, Ingrid, and their two crew joined us on the beach. All we could do now was hope *Schmetterling* would float again despite her being at such a compromising angle. If she failed to rise on the tide, she would be lost. As there was nothing more to be done for several hours, the six of us left our yachts to their fate and went off exploring the park.

We stumbled across a tiny village of mud huts with thatched roofs made from reeds and were startled by the squealing of baby boars with their mother, darting between the huts. Her tusks looked menacing. I took a quick photograph once I realised mother and piglets were running in the opposite direction.

Then came another shock when the low door of one of the deserted huts squeaked open, and a woman with a deeply wrinkled face appeared. She looked just as dumbfounded as we were. Monique broke the ice and said, *'Nos perdimos en el parque'* - 'we got lost in the park.'

The woman smiled. What was she doing here on her own? We were all intrigued.

Monique asked her if she lived there?

The woman explained that the other villagers travelled to various markets in Spain and Portugal during the summer months, selling their wicker baskets and crafts. They stayed in the village weaving their wares for the rest of the time. It seemed incredible that people still lived such a primitive lifestyle, almost like a lost Amazon tribe, only a few miles away from Seville.

We noticed a Land Rover driving down the forest track on our return to the beach. The vehicle quickly pulled up in front of us, and two park rangers stepped out of it smartly. They looked agitated and angry. The men asked for our *'permiso de visita'*- 'visiting permit.' Monique explained we didn't have one.

'How did you get here, and do you carry guns?' the rangers asked in English.

'The only shooting we're doing is with a camera,' I replied, smiling.

They didn't find my remark amusing and told us they were escorting us out of the park.

'We're marooned here,' I pleaded in our defence. 'Our yachts are stranded like whales on the beach until the tide comes in.'

'We command you to return to your boats immediately and refrain from walking in the park. We'll impound your vessels if you don't leave on the next tide.'

We left the rangers, feeling like naughty children scolded for scrumping apples.

To everyone's relief, the sloop lifted with the tide. But Gunter couldn't leave just yet. He wanted to dive over the side to check for any damage from the beaching. We didn't envy him and his crew as they could be stranded if they found the rudder damaged, in which case they would have to face the angry park rangers again. We waved them farewell and headed downriver to the sea.

The Straits of Gibraltar are unpredictable, as Bruce and I knew only too well, having experienced a rogue wave and a near-capsize with the wind coming from the east. It was hard to forget that day. This time, the wind was blowing from the west. It was strong, and the seas were huge. I had to stream long ropes from the stern to stop *Ellis* from turning sideways-on to the mountainous swell. With just a storm sail, we were surfing down the back of waves at six knots. The glorious blue skies helped lessen the drama of sailing in such perilous conditions. Monique seemed calm on the surface, but I wasn't sure what she made of this 'plain sailing.'

The swell subsided when we entered the Bay of Gibraltar, but the wind made it awkward for us to tie up to a pontoon at Shepherd's Marina.

We hadn't even secured our lines ashore when two young Customs Officers jumped aboard. Their forcefulness infuriated me. With the border to Spain still closed, perhaps they thought we were smugglers?

We only planned to stay in Gibraltar long enough to spend our twenty Gibraltarian pounds Hans had given us in payment for the broken mast.

At the Moroccan market by the harbour, we bought vegetables, then later went to the cinema. We had just enough money for the cheapest seats to see 'Bugsy Malone.'

Although the theatre was dark, we could see people in the expensive seats but nobody in the cheaper ones in the front rows, the ones to which the usherette directed Monique and me.

We were so close to the big screen that it made us feel dizzy. I caught the young woman's look of contempt for not paying the small extra like everyone else. Why change our pound sterling or pesetas for the sake of thirty-pence, or bother explaining it to her?

After leaving Gibraltar, we day-hopped along the coast to Alicante, where we left *Ellis.* Then we took a train to Cannes for an interview with the owners of *M.Y. Jesty.* Knox Johnston's charter company had recommended Monique to them after her excellent work on *Spirit of Labrador.* It was a successful interview. Returning to Calpe Harbour, I secured *Ellis* on a mooring and then found a chap called Bill Rodford to look after my boat for the whole duration of our six-month contract as cook and deckhand on *M.Y. Jesty.*

On a sunny April day, we arrived in Cannes, having signed up for an 'Aquatic Upstairs, Downstairs' or as we say at sea: *Topside and Lower Decks.* Would I have to learn to doff my sailor's hat and Monique to curtsy? I think NOT.

20. Spilling the Gin

Was the skipper jesting when he launched a cover-up mission the day after we arrived at the boatyard? He was in deep water, crying out for help to fix the mess. Why had Byron chosen this shipyard for such a luxurious yacht? *Jesty* was like a princess in a white ball gown and tiara at a barn dance amongst the many rusty fishing boats, looking ready to die.

During the next two weeks, Monique and I worked like contortionists and acrobats on the yacht's superstructure, paintbrush in hand, careful not to paint ourselves into a corner! It begged the question as to why Byron hadn't insisted on the workers doing the job properly in the first place. The dockyard painters had left all the awkward areas to get at unfinished. Furthermore, my job description as a steward and deckhand didn't include painting on such a massive scale, and Monique reminded Byron that she was hired as a cook and not a cabin boy wielding a paintbrush!

This outburst won us a day off, which he could ill-afford. The owners were due to join *Jesty* on a holiday cruise to Corsica in a few days. Meanwhile, commuting on the ferry every day between Cannes and Île Sainte-Marguerite gave us a breathing space until we entered the boatyard's gates.

Monique resumed her allocated duties in the evening, cooking for the skipper and me in a rented apartment. With its yellow walls, sunflower motifs, and printed lavender fabrics, the place reflected the influence of Van Gogh. It was a romantic hideaway for a young couple on a honeymoon - but three, as they say, is a crowd.

Byron was keen to pursue his career as a skipper on large luxury motor yachts. Short, with mousy hair, a scraggly beard, and an innocent face, he blushed easily, maybe through shyness. He had a colonial approach to the crew and spoke French with a public schoolboy's accent. It was hard for him to loosen up and see the funny side of life even when we cracked jokes. It was like throwing a custard pie that missed. Maybe being in charge of *Jesty* proved more challenging than he had anticipated.

The yacht was twenty-three metres in length with two staterooms, a double-cabin and a single one, all with en-suite showers and toilets. Her large saloon with beautiful dark mahogany-panelled walls and trim opened into a generous aft-deck patio where one could set up a dining table, sitting ten guests comfortably, either inside or on the open aft-deck. In addition, the saloon had a white leather u-shaped settee, a drop-sided table, an ice-maker, a cocktail cabinet, and elegant brass lamps.

The gin palace promised opulence, but Monique and I were disappointed when we moved aboard. Our cabin was a rabbit hutch with a two-tier berth, a small desk, and a built-in wardrobe. The dark mahogany-lined walls were beautiful but made the inside feel oppressive. Only one person could dress at a time, and if we felt amorous, we had to be creative.

Byron's quarters were in the forepeak, and ours directly opposite the deep freezers, the industrial washing machines, and dryers. This layout left us under no illusion of our status and pecking order. After all, we had signed up for an Aquatic Upstairs, Downstairs!

Getting the yacht shipshape, Bristol fashion in time to be launched proved a major rescue operation. We did it, but at what price. We were exhausted, dusty and smelling of paint when we motored out of Île Sainte-Marguerite to the yacht's home, five miles away. *Jesty* looked impressive in her berth, but La Napoule Marina was a long way from the glitz of Monaco.

After settling in, we provisioned the yacht. Byron went hunting for meat to fill the two huge freezers, using the best butchers in Cannes. Monique, as the cook, took no part in this expedition. It was common knowledge for skippers to receive ten per cent from traders except for supermarkets. Stocking up at the *'Mammouth'* hypermarket came last. We filled trolleys full of fresh food, rice, pulses, condiments, flour, and toilet rolls. Then Monique and I spring-cleaned the owner's quarters once more. Cleaning had become an art form, doing the finishing touches with a toothbrush and a magnifying glass. We were like villains trying to wipe out our fingerprints from a crime scene. Byron had warned us the owners were fussy. They expected bedding and towels replaced every day and would only use Evian water to brush their teeth.

When Claudia, Frederik, and Annika arrived, it was hard for us to hide our sweating brows. The June sun was beating down hard on the Côte d'Azur. That day, there wasn't even a fluffy cloud in the sky to break the Mediterranean perfection.

Skipper, deckhand, and the cook stood on deck in a line, wearing navy shorts, matching deck shoes, and white T-shirts. Byron and I picked up the Gucci luggage from the taxi and brought it on board.

The scent of expensive perfumes wafted through the air. The scene was reminiscent of the gentry pompously dismounting from their carriages while butlers, cooks, and upstairs maids stood poised to welcome their employers to their country retreats.

Claudia was a German heiress to a brewery and *Jesty's* owner. Tall and skinny with brown frizzy hair, she was no Jackie Onassis! However, what Claudia lacked in charm and looks, her husband Frederik more than made up for. He was tall with dark-hair, blue-eyes and a Spanish complexion. Byron had mentioned Frederik was an out-of-work actor who seemed set on making it in the film industry - maybe with the influence of his wife's money?

Their teenage daughter Annika looked innocent. She had long blonde hair and a delicate frame, and unlike her mother, she was pretty. She seemed disengaged. Perhaps she was shy, though her face appeared to say, 'It wasn't my idea to come on this trip.'

As soon as they made themselves at home, Claudia was ready to celebrate. Frederik opened a magnum of champagne and invited us to join them for a glass before dinner. Monique and I were flattered by their invitation. With Byron press-ganging us into hard labour, their approach seemed a more civilised way of building a working relationship from the outset. And it helped somewhat to have a Swiss cook, seeing as Claudia had been to a finishing school in Switzerland. She also liked having a straight-talking Yorkshire man as steward and deckhand.

Two guests arrived in the early evening. Achillios was a Greek shipping magnate in his late fifties and still dashingly handsome. Dressed in expensive red yachting trousers with a blue and white striped shirt and a gold-buttoned blazer, I thought he must have gone to a top yachting chandler to be wearing such an extravagant ensemble.

His companion, Françoise, was a dark-haired Frenchwoman in her mid-forties with feline green eyes and a body and legs fit for the catwalk. She stepped onto the gang-plank in her silky lily-white dress, then paraded about the decks like a celebrity. She flirted with Byron and me as a courtesan would - maybe she was one.

We set off from La Napoule the next day to trendy Antibes, thirty miles away. The conditions were *mer belle* and light winds.

On the way, our hosts and guests requested a *Salade Niçoise* for lunch, served on deck with a light white Côte de Provence as an accompanying wine.

Claudia was impressed with the lunch and flatbread Monique had baked especially, but the French dressing didn't meet with her approval. It needed to be thicker with more Dijon mustard. She came to the galley to show the cook how to make it, which infuriated Monique.

Boiling the eggs for breakfast a few seconds too long spoilt Claudia's joie de vivre the following morning.

Working on a gin palace was no glamour for the crew.

The owners knew I wasn't a trained steward - I could never be a head waiter in a million years. However, Claudia and Frederik didn't seem to mind too much. 'Peter, just leave everything on the table, and we'll help ourselves,' they would say. Monique was nervous each time I left the galley, juggling a tray full of food. 'Peter, please be careful,' she would beg me. Although I can be rather clumsy, I managed to avoid decorating the saloon's deep-pile white carpet with food. Catering wasn't my thing, but I had helped my parents in the pub and hotel as a boy, thrown into a harsh environment, working far too hard for my age. It is no wonder I don't particularly like going to pubs.

In the summertime, after lunch, I would spray the beer barrels with water to keep them cool before going back to school. At eleven o'clock closing time, I washed glasses, emptied ashtrays, filled shelves with bottles, and finally swept around. I often found money under the tables. Bill Goodwill was a frequent *lock-in* customer. At times, he dropped coins on purpose for me to find. I think he took pity on me as a seven-year-old boy working so hard. I was always shattered going to school in the morning and only arriving at the playground gates just in time to hear the whistle blow.

After hours, regulars came up into our lounge in the wintertime to play 'seven card brag.' I joined them after my chores to watch.

One night, a player needed the toilet, and as no one wanted to interrupt the game, they asked me to take his place. Because I excelled at mental arithmetic and had a sharp memory, the men realised I was as skilful as them. So they invited me to sit in when they were short-handed. After that, I played regularly with my parents grubstaking me. Sometimes, I won the equivalent of a working man's daily wage, and it was rare that I lost money. None of the players ever complained about a boy sitting in on their game. Although we only gambled for pennies, it soon mounted up as we played for hours. I never went to bed before two or three in the morning on a Friday or Saturday night and at midnight during the week.

My other job was to open the bar up at five-thirty. I lit the central heating boiler with kindling wood and paper, and when the fire built up, I added coke. I did the same for the bar's open fire, using coal instead. Mr Franklin visited the pub two nights a week. He always arrived early. By that time, the fire was already blazing. He would order a pint of Guinness and place the poker into the burning heat until it glowed red hot before plunging it in his stout. He believed it was his anti-cold remedy. After that, he challenged me to a game of dominoes *five and threes*. I often won. Once the bar started to fill up, I rang the bell upstairs and either my mother or father took over from me.

Charlie Watson was a regular visitor. He spent his holidays at the Wellington Hotel at the same time every year. He came from the West Riding. Small and almost bald, what hair Watson had left at the sides he combed over his bare patch. His eight pints a night drinking habit strongly reflected on his ruddy nose and complexion. Watson enjoyed telling stories of his days as a foreman, working at the mill in the weaving loom machine shop.

Although friendly, I never liked him. However, I had learned to be courteous to all our guests and customers no matter what.

I had only just finished work that night and was now snug under the covers when I heard my bedroom door slowly open. Who could that be? My parents never came to my room. I recognised who it was by the light shining in from the landing. Why was Charlie Watson entering my room? He quietly shut the door behind him, and I saw him undressing down to his vest and pants, illuminated by the street lights coming through the gap in the curtains. Were my parents expecting me to share my bed with Watson because all our rooms were occupied?

Although I was far from happy about it, it didn't seem particularly strange to me. I often slept with my parents or other children when we stayed with friends and relations. We couldn't afford holidays in hotels, even though we ran one.

Watson drew back the covers and got into bed next to me. I quickly moved over to give him more space. The next thing I knew, his hand was sliding inside my pants. I sat up and pushed Watson out of bed, yelling, 'NO, NO get out.' Nobody had warned me about this kind of behaviour.

Watson didn't try touching me again. People were bound to hear me shouting from the room next to mine. Fearful of being caught in my bedroom without trousers, he hurriedly left.

After such a shock, sleep was hard to find, and I felt deeply humiliated. Why had I allowed this man into my bed? I should have known something was amiss beforehand, but I was a naive ten-year-old boy. Would he come back, I wondered, terrified at the prospect? So I left the light on all night and locked my bedroom door for the first time.

The next day, Watson was all smiles, making a fuss of me. I kept my distance without appearing impolite. I couldn't tell my parents. I never confided in them at the best of times. They knew I disliked Watson, and if I told them what he tried to do to me, they might have thought I was lying, just to be spiteful. As for him, all he needed to say to save his skin was that he had drunk one too many and staggered into the wrong room!

The following night, Watson tried opening my door again. Thankfully, I had locked it. Still undeterred, he began tapping and whispering loudly: 'Peter, Peter, let me in.'

I ignored him, but he begged me until I couldn't bear it anymore, so I screamed, 'Go away.'

Not wanting to arouse curiosity with the guests in the next room, Watson finally abandoned his pursuit, and I could go to sleep.

After an agonising week of giving him dagger looks and refusing to serve him at the bar, his holiday ended. I wanted my parents to ask me why I was rude to him. If only they had, I could have told them, and it wouldn't have looked as if I was telling tales.

Watson arrived at the Wellington Hotel for yet another holiday the following year. I was shocked and horrified by how warmly my parents greeted him. The season was hectic; my parents and I had already given up our rooms to visitors to sleep in the attic.

The Wellington used to be two separate dwellings. To get to my parent's bedroom, I had to climb down a flight of stairs and walk through a short connecting passage and up another flight. My bedroom had no lock on the door, and I had seen watching films how someone would wedge a chair under the doorknob to prevent access. I was terrified at the likelihood of Watson breaking into my room. I had to prepare myself just in case.

I got into bed at 1 am after I finished washing glasses and sweeping up the floor and had only just settled down when I heard my door handle turn. I assumed it was Watson. He started tapping, and then he tried pushing the door. I remained quiet, but my heart was racing. I felt sure Watson could hear my shallow breathing and sense my panic.

For ages, he begged me to let him in. He knew he was out of earshot of my parents and must have felt safe trying to force himself upon me. But why were the young miners in the two other bedrooms on the landing choosing not to intervene? No doubt, they would have heard the noise. The men were regular visitors like Watson. Maybe they thought it might be my father wanting to enter my room, and they had no place to interfere.

Finally, I heard the stairs creak. Watson had abandoned his pursuit and was returning to his room.

The whole week, I barricaded myself in each night, ready for him. Watson didn't try my door again, nor did he return to the Wellington Hotel for another holiday. If only I could have told my parents about him trying to abuse me, but they would probably have accused me of lying? So I kept this terrible secret to myself until I met Monique.

Jesty was cruising at eight knots towards Antibes, but she was capable of fourteen. Her navigation console was an impressive arsenal with radar, sonar, autopilot, log, VHF radiophone, computers, and plot devices. Although the yacht's fuel tanks gave her a range of one thousand two hundred nautical miles, her playground was unlikely to stretch beyond the South of France and Corsica. It was a leisurely passage with no rocks or tide to worry about, and the sea looked as if God had ironed every ripple out. Byron just needed to follow the coast, but he looked tense in his captain's hat.

This is no bloody Cape Horn, I wanted to say!

On our way, Claudia and Françoise paraded in various long flowing dresses. They paced up and down from their cabins to the upper decks as if they were on the catwalk, hoping the crew would notice them as they walked past the galley. Were they relieving boredom by obsessively changing their clothes?

When we docked in Antibes, Frederik insisted that we moor astern to the quayside. Byron warned him about the lack of depth and his concern about possible damage to the propellers.

Frederik overruled him. It was Claudia's wish for *Jesty* to lay astern, and what she wanted, she got! Mooring *Jesty* bow-to would have been safer, and with more privacy on the aft deck. On the other hand, berthing stern-to would enable them to sip their champagne by candlelight and flaunt the lifestyle to strollers striding up and down the quayside. What was the point of owning a gin palace and not showing it off!

The depth was shallow, just as Byron had warned Frederik. We heard some ominous rumbling from underneath the keel as we approached the quayside. It seemed the props were hitting something.

Antibes is the 'Mecca' for posers; maybe it was all worth the risk for the millionairess and her handsome husband actor to be seen sipping champagne on the aft-deck no matter what.

The following day, Byron arranged for two divers to check the propellers. They found one bent, removed it and took it away for repairs. It was put back in place twenty-four hours later. I didn't see the bill but guessed that the underwater damage must have made the candlelit dinner on the aft-deck expensive.

We spent a few days in buzzing Antibes. Monique and I were busy housekeeping while the skipper applied himself to hosing down the teak deck, posing as if he was the owner of this gin palace in need of some physical exercise. Claudia, Frederik, and their guests went out to dinner some nights, but Annika insisted on staying aboard. They weren't abandoning ship because of the cook's performance; they wanted to sample exclusive restaurants and be seen.

Monique still cooked for Annika. She loved wiener schnitzel and chips and ate in the galley. She didn't like sitting alone in the large empty saloon. When Annika finished her meal, Monique and I went out to dinner, courtesy of Claudia and Frederik, who gave us two hundred French francs for the restaurant bill. We had to spend it and present a receipt to Byron after. We couldn't save the money and eat on board. So we had our own candlelit dinners in excellent restaurants. Who was posing now!

We left Antibes four days later on an overnight passage to Corsica. The wind was light, but the groundswell seemed to come from nowhere, making *Jesty* roll awkwardly. Owners and guests kept to their cabins until the morning.

They were delighted when we anchored in a sheltered, secluded bay and the noise of the turbo-diesel engines finally stopped. After we finished serving breakfast and had cleaned the cabins, Monique was already rushing to prepare Claudia's request for lunch:

Osso buco à la Milanese
Pommes de terre Mousseline
Salade de fruits and glaces fait-maison

The skipper, Monique, and I shared the same food. However, we ate our meals in the galley after the owners and guests had finished theirs. Frederik often brought the main dish to us himself and would say, 'Eat it while it's still warm.'

But the 'upstairs downstairs' status didn't stop there. Everyone had an allocated space on the ship; the crew lounged around on the foredeck while the owners and guests used the upper deck. So whenever Byron and I went to winch down the ski boat, we had to stride over the beautiful Françoise in the nude. She had a mischievous smile each time duty called us up there.

She knew when we were coming. Byron would shout ahead for permission to lower the tender. 'Just pretend Françoise is fully clothed,' he would say. How could I? I needed to acknowledge her presence to avoid stepping on her accidentally. It wouldn't have been so bad if she had laid on her stomach. And if I were to stumble and fall on top of her? Monique might even think I did it on purpose.

In the afternoon, Frederik went scuba diving. He could refill his oxygen bottles on board as he owned a special licence. He looked like Neptune, ready to wreak destruction on wayward sailors when he emerged from the water. As Byron and I helped him off with his diving gear, Frederik asked, 'What kind of a shipyard have you taken *Jesty* to? The anti-fouling paint is peeling off in big patches. As soon as we finish our holiday, I want you to take *Jesty* back to the shipyard and get her sorted.'

Byron's face looked like a red snapper, opening and closing his mouth with no words spilling out. He didn't dare ask about the repairs on the propellers to avoid further angry outbursts. Would Byron be forced to give his ten per cent commission back to the shipyard?

The mood on *Jesty* soon lightened up. In this perfect setting, there was only room for indulgence and pleasure. Claudia spent a short spell on the water skis, fell a few times, and gave up. Frederik, more experienced, had a good half hour, jumping across the ski boat's wake like a pro. Françoise and Achillios opted for an afternoon nap. Monique went for a swim to a nearby beach while I sketched various yacht designs. I longed to be getting on with my project; this theatre of decadence didn't impress me much!

Then Claudia announced she was inviting the crew to an exclusive restaurant. She explained we could only gain access to the place by yacht; therefore, the dress code needed to be casual. We would anchor *Jesty* two hundred yards away from the restaurant and land on a private beach with the inflatable ski boat. Annika decided not to come. She was happy spending the evening reading. Once again, Monique cooked her wiener schnitzel before we set off.

As soon as the ski boat bow touched the shallow water, Françoise was over the side, lifting her yellow skirt high enough to reveal her long legs and white lace panties. She paddled to the shore, happy to exchange the red carpet for a pale sandy beach.

A short distance away were some stone steps, bordered on either side by dry-stone walls with cascading flowers and foliage. The steps led to the restaurant terrace, which was surrounded by a stone balustrade and exotic blooms flowing out of large Greek urns.

Underneath the grapevine-covered pergola was a long table set up with Indian linen. Each placement had a serviette fashioned into a swan. The gleaming silver cutlery and candelabra would have made a scrap dealer's eyes pop out of his head. Our elegant table was the only one laid out and included the most exquisite bouquets. We must have been the sole guests expected that evening.

As dusk fell, waiters lit hundreds of candles and lanterns. They served us the hors-d'oeuvres and aperitifs with great reverence. The sumptuous setting and the seven-course banquet were deemed fit for Royalty. We ate monkfish, lobster, coquilles St Jacques, mussels, prawns, and crustaceans I didn't recognise. A different wine accompanied each course. For dessert, we had Tarte-Tatin, which elevated my taste buds to a whole new level.

When we finished our coffee and liqueur, a waiter offered the men Havana cigars. I had never smoked in my life, so I declined. Françoise volunteered to have my cigar. We all drank and ate far too much, mingling as though we were the best of friends.

When we left the restaurant, Françoise was so unsteady on her legs that she put her arms around me to support her back down to the beach.

Monique looked at me disapprovingly. 'Either she fancies you, or she's trying to make Achillios jealous,' she said. 'He might not like it.'

Everybody thankfully made it safely back to their cabins that night. *Jesty's* sturdy boarding platform and steps amidships were a godsend in the state some of us found ourselves in. Falling in the water could have been disastrous.

Achillios and Françoise left *Jesty* two days later. Then Claudia and Frederik ran out of patience, waiting for the Mistral to ease. They decided to fly back to Germany from Ajaccio.

As I ferried them ashore in the ski boat, Claudia lost her temper when a tiny splash of spray landed on her long white skirt. She looked at Frederik as if it was all his fault.

After they left, the crew waited for the force six wind to ease off. It would have been a fast passage back to La Napoule for my *Sadler 25*. Byron was anxious about the weather. The yacht had two turbocharged engines of 650 hp each. What was his problem?

So we waited and spring-cleaned all the cabins until Monique had another tantrum, and we were allowed a day off.

As soon as the wind eased we set out, ploughing into a cobalt sea with just a few white spumes breaking the surface. The shimmering light and the colour-rich Mediterranean coast are a magnet for artists. I took hundreds of pictures with my eyes.

When we made landfall eleven miles south of La Napoule, Byron was proud of his accurate navigation, but it was just an easy one-hundred-mile passage. I couldn't help wondering how he would have managed twelve days at sea, running before a storm under jury rig with only a sextant and a Radio Direction Finder. If he had been crossing an ocean, he might have found himself on the wrong continent!

Two days later, we left La Napoule for the short journey to the shipyard. In no time, *Jesty* was gliding into the haul-out cradle. I made her fast to the four supporting posts, and then Byron switched the engines off and rejoined us on the starboard side deck as the boatyard staff started to winch her ashore.

'Look at these rusty posts,' Monique said, pointing at them. 'Are they strong enough to keep the ship upright?'

'They know what they're doing,' Byron replied with a condescending smile. 'It's just a bit of surface rust. Anyway, *Jesty* was hauled out with the same cradle weeks ago.'

'I think she's going to collapse and fall over,' Monique declared.

Her warning rattled Byron's cage, and he went to check the lashing on the port side, leaving us leaning on the highly varnished wooden rail of the starboard bulwark. I tried hard to appease Monique, but I was equally apprehensive.

As the winch continued pulling the cradle and *Jesty* up the slipway and her propellors emerged from the water, we heard a sickening crack like both barrels of a shotgun going off at once. And before we had time to react, *Jesty* was rolling to port like a stranded whale desperate to get back out to sea. Monique yelled: 'What do we do now?'

'I don't know how far she'll go, but we've got the upper deck above us,' I said. 'We'll have to follow *Jesty* round like a hamster in a treadmill. We might even find ourselves standing upright on the cabin wall.' Byron, on the port side, was in more danger than us. If *Jesty* were to keel further over, he could be crushed by the hundred and twenty-five-ton boat.

Luckily for the crew, *Jesty* halted her capsize at a 60° angle, but we still held onto the handrails, afraid that she might topple further. By then, Byron had scrambled ashore.

'Peter, Monique, are you all right?' he called out in a heavy whisper as if he was afraid to shout too loudly and cause *Jesty* to collapse further onto her side. 'Don't bother taking anything with you. Just get off the boat as fast as you can.'

Jesty was leaning at such an angle that we had to slide down the foredeck on our backsides. When we reached the port bulwark, I jumped over the side rails, dropping six feet down to the concrete slipway, and then I quickly helped Monique. At this point, if our action had tipped the yacht's balance, we could have been the next day's front-page headlines: *Two crew aboard a super-yacht crushed to death. It may be weeks before their bodies are recovered.*

It still looked as if *Jesty* could complete the roll at any moment. We saw Byron standing rigid at the top of the slipway. His suntanned complexion had turned a ghostly white. No one spoke. We were far too traumatised to find words or make sense of what had happened. As I glanced at the yacht, I shuddered at the thought of being buried under her.

I took Monique aside, leaving Byron to work out his next move and the mortifying task of informing Claudia and Frederik about the little mishap! I doubted he would say: 'I've got good news and bad news for you! You'll have to cancel your next holiday on *Jesty*, but the good news is that Thompson is doing an all-inclusive cheap deal in Benidorm.'

We were now shipwrecked and left *Jesty* with only the clothes on our backs. It felt like we had woken up from a bad dream as we waited for the ferry to take us to Cannes. Everyone around us was laughing and in holiday mode, but for us, our narrow escape from being buried under the gin palace had been far too close for comfort.

Byron rented a two-bedroomed apartment which the three of us moved into without luggage. We were like *un mariage à trois* checking into a hotel for an afternoon of passion. Byron never said anything about his conversation with the owner of *Jesty*, apart from the fact that he was told to find us some accommodation ashore for the time being. I wondered about the workmen's reaction to the cradle collapsing. No doubt there were much stronger words used amongst themselves than just *Sacrebleu!*

After the shipyard had shored *Jesty* up with timber props and secured her from falling on her beam ends, Byron gave us permission to go and retrieve our personal belongings. Monique and I took the ferry to the island, and as we walked through the shipyard gate, we weren't sure what to expect. Then when we saw *Jesty* on the slipway, she looked like a giant discarded toy.

'The gin has definitely run out of this palace,' I remarked to Monique as we clambered on our hands and knees up the near-vertical foredeck. She was too busy keeping a grip to laugh.

Once inside, it felt as if we were actors in The Poseidon Adventure. Everything was *topsy-turvy,* forcing us to toboggan down the wall on the left-hand side of the companionway. There were no level surfaces anywhere to hang on to; Monique and I had to support each other like two drunken sailors. It was the most disorientating, head-spinning experience I had ever encountered.

When we reached our cabin, I had to open the door like a submarine's conning tower hatch to get inside. Our bunks now hung off the ceiling while the wardrobe lay on its side, with one door flopped open. I had to prop the other up like a car bonnet to retrieve our clothes. Then, when I opened the upended drawers, everything fell to our feet.

While we were inside, Byron suggested that we extract as much frozen meat as we could carry from the chest freezers as it would all defrost and go to waste. Had he any idea how challenging this would be? First, we had to stand on the side of the units like stunt performers in a movie. Despite our balancing act, we managed to fill up several bags, and then Monique and I handled them one by one onto the deck, along with our backpacks.

When we emerged into the light, we still saw the world at the wrong angle, feeling dizzy and thoroughly disorientated. Finally, we slid our cargo down across the foredeck, and Byron caught each item at the bottom before they could smash into the bulwark. The deck was steeper than a ski jump launch, so we slid down on our backs as if we were on a near-vertical playground slide.

It was a relief when we reached 'terra firma' - the more 'firma,' the less terror! Then as Monique and I walked away with our bounty, I couldn't help saying to Byron: 'At least it would be easier to paint *Jesty*'s bottom now!' He didn't appreciate my Yorkshire sense of humour.

There was nothing else to do for the moment, apart from waiting for the insurance company to establish who was accountable for the accident and whether *Jesty* would be a total write-off. Meanwhile, we were still on full pay with all our incidentals covered, but I was getting restless. Although Monique and I soaked up the sun on Cannes beaches for a few days, we couldn't relax. We were far too preoccupied, not knowing which course to steer. *Jesty's* demise had jeopardised all our plans. Moreover, I was concerned about *Ellis* anchored in the harbour at Calpe. Maybe this was a sign for me to get back to my boat.

I told Monique I was quitting and ready to sail back to England. Once there, I would start building my yacht *Capricorn*. I needed to be single-minded without the distraction of a relationship. I admit it was brutal. Monique would lose her job on *Jesty;* the owners had hired us as a couple, but we would be dismissed anyway if the insurance company wrote off the yacht.

Monique was heartbroken and angry with me for leaving her. Anybody would have thought I didn't care. But I must confess, when confronting my emotions, my trigger would always be to shut off. I had paid such a high price when I accepted Elisabeth's marriage proposal, only for it to end in disaster. I was scared of being hurt again. Everything felt so confused, just like *Jesty* wrecked on the shore of the Île Sainte Marguerite.

Monique then decided to look for another job. Byron lent us the ship's motorbike, and I took her around nearby marinas. She found a position as cook on the thirty-five-metre yacht, *Kovalam.* The cruiser was built like a mini-liner and owned by a French couple. The man dealt in armaments. The last cook had only just left the yacht, hopefully not at gunpoint! There were five crew on board; the captain, two deckhands, the engineer, and a stewardess. The vessel was due to sail to the Balearics and then to Malta. So once again, Monique and I would be two ships passing in the night. Of course, deep in my heart, I still hoped it wouldn't be the end of our relationship, but how could our conflicting visions of the future be compatible, with Monique hopes of a career in the music business and my ambition to build a yacht and sail the seven seas. Maybe it was best for each of us to chart our separate ways. But did I truly want that?

21. Farewell

Was I in for an unpleasant surprise, I asked myself when I arrived at Calpe Railway Station? As I walked towards the marina, I could see a forest of masts in front of some single-storey buildings with the Rock towering above. I wondered if *Ellis's* mast was amongst them? I had left her on a mooring three months earlier.

When I turned the corner and entered the harbour, I quickened my pace. Had Bill Rodford kept an eye on my boat? It shouldn't have been difficult for him as his house overlooked the harbour.

The sea of doubt lifted when I saw *Ellis* gently tugging on her mooring. Luckily she hadn't dragged the anchor I had set from the stern to stop her coming closer than three feet to the shore. However, to get aboard was a tug of war between a two-ton boat with a well-dug-in anchor and me, weighing seventy-five kilos. I pulled *Ellis* close to the quayside, let the shoreline rope go and then jumped onto the pulpit before she could catapult away. Had I not been quick enough, I would have fallen into very murky waters!

At first glance, the boat seemed fine except for the decks. The seagulls must have been roosting in the rigging during my time away. As for *Ellis's* waterline, the seaweed clinging below would have put the *Hanging Gardens of Babylon* to shame!

I spent time scrubbing the decks and scraping the underneath of the hull as far as I could reach from the dinghy. After hours of elbow grease, I decided to leave the rest for later. I put everything back in place, including the sails and the outboard engine, then stocked up. I never saw Bill Rodford but left a cheque for him with his neighbour.

At 8 am on 26 July 1979, I lifted anchor and let the two shorelines go, trusting that Providence would grant me a safe passage back to England this time. However, losing my mast still haunted me. Although the Atlantic route back to *Blighty* through the Straits of Gibraltar would be the fastest way home, the shortest route in miles was via the Canal du Midi and Canal Latéral from Sète to Bordeaux. Then I could coast-hop around the top half of Biscay before crossing the English Channel.

I set off in an easterly direction, intending to day-sail along the Spanish coast - however, the wind was so light that it hardly fluttered the ensign. I was close to a beach when I started a conversation with a couple on a pedalo. 'Where are you heading for?' the young man asked.

'Back to England,' I replied.

'But aren't you going in the wrong direction?'

'I'm sailing back via the Canal du Midi,' I replied.

The man found it incredible to be paddling alongside a sailing boat in a pedalo, chatting to a sailor on his way back to *Blighty*. When we bid each other farewell, I warned the pair about the danger of being so far out from the shore. Then, as I drifted away in the opposite direction, I saw them heading back to the beach, their legs pumping away as if they were competing in an aquatic Tour de France.

The flag received a good beating, crossing the Golfe du Lion, which fully lived up to its reputation. I sailed close to the wind, decks awash with spray. Although I enjoyed the exhilarating passage, I sighed with relief when I arrived in Sète and moored *Ellis* amongst other yachts near the entrance of the first lock. It was hard not to notice all the car tyres strung down on either side of some boats. Were their owners preparing for a bumpy ride in the locks? I started to wonder if I would be able to cope single-handedly.

When I spoke to a sailor working on his deck, he said, 'It was bloody hard to negotiate the locks alone.' He had travelled down the Canal du Midi from Bordeaux, and his white fibreglass yacht *Fair Wind* looked scratched and battered. Hearing his woes, I thought of Roy, my 'gin and tonic,' friend, who had kept my morale up when I was building *Ellis*.

I decided to call him to ask if he fancied a trip through the canals. Roy jumped at the opportunity and arrived in Sète three days later. Then I arranged to lower the mast at the local yacht club at 10 am the following day.

We rendezvoused on the dot by the harbour crane and waited for half an hour, but no one came. Being mischievous, Roy decided to play with the crane while I double-checked that I had loosened every rigging bottlescrew. Then Roy said, 'Look Pete, there's a handle on the side and the crane isn't locked.'

'Okay, Roy, we'll lower the mast ourselves.'

Within ten minutes, it was down and across the deck. While I was coiling up the rigging, a man with a peaked cap appeared from nowhere. He looked official. There was a storm sweeping over his face. He started shouting at us, pointing at the crane and gesturing wildly. We guessed he was scolding us.

'Roy,' I said, 'your French is better than mine.' His only word was *Sacrebleu*. 'See if you can pacify him with this bottle of wine.'

The man's expression never altered when he took it from Roy. We left him locking up the crane while we carried on clearing the decks. After folding the sails, *Ellis* was ready for her new role as a canal boat. The English ensign would be flying from the end of the mast, which now laid across the deck, like a dipped flagstaff at a cenotaph. Then my two horsepower outboard motor would have to *putt-putt* the three hundred and twelve-mile journey from Sète to Bordeaux with one hundred and thirty-nine locks to negotiate on the way - yes, a doddle!

The Canal du Midi traverses aqueducts that span lush valleys beneath turbulent rivers. Flanking the canal were elm, ash and oak trees. The waterway resembled scenes from the Lord of the Rings in the early mist. Once the sun rose above the distant hills, alleys of trees reflected on the water like pillars in a cathedral.

It was hypnotic, and I felt as if I were in a trance. There were sleepy villages dotted along the way and beautiful lock-keepers' dwellings with hanging baskets of colourful flowers and neatly trimmed lock-side lawns. I wondered if living by the canal could be for me, but seeing the snowbird sailors heading south in autumn, I knew I wouldn't be able to resist becoming a stowaway.

It was a shame we had to rush through such picture-postcard places. Roy couldn't afford much time away as he had left his wife, Liz, alone running their nursing home.

We set off every day as soon as the locks opened, taking turns at the helm and operating the sluices and lock-gates. It was laborious to manoeuvre through them, especially in the August heat. Only a few locks were fully automated. One afternoon as Roy was at the tiller, shading himself under a black umbrella, a French motorboat passed us, heading the other way. 'You must be English,' the skipper hailed.

'*Oui*, *Monsieur*,' Roy replied, raising his gin and tonic and grinning triumphantly. It was easy to converse with other boats on the canal, travelling at the speed of a pedalo, and this time nobody said I was going the wrong way!

Every paradise has its drawbacks, and on this slow-paced journey through history, mosquitoes were eating us alive, particularly at night. As I didn't have any remedy aboard, we stopped at the next village.

We found an old-fashioned store down a narrow cobbled street that offered various goods and hardware. There were numerous items on shelves behind the counter or in a back room. An elderly lady was tending the shop. She was dressed in black and wore a scarf tied under her chin. As we approached the counter, the woman quickly drew her matching shawl across her chest as if she was adjusting the breastplate of a knight's armour.

'*Qu'est-ce que vous voulez?*' she asked scornfully.

Roy said, 'Fly killer, *S'il vous plaît*.'

The woman shrugged her shoulders with a disinterested look on her face.

Roy repeated 'Fly Killer' a few times.

Her answer was a scowl.

Roy tried miming the action by pressing an imaginary aerosol can and going 'Sssssh.'

This charade didn't work, so I decided to join in. I lay on the floor and started to wave my arms and legs in the air, mimicking a dying fly going 'buzz, buzz,' while Roy pretended to be squirting me with a deadly hiss.

The woman's expression never altered. She merely picked up an aerosol spray from the shelf behind her and slapped it down on the counter as if she wanted to use it as a rubber stamp to censure our humour. She remained grim-faced and thoroughly unimpressed by our antics. Roy and I were hysterical and couldn't restrain ourselves, no matter how hard we tried. We quickly paid and left before the woman could attack us with a stale baguette.

Three weeks later, we entered the River Garonne and the Gironde estuary. We then stopped in Royan to erect the mast. This time there was somebody to operate the crane! Next, we sailed to Les Sables-d'Olonnes with a fair wind.

As we approached the marina pontoon, we saw a man with a beret standing by. How strange - he had a ticket machine hanging across his chest like the old-fashioned tram 'clippy.' He waited until we tied up before winding the handle on his device to produce a ticket. I looked at the price before I took it from him. 'This is extortionate,' I said, turning to Roy. 'I feel like carrying on but it's a night sail to Île d'Yeu.'

'It's up to you,' he answered. 'How much is it?'

I told him the price, and without a word, Roy cast off. I gave *Ellis* a good push away from the pontoon and raised the headsail swiftly while he steered us towards the marina entrance. The Frenchman watched us sail into the sunset, still holding the ticket in his hand. He looked puzzled as to what to do with it. We could have given him some suggestions!

After a few stopovers on the way, Roscoff was our last port of call before crossing the English Channel. It was dark when we approached the marked channel to the harbour entrance. Although I didn't have a detailed chart to guide us, I had written directions in the Cruising Association Almanac. 'Don't worry,' I said to Roy, 'I'm sure we'll manage with these instructions. After all, Cross Channel Ferries operate out of Roscoff. Take the tiller and I'll direct you.'

Roy knew I was a stranger to caution, but he still had confidence in me as a skipper. So I told him to keep the first two leading lights in line.

Roy held his course. Then he yelled: 'Bloody Hell, Pete, there're rocks on the port side, twelve feet away.'

'Roy, don't look at them, just steer towards the lights until I tell you.'

'You're the Captain.'

They looked menacing with the red reflection from the port navigation lights.

'Okay, turn hard to port and keep the next two leading lights in line,' I said as I pointed them out. 'We're nearly there, but don't stray for goodness sake!'

While Roy took up the new transit, I let the lee sheet go and pulled the sails in and over to the other side.

Entering Roscoff was proving trickier than I had anticipated, but I still managed to hide my concern from him. Then after a few more agonising minutes, we entered the harbour under full sail, with water lapping over the lee-rail.

Once we were in, I told Roy to round *Ellis* up into the wind while I dropped the sails onto the deck. Then I started the outboard and motored up to the quayside, where there were several French yachts already moored. People were partying on one of them, and above the merriment we heard somebody shouting: 'Well done English,' followed by rapturous clapping and cheering. It seemed these revellers had interrupted the party to watch us come in. It made us proud to be applauded by French yachtsmen, although we didn't feel we had done anything heroic.

At low tide the next day, we looked over the harbour wall, and from where we stood, the approach to the entrance seemed impossible to do. How did we manage to navigate in the dark, zigzagging our way through the rock-strewn channel under full sail? Then I found out later that the Cross Channel Ferries were operating from a deep water jetty around the corner!

While storm-bound in Roscoff, Roy decided to fly back to England, leaving me to wait for a break in the weather. When it came, I prepared a huge beef and vegetable stew I would eat during my night-crossing. I needed the food to keep me awake during the 103-mile passage to Dartmouth. The English Channel is one of the busiest stretches of water in the world, and I just hoped there wouldn't be another ship like *The Mineral Alegria* out there with *Ellis's* name on it!

At daybreak, in an easterly wind, force 4, I weaved my way through the shipping lanes like a Harlem Globetrotter dodging his opponents. I stayed awake for nineteen and a half hours and arrived at the entrance to Dartmouth at 07h15 the following day. I made a few tacks up the estuary against wind and tide before mooring to a buoy. '*Blighty* at last,' I sighed.

When I arrived in Southampton, I read in the newspaper about the dispute that had flared up after Margaret Thatcher decided to reduce quotas on the number of herrings French fishing fleets could land in UK ports. After spotting an English sailing boat tied to the quay in Roscoff, some protesting French fishermen tipped a lorry load of rotten-stinking herrings over the quayside and onto their deck. It could have been *Ellis* if I had stayed there longer. What a narrow escape - besides, I don't like herrings; they have too many bones!

While I was here, The Southampton Boat Show was currently in full swing. It is a pilgrimage for sailors from all walks of life. I thought it would be the perfect opportunity to buy plans to build my new boat and was still interested in a modern French design with a lifting keel. However, that day I stumbled upon the exhibition stand of the marine architect Bruce Roberts. I explained to the representative what I was looking for.

'I've got just the plans for you, on special offer for the show only,' the man said. 'Surely, you've heard of *Joshua Slocum* and his boat *The Spray*. He was the first yachtsman to sail around the world single-handedly at the turn of the nineteenth century.'

He paused, then looked at me with an expression that seemed to say, "Do I have a buyer?" 'These plans are a steel adaptation of *Joshua Slocum's* wooden boat,' he explained. 'During *Slocum's* circumnavigation, he sailed three thousand miles across the Pacific, never touching the tiller once. Then, the ghost of the navigator on the *Pintar*, who had reputedly accompanied Christopher Columbus aboard the Santa Maria, suddenly appeared to *Slocum*. At the time, he was delirious and incapable of handling his boat. In his book, "Sailing Alone Around The World,"

Slocum wrote about the ghost who had steered his boat until he was well again.'

The exhibitor had won me over by the time he had finished telling me about *Joshua Slocum.* I bought the plans solely on a romantic whim, despite my original intention of building a modern French steel design.

Ever since we parted in Cannes, Monique had remained very much on my mind. I had given her my temporary address at my sister Eileen's, and she wrote suggesting she could visit me in Southampton after she finished her contract as a cook on the mini-liner she had signed up to.

It was a strained atmosphere when she arrived aboard *Ellis.* I was in an odd space in my head. Monique met my mother at Eileen's house, where we had dinner together, and she stayed overnight with me. I thought she was disappointed at my aloofness towards her.

The following day, we gave each other a quick kiss before she left on the train to visit her friend Felicity in Dorset. After that, neither of us knew whether we would see one another again.

I had been five weeks in Southampton, preparing the boat for sale and waiting for an answer to my advertisements in Yachting Magazines. Then a couple contacted my sister, whose telephone number I was using. They wanted to see the boat at the marina, half a mile up the Itchen River.

That afternoon, my outboard motor was particularly obstinate, refusing to fire up. After all, I had used safety pins and sticky tape the whole way through the French canals to keep it going. Before then, I had sailed everywhere, even into harbours and right onto the quay, dropping the sails at the very last moment.

Eventually, I got the ailing outboard engine ticking, but I was a quarter of an hour late for the rendezvous. Nobody was waiting on the pontoon except a chap on his boat near to where I tied up. 'Are you looking for a young couple?' he shouted over to me.

'Yes,' I replied.

'Oh, they were extremely upset with you for not turning up. They waited an hour, then went.'

I rushed to the nearest telephone box and called them. The woman was very off-hand and, in no uncertain terms, told me to get lost. Before she could put the telephone down, I asked her, 'Can you tell me what the time is please?'

'I beg your pardon,' she retorted abruptly.

I repeated my question.

'It's two o'clock,' she snapped.

I explained that she must have forgotten the clocks had gone back. She apologised and asked me to hold. When she came on the line again, she said, 'my husband and I would like a survey on *Ellis.* Could you ring me back tomorrow to make arrangements?'

I arrived at the marina at the appointed time a few days later. *Ellis* was hauled out, just long enough for a surveyor to check her over. The assessor had some criticisms. First, he pointed to some marks on the hull.

'I had a try at sinking a sixty-five-thousand-ton ore carrier in the English Channel!' I said, out of earshot from my potential buyers.

He thought I was joking and made no comment. Then he asked how much I wanted for my boat. With the price I gave him, he told his clients to shake hands on it. We agreed on the deal, and the couple paid me by cheque.

Next, I bought an old Fiat from Eileen's husband's younger brother. He wanted £350 for the car. I went into my car salesman's mode and got it for £75. He thought the ticking noise from the engine was the big ends going when it was the speedo cable rattling - but I forgot to tell him that. I loaded the car up with all my belongings and drove away. I had mixed emotions about parting with *Ellis.* Despite my healthy bank balance, it felt as if I had sold a faithful friend for a few coins of silver.

I wrote to Monique when I returned to Scarborough, inviting her to sail with me when I finished building my boat *Capricorn,* though I couldn't tell her when this would be. Would she wait for me until then, I wondered?

Sometime later, she answered my letter and wrote: 'Love isn't like money you put in the bank waiting for it to gather interest.' She mentioned she would be looking for adventure in the Caribbean, and I feared she was writing me off!

I continued burying myself in my project to block out my turbulent emotions, but I wasn't coping well. I missed Monique too much and had to remind myself that I had a boat to build. There was so much to think about and organise. House-sitting for my mother proved a godsend as I had a place to stay. She had flown to Australia to visit Eileen, who had recently emigrated near Sydney with her third husband.

Next, I rented a piece of land from my friend Alex, who had done joinery work in the bungalow I built in Lebberston. I bought the steel, the oxyacetylene bottles, a welding plant, and other heavy-duty power tools. Then I erected a forty-foot long building frame and had just completed it when a violent storm swept in that night.

I arrived on-site the following morning to find the complete structure had collapsed onto some old outbuildings. Luckily, nothing got damaged apart from my pride. But was this an omen telling me to abandon the project and do something else? I am not a man who gives up easily, so the frame was soon re-erected and strengthened. Everything was now in place for me to build my thirty-three-foot ocean sailing yacht single-handedly.

I started by making the boat's ribs and hung them from the frame. Then, I connected horizontal round steel bars called *stringers* to each rib, creating a skeleton I would later clad with steel plates. It was all taking shape.

Despite progressing well, I felt like a ship without a rudder. I couldn't get Monique out of my mind. After six months of toil, the boat's skeleton was sheathed in its steel skin. It was a big learning curve, and everyone who saw my project thought I had bitten off more than I could chew. Their comments worsened my feeling of loneliness, although I had never felt lonely before, and it wasn't the hard physical work of boat-building that caused me such distress. I love ambitious challenges, but I needed Monique to believe in me and my dream. Was I going to let her go?

What a fool I've been, I thought as I mulled over Monique's words: 'Love is not like money you put in the bank waiting for interest.' I suddenly felt like a man condemned to a life without the woman he truly loves.

Was I about to lose Monique for good? Maybe I had lost her already. I had a vague idea that she might be in Martinique or Guadeloupe by now. Hopefully, she would have left a forwarding address with her parents. Would they send on my letter or put it away in a drawer as Monique once told me they did with her mail?

I was nervous when I started writing. My fate could be determined by the words I chose. Undoubtedly, the odds were stacked high against me.

The weeks dragged painfully on, and still, no letter arrived from Monique. I became more and more despondent. Then one morning, I was unusually late setting off for *Capricorn* when I heard the telephone ring. I rushed to answer, wondering who it might be.

My dark mood instantly lifted when I heard Monique's voice, saying, 'Bonjour Peter,' with her alluring French accent. I felt a wave of excitement racing through me…

Slow Boat to Nashville

is the sequel to

'Stranger to Caution'

Monique asked Peter, 'What are you looking for in life?'
'Contentment,' he replied. Will they find it together sailing the Seven Seas?

ACKNOWLEDGEMENTS

I want to thank my long-standing friend Felicity Redman for all the support, help and encouragement she offered during the journey of writing Stranger to Caution. Her patience, skills and input have been invaluable. Special thanks also to my friend Joan Wright for reading my earliest drafts. Sadly, she passed away before she could see the book in print. I would also like to mention Vanessa Schäffeler for the creative use of her red pen and valuable critiques, not forgetting my friend Dr Alan Dodson for his helpful suggestions. But above all, I would like to thank my husband, Peter, for his bravery in revisiting painful memories. His extraordinary story has helped me understand and love him even more.

Stranger to Caution

Self Published 2023
ISBN: 978-1-7391967-0-7

Printed in Great Britain
by Amazon

17606841R00210